Entrepreneurial Strategic Decision-Making

Entrepreneurial Strategic Decision-Making

A Cognitive Perspective

Edited by

Patrick A.M. Vermeulen

Associate Professor, Department of Organisation Studies, Tilburg University, The Netherlands

and

Petru L. Curşeu

Associate Professor, Department of Organisation Studies, Tilburg University, The Netherlands

Edward Elgar

Cheltenham, UK • Northampton, MA, USA

Published by
Edward Elgar Publishing Limited
The Lypiatts
15 Lansdown Road
Cheltenham
Glos GL50 2JA
UK

Edward Elgar Publishing, Inc.
William Pratt House
9 Dewey Court
Northampton
Massachusetts 01060
USA

Paperback edition 2010
Paperback edition reprinted 2014

A catalogue record for this book
is available from the British Library

Library of Congress Cataloguing in Publication Data

Vermeulen, Patrick Alexander Maria, 1970–
   Entrepreneurial strategic decision-making : a cognitive
perspective / Patrick A.M. Vermeulen, Petru L. Curseu.
       p. cm.
   Includes bibliographical references and index.
1. Entrepreneurship—Decision making. 2. Decision making. 3.
Strategic planning. I. Curseu, Petru Lucian, 1975– II. Title.
   HB615.V443 2008
   658.4'03—dc22

2008023885

ISBN 978 1 84720 903 0 (cased)
      978 1 84980 158 4 (paperback)

Printed in Great Britain by Berforts Information Press Ltd

Contents

Figures

Tables

Contributors

René M. Bakker worked on research projects at the University of Arizona (USA) and the University of Pretoria (South Africa) before acquiring his Research Master's degree in organization studies (MPhil) from Tilburg University in 2007. He is currently a PhD candidate at the Department of Organization Studies at Tilburg University. His research interests include temporary organizations, organization theory, inter-organizational relations and networks.

Sjoerd Bosgra has a Master's degree in organization studies and a Bachelor's degree in business administration. His Master's thesis was on the effect of cognitive complexity on risk-taking behaviour. After working as a service manager in China and the United States, he is currently employed as a management professional at Schiphol Group, in the Netherlands.

Petru L. Curşeu is Assistant Professor in the Department of Organization Studies at Tilburg University. He received his PhD from Tilburg University and he teaches courses on Organizational Behavior and Complexity within Organizations. His research interests include team dynamics (with a special focus on team cognition), social cognition (in particular the study of stereotypes and prejudice in organizational settings), as well as decision-making in organizations. He has published papers on related topics in the *Journal of Information Technology*, the *European Journal of Social Psychology*, *Group Dynamics*, *Group Decision and Negotiation*, *Studia Psychologica* and other journals.

Marijn J.J. de Kort has a Master's degree in organization studies from Tilburg University. His Master's thesis was on types of entrepreneurial decision-makers and the use of biases and heuristics in making strategic decisions. Currently he is travelling and working around the world in order to experience many cultures. In the near future he will be applying for a challenging job.

Petra Gibcus graduated in econometrics and operational research from the University of Groningen in 2002 with a specialization in econometrics and statistics. After her graduation, she joined the independent research and consultancy organization, EIM, where she works as a researcher. She participated in a wide range of projects on firm dynamics, entrepreneurship, innovation and market competition. Her topics of interest are decision-making in SMEs and the growth of enterprises.

Dinie Louwers has a Master's degree in organization studies and another in human resource studies, both from Tilburg University. Her Master's thesis was on the mediating role of cognitive representations in the relationship between entrepreneurial experience and organizational innovation. She works as an temporary employee for public organizations for the company XOPP, based in Amersfoort, the Netherlands.

Gerardus J.M. Lucas is a Research Master's student (MPhil) at both the Department of Organization Studies and the CentER Graduate School, Tilburg University. Currently, he is in the final semester of his studies and plans to continue into the PhD stage. His research interests are entrepreneurship, decision-making and innovation. Besides being an aspiring researcher, he is also an entrepreneur.

Elissaveta Radulova is a PhD candidate at the University of Maastricht in the Netherlands. She has studied in Sofia (Bulgaria), Nice (France) and Maastricht, and holds a BA in business administration, an MA in international relations and an MA in European public affairs. She is currently working on her PhD project on the effectiveness of the open method of coordination of the European Union in the field of gender equality.

Jaap van den Elshout has a Master's degree in organization studies from Tilburg University. His Master's thesis was on the involvement of different stakeholders in the strategic decision-making process in SMEs. Currently he is working as a project manager with the Department of Business Development at Royal BAM Group, Bunnik, the Netherlands.

Daniëlle G.W.M. van Gestel has a Master's degree in organization studies from Tilburg University. In her Master's thesis she studied the relationship between social capital and the innovative performance of SMEs. Currently, she is working as a project manager at the N.V. Noord-Brabant Development Agency (BOM) in the Netherlands. Situated at the BOM Centre for Start Ups, she is involved on a daily basis in projects which support the coaching and advising of individual innovative entrepreneurs aiming to start a business based on technical inventions, and spin-off activities from established businesses.

Peter van Hoesel graduated in psychology in 1970 and was awarded his PhD in social sciences in 1985 on the subject of policy research. Currently he is director of the research company Panteia at Zoetermeer and Professor in Applied Policy Research at Erasmus University, Rotterdam.

Patrick A.M. Vermeulen is Associate Professor of Organization Studies in the Department of Organization Studies, Faculty of Social Sciences, at Tilburg University. He received his PhD from the Nijmegen School of Management and previously worked at the Rotterdam School of Management. His main research interests focus upon processes of institutional change, strategies for the Base-of-the-Pyramid (BOP), and strategic decision-making. His work has been published in *Organization Studies*, the *International Journal of Research in Marketing*, the *Journal of Small Business Management, Long Range Planning*, the *International Small Business Journal, Technovation* and several other journals. He serves as the academic director of the BOP learning laboratory™ for the Benelux.

Preface

Entrepreneurial cognition is an emergent and promising field of research. The most distinctive feature of this new domain is that concepts and methods developed in cognitive sciences are used to explore highly relevant research questions raised in the entrepreneurship literature. For example, cognitive concepts and methods have already been used to explore the factors that lead to the start of new ventures. Nevertheless, little to no attention has been paid to the way in which entrepreneurs make other strategic choices, after the business is up and running. The main aim of this book is to fill this gap in the entrepreneurial cognition literature. Therefore, this book addresses the way in which entrepreneurs make strategic decisions.

Organizational decision-making is inherently bound to two important concepts: strategy and cognition. In all organizations, decision-making is a strategic activity. It is related to setting out specific courses of action to reach strategic goals. The process that leads to the choice of goals and means and the way in which these means are effectively deployed is the strategic decision-making process. Cognition is the second relevant facet of organizational decision-making. It refers to the way in which decision-related information is represented in the human cognitive system and to the way in which these representations are transformed. The accuracy and quality of the decision-making process depend on the cognitive underpinnings of the strategic process.

We have been fascinated by the idea of combining the insights from the strategic decision-making literature and cognition in entrepreneurship. Cognitive scientists have so far shown little interest in addressing highly relevant questions related to entrepreneurship (for example, what cognitive factors drive strategic choices in entrepreneurship?). Rather, strategists were interested in exploring strategic choices in large corporations and little attention was paid to how these decision processes unfold in small and medium-sized enterprises. Finally, although the need for a cognitive perspective has been raised before in both the entrepreneurship and strategy literature, there is a lack of consistency in the way in which cognitive concepts and research methods have so far been applied. These three reasons triggered us to write this book, which is the result of an enduring unsatisfactory feeling with these bodies of literature. As such our book contributes to the research on entrepreneurial strategic decision-making (ESDM) by combining concepts, theories and methods developed in cognitive sciences and organization studies.

This book is the result of a collective effort. Therefore, a special note goes out to our co-authors. Whereas we value the input of each and every one of them, we would especially like to thank our (former) students: Daniëlle, Dinie, Gertjan, Jaap, Marijn, René and Sjoerd. Working with you has been a great experience for us. This book is truly a collective effort that has blended our teaching and research activities to a large extent. Your perseverance in working with the data, continuous enthusiasm to reflect on our ideas and stimulating questions during the group meetings brought this book to a higher level. In fact, we wonder whether there would have been a book at all if it weren't for your entrepreneurial spirits! We are convinced that each of you will pursue an exciting career.

We would also like to show our appreciation to the entrepreneurs who gave generously of their time and patience while the data on which this book is based were collected. Furthermore, the ideas presented in this book also benefited from discussions with and feedback from many colleagues. We wish to mention a few in particular: Smaranda Boroş Oana Iederan, John Goedee and Jeroen de Jong. We would also like to thank Alice de Kok and Helen Pluut for their support in the tiresome but necessary editing and referencing work.

And what would a preface be without thanking those that matter the most. Patrick would like to thank Afke, Hugo and Simon for sharing their unlimited love. Petru would like to thank Alina, Dragoş and Antonia for their unconditional love and support. Now that this project is finished there is a lot more time to play!

Petru L. Curşeu
Patrick A.M. Vermeulen
Tilburg, January 2008

Acknowledgements

The authors would like to express their gratitude to EIM Business and Policy Research for so generously allowing us to experiment with the data they have collected over the last few years. EIM Business and Policy Research (EIM BV) is an independent research and consultancy organization based in the Netherlands with about 80 regular employees. It is part of Panteia. EIM has been carrying out policy research on enterprise issues for 75 years in various fields such as entrepreneurship and business development, employment, information and communication technology, innovation, internationalization and administrative burdens. EIM conducts the 'SMEs and Entrepreneurship' Programme (www.entrepreneurship-sme.eu) on behalf of the Ministry of Economic Affairs. We especially want to thank Petra Gibcus and Peter van Hoesel who designed most of the decision-making project. All the empirical chapters have used data from EIM. More information about the various stages of data collection can be found in the Appendix.

1. Entrepreneurs and strategic decisions

Patrick A.M. Vermeulen and Petru L. Curşeu

1.1 INTRODUCTION

Making decisions is a daily routine. We make decisions that involve our private life (for example, what we eat, how to dress, what to do in our free time) as well as specific decisions related to our work. Decision-making is a cognitive process that involves the selection of a specific course of action that is supposed to bring us to a certain result. The fact that there is selection in decision-making implies that there are alternative choices to be considered. Often, we do not know the exact outcomes of these alternatives and thus one of the key challenges in decision-making is the reduction of uncertainty. One way to reduce uncertainty is to gather relevant information before we make a decision. We use the specific information to fill in the cognitive gaps and choose the most suitable alternative for our purposes. For example, if we want to make a choice about what to wear, we might check the weather forecast, look at our agenda for important meetings, or ask someone for advice. On the basis of this information we look over our alternatives and make a choice. Another way to reduce uncertainty is to apply pre-existing heuristics (cognitive short cuts developed through experience) and to use just a minimal number of cues when making a choice. In the example above, we might decide to take our jacket as well as an umbrella, simply based on the observation that so far this has been a wet autumn. In organizations we are also confronted with various decision situations that involve varying degrees of uncertainty. Whereas these might be more complex, the steps of the underlying process will be similar: we recognize a problem situation, we generate alternatives, we evaluate the various alternatives and based on these evaluations we select the one that best satisfies our evaluation criteria (Simon, 1965).

This book addresses the way in which entrepreneurs make strategic decisions. We therefore face a twofold challenge in that entrepreneurs are a special type of decision-maker and strategic decisions are a particularly important type of decision. Entrepreneurs are those individuals who start

and run their own business and are often believed to have specific characteristics that influence the decision-making process (Brouthers et al., 1998;
Mador, 2000). They are also described as being distinct from other people
(Low and MacMillan, 1988) in that they are 'decisive, impatient, action ori-
ented individuals' (Smith et al., 1988: 224) and have also been called
'rugged individualists' (McGrath et al., 1992). Although newly started businesses can grow into large ones, we are interested in strategic decisions in
small and medium-sized enterprises (SMEs).

Entrepreneurs in SMEs are often confronted with a myriad of important
issues that require decisions to be made. Examples include the shutting
down of a manufacturing plant, moving to a new location, extensive
collaboration with former competitors, developing new products, or the
redesign of internal work processes. Decisions with major consequences for
the SMEs are labelled 'strategic decisions'. The success of small firms is to
a large extent dependent upon strategic decision-making practices
(Robinson and Pearce, 1983). Strategic decisions made by SME owners
form the heart of entrepreneurship and can therefore be considered essential for economic development. Hence, a study on their decision-making
processes will enrich the knowledge of mechanisms that drive these companies to participate in the economy, thus creating growth and prosperity
for society.

The book contributes to the research on entrepreneurial strategic
decision-making (ESDM) in several ways. First, it reviews the current body
of literature on the factors associated with ESDM by looking at both the
attributes of the decision-maker, as well as situational constraints.

Second, it fills a gap in this literature, by addressing the lack of integration between the distinctive personal features of entrepreneurs and information processing in explaining the entrepreneurial strategic choices. In
this respect we develop an integrative model for entrepreneurial decision-
making based on a dual-processing approach. The model integrates personal attributes, cognitive factors and emotional reactions into a unitary
framework. One of the unique aspects of our book is that we have been for-
tunate to be able to test parts of our model empirically. The results show
the potential of the model for setting up interesting research agendas.

Third, we introduce the concept of cognitive complexity, defined as the
richness of entrepreneurial cognitive representations, to explain ESDM
effectiveness. We argue that the cognitive representations developed by the
entrepreneur can be elicited and represented in the form of cognitive maps,
and we use the structural complexity of these maps as an indication of cognitive complexity. The conceptual contribution is therefore supported by
the discussion of a valid elicitation and representation method that can also
be used as a diagnostic and research tool.

1.2   STRATEGY AND COGNITION

Organizational decision-making is inherently bound to two important concepts: strategy and cognition. In organizations, decision-making is a strategic activity. It is related to setting out specific courses of action to reach strategic goals. The process that leads to the choice of goals and means and the way in which these means are effectively deployed is the strategic decision-making (SDM) process (Noorderhaven, 1995). Strategic decisions are crucial to the viability of firms and are defined as 'intentional choices or programmed responses about issues that materially affect the survival prospects, well-being and nature of the organization' (Schoemaker, 1993: 107). As such they are 'important in terms of the actions taken, the resources committed, or the precedents set' (Mintzberg et al., 1976: 246). Strategic decisions are the infrequent decisions made by the leaders of an organization that critically affect organizational health and survival (Eisenhardt and Zbaracki, 1992) and guide the organization into the future and shape its course.

According to Noorderhaven (1995), strategic decisions share four fundamental characteristics. The first of these concepts is the degree of *complexity* involved in the decision situation, which equals the amount of differentiation in the knowledge domain of the decision. A complex decision situation involves a large number of facts, variables and contingencies that are relevant for the decision at hand. When a situation is simple (that is, consisting of only a limited number of variables and contingencies), SDM becomes trivial (Winter, 1987). The second concept described by Noorderhaven is *uncertainty*. Most strategic choices are made without knowing all possible alternatives and all the possible outcomes associated with these alternatives. There is therefore, a high degree of uncertainty involved in SDM. If decision-makers could calculate the odds of success for all of their options, it would probably take them a considerable time, and in the end they may still not be able to find the single best undeniable option, based on mathematics (see, for example, problems with no optimal solution or no solution at all). In SDM, decision-makers operate with uncertain information and mathematical models are seldom used.

This brings us to the third concept used by Noorderhaven to define SDM, namely *rationality*. By claiming rationality as one of the four basic concepts of SDM, it is assumed that there is some intention behind the decision, in other words: the decision-maker is trying to reach a specific goal by making the decision (an instrumental perspective on rationality). In this respect, the cognitive processes involved in SDM are rational because they help the decision-maker to achieve an important organizational goal. The fourth and final concept we mention here is *control*. The concept of control in SDM refers to the intentional character of the strategic choice. SDMs results from intentional and deliberate actions of decision-makers (Noorderhaven, 1995). To summarize, SDM is the intentional and goal-directed cognitive process of selecting an alternative from several available, when only incomplete information on the alternatives and their possible outcomes is available and the facts, variables and contingencies involved in the decision situation are highly complex. The outcomes of these decisions are often unknown, meaning that there is uncertainty involved in decision-making processes. As such, the decision-making process consists of a set of mental activities, which implies that decision-making cannot be separated from cognitive processes.

Cognition is the second relevant facet of organizational decision-making. It refers to the way in which decision-related information is represented in the human cognitive system and to the way in which these representations are transformed. The accuracy and quality of the decision-making process depend on the cognitive underpinnings of the strategic process. Several factors (for example, political, norms and procedures, social dynamics) impact on strategic decisions in large firms, while in SMEs it is often the entrepreneur, alone, who makes the strategic choice. Therefore, to a certain extent, ESDM can be seen as a less rationalized and political process than SDM in large firms. This is one reason why scholars have argued that stressing the role of cognition has the potential to make a significant contribution to the studies of entrepreneurship (Baron, 1998; Mitchell et al., 2002). The cognitive approach offers multiple mechanisms, both theory driven and empirically robust, to build a better understanding of how we learn to see opportunities and further assess our skills and abilities along the entrepreneurial process (Barbosa et al., 2007). A first important stream of literature emphasizes the way in which entrepreneurs represent decision information and it also stresses the role of oversimplification played by the use of general cognitive heuristics. A core argument in the literature on entrepreneurial cognition is that the use of cognitive heuristics and biases enables fast decision-making (Busenitz and Barney, 1997; Busenitz, 1999; Keh et al., 2002) and this is a distinctive feature of entrepreneurial strategic decisions. A second stream of literature emphasizes the role of specific entrepreneurial traits (for example, risk-taking propensity, self-efficacy, need for achievement) on decision effectiveness and particularly on the decision to start a new venture. These specific entrepreneurial traits impact on the way in which entrepreneurs acquire, store, transform and use the decision-related information (Baron, 2004).

1.3 ENTREPRENEURS AND SMALL BUSINESSES

Strategic decision-making has been studied in a wide variety of settings, and has attracted widespread research attention from a broad array of scholars in different fields. Entrepreneurs are a particular category of strategic decision-makers, but a universally accepted definition of entrepreneurs is lacking (for example, Stewart and Roth, 2001). Entrepreneurs have, for instance, been deemed risk takers and rugged individualists (McGrath et al., 1992) and as being a breed apart (Ginsberg and Bucholtz, 1989). Yet other definitions have focused on founders of new ventures (for example, Begley and Boyd, 1987a) or owners of small businesses (Masters and Meier, 1988). Douglas and Shepherd (1999: 232) mention that entrepreneurs have been characterized as 'people who respond to opportunities for creating new products and services that arise due to technical progress'. In this book we shall stick to one of the most widely used definitions of an entrepreneur (Stewart and Roth, 2001), namely: 'an individual who establishes and manages a [small] business for the purposes of profit and growth' (Carland et al., 1984, in: Jenkins and Johnson, 1997: 895).

Entrepreneurs are a particular group of strategic decision-makers that are especially important for three reasons. First, in recent years, entrepreneurial ventures have been responsible for 65 per cent of the net employment growth in the US (Lyon et al., 2000). However, studies show that around 61 per cent of SMEs exit the market in their first five years and almost 80 per cent after 10 years (Camerer and Lovallo, 2000). These facts make the concept of SDM in SMEs of vast economic importance. Second, entrepreneurship has evolved into a broad field of research, attracting widespread research efforts from scholars in different fields (Jenkins and Johnson, 1997). Third, there is agreement on the clear need for explaining entrepreneurship from both a theoretical and a practical point of view (for example, Low and MacMillan, 1988), especially because most of the previous research on SDM focused on managers of large multinationals (Forbes, 1999).

From another perspective, the focus on entrepreneurs in SMEs is relevant because SMEs play a key role in the modern market economy and are fundamental to every prosperous economy. Individually, these enterprises do not have a major economic impact, but combined they play a key role in the modern market economy. They possess a number of advantages, which place them at the centre of the economic and social goals of society. They are believed to provide high employment rates, regional cohesion and sustainable development, diversification of the economy structure, social inclusion and new technologies for the knowledge-based society. Moreover, they tend to be innovative, introducing new products and services, and exploit new business opportunities (Brouthers et al., 1998). SMEs constitute at least 95 per cent of all businesses in the European Community (Storey, 1994). In 2006, nearly 3.8 million people worked for an SME in the Netherlands, about 300,000 more than work for large companies. SMEs in the Netherlands account for 99 per cent of all registered businesses.

In the entrepreneurship literature two specific features are identified concerning the context in which small entrepreneurial firms operate. First, it is argued that these firms often face a hostile or uncertain environment in their decision-making activities (Hambrick and Crozier, 1985; Covin and Slevin, 1989). Unlike managers in large firms, for instance, they do not have access to extensive information sources. Managers of large firms tend to be supported by staff members who continuously monitor the environment and gather information (Busenitz and Barney, 1997). Second, the environment of small firms is dynamic and complex (Covin and Slevin, 1991). As a result, entrepreneurs tend to simplify it and often they make decisions on the basis of cognitive heuristics (Busenitz and Barney, 1997). Furthermore, in a more dynamic and complex environment it is believed that the comprehensiveness (or rationality) of strategic decision processes tends to be lower (Fredrickson, 1984; Fredrickson and Mitchell, 1984) and cognitive issues become more important (Forbes, 1999). However, the degree of uncertainty, dynamism and complexity will vary to a large extent depending on the industry in which the small firm operates. Hence, not all small-firm owners operate under similar circumstances. The environment in which a small firm operates might affect the propensity to exhibit certain cognitive biases (Baron, 2004), which will affect decision-making processes. In line with previous research (Forbes, 1999; Gustafsson, 2006; Gibcus et al., 2008) we argue that there are indeed many different types of entrepreneurs and that we should further explore the cognitive differences among them.

1.4 OVERVIEW OF THE BOOK

This book has two main parts. Part I gives an overview of the decision-making literature. As such it provides the theoretical background for Part II, which contains the results of several empirical studies. Chapters 2, 3 and 4 set the stage by explaining some of the basic decision-making concepts. For those readers who are new to the field, we have deliberately provided more details on some of the key concepts in ESDM in the first part. More experienced readers might find these chapters useful to obtain an overview of the extant literature. We start with a brief survey of more rational approaches to decision-making in Chapter 2. In this chapter we also outline a strategic framework for decision-making. This framework consists of three components: the entrepreneur, the decision environment and the decision-making process, each of which is elaborated on. In Chapter 3 we turn to the psychological perspective on decision-making. This chapter provides an extensive overview of the factors related to ESDM, from personal attributes of the decision-maker to emotions and cognitive biases and heuristics. We also develop an integrative ESDM model based on dual information processing models of cognition. The model integrates personal attributes, cognitive factors and emotional reactions into a unitary framework of ESDM. Chapter 4 introduces the concept of cognitive complexity to the field of decision-making. The chapter gives both a conceptual account of the implications of cognitive complexity for ESDM as well as a method illustration, describing the cognitive mapping as a valid technique for eliciting and representing cognitive representations. We explain this important method in detail, since several of the empirical studies involve the role of cognitive complexity in decision-making processes.

After we have presented an overview of the decision-making literature and elaborated on cognitive complexity, we shall empirically investigate many of the issues discussed in Part I. In order to avoid unnecessary overlap in terms of the theory used, we have limited the theory sections in these chapters to the development of hypotheses since they all draw from the theory described in Part I. In Chapter 5, we present the results of an inductive qualitative study in which the decision-making process of entrepreneurs is described in detail. On the basis of a first pilot study the process is described in terms of three distinctive stages and two decision moments. A second pilot study is used to test four preliminary hypotheses. In Chapter 6 the cognitive dimension of the decision-making process is explored. On the basis of an existing taxonomy of types of entrepreneurs, the authors explore specific cognitive strategies used by different types of entrepreneurs when making strategic choices. Chapter 7 provides more insight into the relation between different types of entrepreneurs and the use of cognitive bias and heuristics (overconfidence bias and representativeness heuristic) in making strategic decisions. Chapter 8 explores the mediating roles of stakeholders' involvement in the relationship between perceived risk and uncertainty on the one hand and ESDM outcomes on the other. Chapter 9 describes two empirical studies that explore the mediating role of cognitive complexity in the relation between the demographic attributes of the entrepreneur on the one hand and ESDM outcomes and innovation on the other. Moreover, the chapter explores the detrimental role of general cognitive heuristics and biases for cognitive complexity in ESDM. Chapter 10 demonstrates the positive influence of social capital on cognitive complexity and explores the effect of these on the innovative performance of SMEs. Chapter 11 demonstrates the moderating role of industry dynamism in the relationship between cognitive complexity and risk taking in ESDM. Finally, Chapter 12 concludes the volume and discusses a set of nine key issues explored in the book, and presents proposals for future research in the vein of the theoretical arguments and empirical results presented so far.

PART I

Overview of the literature

2. The decision-making entrepreneur: a literature review

Petra Gibcus, Patrick A.M. Vermeulen and Elissaveta Radulova

2.1 RATIONALITY AND GENERAL DECISION THEORY

In this section we shall elaborate on the general theoretical approaches in decision-making from a rationality perspective. An important part of the literature on strategic decision-making assumes that it is an inherently rational process. 'Rationality is the reason for doing something and to judge a behaviour as reasonable is to be able to say that the behaviour is understandable within a given frame of reference' (Butler, 2002: 226). Economists equate rationality with utility maximization, an assumption in which individuals maximize their expected utility (Bell et al., 1988). This implies that decision-makers are able to choose the most optimal alternative and always strive for utility maximization, hence the decision-maker acts purely instrumentally. Rationality is strongly related to behaviour that is calculated and instrumental. Thus, rational behaviour is that type of behaviour which is sensible or logical in pursuing goals (Dean and Sharfman, 1993). There are different types of rationality distinguished in the literature. Noorderhaven (1995: 47) presents some of the most important:

- *Substantive rationality*: the alternative that is objectively best is chosen. No imperfections or logical errors are assumed.
- *Instrumental rationality*: the right means are chosen in relation to an end, given the decision-maker's belief system. Logical errors are not assumed, but the decision-maker's belief system does not necessarily correspond to objective reality (Walliser, 1989).
- *Procedural rationality*: the extent to which the decision process involves the collection of information relevant to the decision and the reliance upon analysis of the information in making the choice (Dean and Sharfman, 1996: 373). On the basis of available information, reasonable decisions are made.

The definitions presented in these types of rationality reflect the distinction between the rationality of the decision-making process and rationality concerning the outcome of the process. In the field of organization studies, Simon's concept of 'bounded rationality' has frequently been used to indicate that 'people act intentionally rational, but only limitedly so' (Simon, 1957: xxiv). In the remainder of this section we outline some of the key premises of classical, bounded and neoclassical rationality perspectives in decision theory.

Classical Rationality

Until the 1970s, the ruling paradigm was that of *homo economicus*, the 'rational economic man'. The classic theory of rational choice suggests that people are driven in their economic actions by pure rationality, hence are able in every given situation to rank their preferences with almost mathematical precision and to pursue the optimal outcome. Rational decision-making is choosing among alternatives in a way that 'properly' accords with the preferences and beliefs of an individual decision-maker. Shaver and Scott (1991) claim that behaviour is influenced by the way in which the external world is represented in the mind and by the individual's exercise of choice. Hence, according to the rational approach, once the characteristics of the environment are identified and studied, behaviour is easily predictable under the assumption of perfect rationality (Simon, 1979).

The theory of rational choice developed intensively during the first half of the 20th century. In particular, the theory of subjective expected utility and game theory were largely accepted as models of rational choice. Utility theory is a branch of decision theory concerned with measurement and representation of preferences. Models of this theory were elaborated in the economics literature by John von Neumann and Oskar Morgenstern (1944). Utility theorists focus on accounts of preferences in rational decision-making, where an individual's preferences cohere with associated beliefs and actions. 'Utility' refers to the scale on which preference is measured, thus the utilitarian definition of rationality is the maximization of 'utility' (Wilson and Keil, 2002). Game theory is a mathematical framework designed for analysing the interaction between several agents whose decisions affect one another. In a game-theoretic analysis, an interactive situation is described as a game: an abstract description of the players (agents), the courses of actions available to them, and their preferences over the possible outcomes. The game-theoretic framework assumes that the players employ rational decision-making, that is, they act so as to achieve outcomes that they prefer. Typically, preferences are modelled using numeric utilities, and players are assumed to be expected utility maximizers. Game theory is a tool that can be used to analyse strategic problems under the condition of a number of simplifying assumptions (Noorderhaven, 1995).

In the first half of the 20th century, rational theories of decision-making flourished, leaving no space for other explicative frameworks of the decision process. Managerial decision-making was considered to comprise nothing more than calculating the output of these normative models. While in reality the vast majority of managers do attempt to make optimal decisions, there are numerous impediments preventing them from actually doing so. The behavioural decision theory and cognitive psychology literatures have outlined numerous deviations from perfectly rational behaviour (Tversky and Kahneman, 1986; Poulton, 1994). One of these deviations is that people do not weigh probabilities linearly but tend to overweigh small and underweigh large probabilities (Tversky and Kahneman, 1992). This overweighing of small and underweighing of large probabilities implies diminishing sensitivity. Hence, increasing the positive probability of a new strategic move may explain the entrepreneurial actions despite the availability of obviously highly probable negative outcomes.

Bounded Rationality

Further anomalies of rational choice have been observed in nearly every aspect of economic activity (Simon, 1986). Consequently, at the beginning of the 1950s the foundations of rational decision theory began to crack. As the environment was uncertain and market conditions far from perfect competition, the model of bounded rationality emerged as an alternative to the classical rationality concept. The call of rationality to compare all the consequences of a certain choice was deemed infeasible, since it would require measuring the probability of all possible eventualities (ibid.). This requirement is too stringent to permit accurate description of the real behaviour studied in economics or psychology.

The limits of the classical approach are quite obvious, since the identification of all alternatives is impossible, given the intensively moving (and rapidly changing) factors of the environment. According to Simon (ibid.) economic agents do seek to maximize utility, but within limits posed by incompleteness and uncertainty of the information available. The notion of bounded rationality was born. It refers to the rationality that decision-makers with limited abilities (due to incompleteness and uncertainty of information) demonstrate. Furthermore, in order to cope with the not fully computable circumstances, decision-makers are able to adopt several approaches that all explain a mechanism of bounded rationality (Simon, 1979, 1986):

- to determine certain levels of preference and, as soon as a choice that satisfies the required criteria becomes available, to accept it. This mode looks for satisfactory choices, not for optimal ones;
- to simplify the complex, uncertain situation into smaller easily observable and controllable outcomes; and
- to delegate and distribute the decision tasks between several specialists who are able to grasp all the aspects of the issue.

Thus, the traditional paradigm of maximizing behaviour should be substituted for a more realistic notion of decision behaviour. The satisficing (combination of satisfactory and sufficient) principle asserts that people have only limited problem-solving capacities and often do not have the time, motivation, or ability to imagine all possible decision outcomes in advance. More specifically, decision-makers generally are not looking for the best or optimal, but for a satisfying solution of a decision task (March and Simon, 1993). Thus, they may try to simplify a complex decision by anticipating only a small part of all possible outcomes. The idea of satisficing behaviour of decision-makers demarcated a radical turn in decision theory. Decision-makers were no longer assumed to test all alternatives, but instead to set a level of aspiration and choose an alternative that matches this aspiration.

Moreover, the social psychology literature strongly emphasizes the view of persons as 'cognitive misers' (Fiske and Taylor, 1991), thereby suggesting that people try to minimize cognitive effort whenever possible. The view of people as 'cognitive misers', taken together with their more distinct sensitivity to changes than to non-changes, offers the hypothesis that decision-makers would be able to simplify the decision task by just anticipating gains or losses but ignoring non-gains or non-losses, that is, to be partial in their planning.

Neoclassical Rationality

The theory of 'bounded rationality' was studied and empirically tested by the followers of the neoclassical rational approach, who tried to overcome the gaps of the classical theory in order to create a new rational model. Since the mid-1970s, an increasing interest has been taken in the analysis of quasi-rational decision-making under uncertainty and risk. Several formal theories have been proposed, such as Tversky and Kahneman's (1986) prospect theory and regret theory (Savage, 1954; Bell, 1982). Prospect theory is a model of decision-making under risk that explicitly incorporates the cognitive errors that have been found to systematically occur in decision contexts. This theory asserts that people are especially sensitive to environmental changes, that is, persons adapt to the status quo, which serves as a neutral reference point, and then evaluate changes from this neutral reference point. If so, decision-makers may more easily anticipate gains and losses than non-gains and non-losses, because the latter do not constitute changes from their neutral reference point (Wilson and Keil, 2002). According to the adherents of prospect theory, decision-makers first form mental models of a certain situation in which they code outcomes in terms of gains and losses. Subsequently they assess the value of the outcomes on the basis of a value function and a weighting function after which they choose one of the alternatives (Noorderhaven, 1995).

Regret theory assumes comparisons between choices and captures anticipated regret and triumph when one learns that a different choice would have produced a better or worse outcome. Preferences in regret theory are defined with regard to actions rather than to prospects (Loomes and Sugden, 1982). Hence, the choice of a decision-maker depends not only on the outcome of certain actions, but also on the feeling of regret a decision-maker anticipates experiencing when he/she has made a choice and other potential outcomes that were not chosen are revealed (Leland, 1998). Furthermore, recent advancements in management information systems have increased the ability of managers to progress towards optimal decision-making by reducing the two constraints identified by Simon (1979): time (computational processing power) and memory (information storage and retrieval). Decision tools such as cost–benefit analysis, SWOT analysis, net present value technique and so on are associated with the neoclassical rational approach of decision theory.

2.2   AN ANALYTICAL FRAMEWORK OF STRATEGIC DECISION-MAKING

The notion of rationality also holds a central place in the literature on strategic decision-making (SDM) processes (Elbanna and Child, 2007). However, in order to fully understand rationality in decision-making processes, we need to understand the context in which it takes place. Most theories concerning the decision-making process (Mintzberg et al., 1976; Papadakis et al., 1998; Mador, 2000) gravitate around a model of decision-making that consists of three components: the environment, the specific characteristics of the decision to be taken and the entrepreneur him-/herself. These three components are in constant interaction while the path of the decision process is being followed. Papadakis et al. (1998) state that for understanding decision-making processes in-depth, an integrative

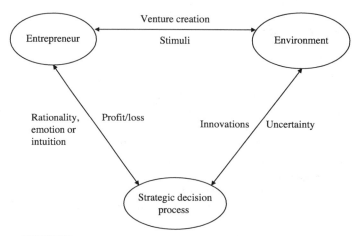

Source: EIM (2004).

Figure 2.1   A framework for entrepreneurial decision-making

model, which includes decision-specific, environmental and organizational factors, is needed. Likewise, Schneider and de Meyer (1991) state that the elements that are expected to influence strategic processes, are the manager's individual characteristics, internal organizational context and environmental factors. Hough and White (2003) argued that each of these contextual factors needs to be taken into account in order to present a complete and accurate picture of the strategic decision-making process. Whereas some of these authors adopted integrative models of strategic decision processes and studied the direct relationships between individual context variables and decision-making process rationality (Papadakis et al., 1998), Elbanna and Child (2007) investigated the overall impact of different contexts on strategic decision-making process rationality. In their study of Egyptian manufacturing companies, Elbanna and Child (p. 563) include decision-specific, environmental and firm characteristics, and indicate which of these perspectives receives the greatest empirical support when considered alongside one another.

From these integrated perspectives it is possible to distinguish three levels of analysis: the individual (the entrepreneur), the environment, and the strategic decision process itself as depicted in Figure 2.1. Such an analytical perspective is based on the same 'triadic reciprocity' mechanism that Bandura (1986) uses, in order to develop his concept of social cognitive learning. Similarly, in Figure 2.1 the three major elements constructing entrepreneurial decision-making are interlinked, and change in any of them reflects a change in the others (compare Bandura's reciprocal causation).

The entrepreneur influences the parameters of the strategic decision process according to the approach he/she adopts (rational, emotional or intuitive). The decision process, on the other hand, will affect the entrepreneur by bringing profit or loss to the business and will thus (possibly) reshape the entrepreneurial knowledge and experience. The entrepreneur influences the environment by the very act of venture creation and by further strategic decisions he/she makes. In the opposite direction, the environment is constantly forwarding impulses for entrepreneurial actions (opportunities, threats and so on). These environmental stimuli act as driving forces for the entrepreneur to make strategic decisions. The strategic decision process influences the environment by introducing advanced new methods of production or innovations (product or market novelties and so on), thus creating economic growth and market diversification. Conversely, the environment brings uncertainty and probabilities of negative outcome that shape the decision process and most often reflect satisfactory rather than optimal decisions.

An interesting question is which of the three elements is more deterministic on the final outcome, that is, whether the nature of the decision problem shapes the process more than the environmental and organizational context through which the process proceeds. According to Papadakis et al. (1998), it is the decision-specific characteristics that determine the final decision. However, they also concluded that decision-making rationality is affected by firm variables. This is in line with the results from the empirical study by Elbanna and Child (2007). Yet, Elbanna and Child's study also indicates that environmental variables add significantly to the prediction of variance in decision-making rationality, albeit less than decision and firm characteristics. In the following sections we review the contributions described in the literature for each of the three main factors determining entrepreneurial decision-making: the entrepreneur, the environment and the SDM process.

2.3 THE ENTREPRENEUR

Whether a new firm is established or not depends on the respective environment and on the founder – the entrepreneur. Usually the entrepreneur does not have perfect knowledge about all critical factors that drive an industry's development. Thus, he/she will have to bear certain risks. A new firm is born only if the dimensions of the perceived risk appear to be sufficient to enter a market and the expected economic future shows promising signals. The act of founding a firm depends on individuals' perceptions and on the evaluation of the current (micro- and macroeconomic) situation. Furthermore, the firm's economic success is determined by the individuals' resources and the specific managerial capabilities. In short, it all depends on the entrepreneur.

Different Types of Entrepreneurs

Although it has been recognized that there are different types of entrepreneurs (Birley and Westhead, 1993; Westhead and Wright, 1998; Wennekers and Thurik, 1999; Westhead et al., 2005a, b; Gustafsson, 2006), little systematic research has been conducted to categorize different types of entrepreneurs and subsequently relate these types to variations in decision-making practices (see Forbes, 1999). Much of the previous work on entrepreneurial typologies builds on the early classification of Smith (1967) who, on the basis of psychologoical traits, distinguished between craftsmen and opportunists. This conceptual distinction did not hold in several empirical studies. Furthermore, the predictive power and comparability of the typology developed by Smith was low (Woo et al., 1991). Gustafsson (2006) argues that the dissimilarity between entrepreneurs is not based on their personality, but instead on their behaviour.

In line with a more behavioural perspective, Gibcus et al. (2008) draw on a dataset derived from 646 owners of small businesses to derive and validate a taxonomy of five distinct types of small-firm owners with significant differences in their decision-making behaviour. They used a number of dimensions on which the owners could differ (frequency of decision-making, dependence on others, confidence, innovativeness, perceived risk, extent of information search, consideration of alternatives, problematic decision-making process and economic situation). The cluster analysis resulted in five types of entrepreneurs: Daredevils, Lone Rangers, Doubtful Minds, Informers' Friends and Busy Bees. Furthermore, a validation analysis was conducted in which it was shown that the five types differed on four other variables that they were likely to be distinct on: the amount of investment, type of decision, degree of radicalness of their innovations and cooperation with third parties. We describe each of the different types below:

1. *Daredevils*   As the label suggests, this type of entrepreneur perceives a high degree of risk in the decision and tends to make an above-average number of strategic decisions. Furthermore, they are above average in innovativeness, information search and consideration of alternatives. They are quite aware of potential problems and bottlenecks, but do not seem to be put off by them. Daredevils are thus best referred to as risk seekers, which is also evidenced by the fact that their decisions involve

cooperation with other firms, takeovers or radical innovation, which often involve substantial sums of money.

2. *Lone Rangers* This type of entrepreneur values his/her independence. Lone Rangers seem to dislike asking for advice or assistance in decision-making. They do not see many problems or bottlenecks that would impair their plans, nor do they find it important to search for information or consider alternatives. They know what to do and how to do it, and want to have it done their way. They do not engage in cooperation to the same extent as the other types.

3. *Doubtful Minds* In contrast to the Lone Ranger, the Doubtful Mind is not at all sure about his/her decision. In some sense, Doubtful Minds see themselves as victims of faith, given that they ascribe much importance to the economic situation. They also perceive a lot of problems and run through a number of alternatives before arriving at a decision. Their propensity to consider many alternatives seems to indicate that they would rather not make a decision. Insecurity about being able to pull it off might have something to do with this.

4. *Informers' Friends* Modesty seems to be the main characteristic of this type of entrepreneur. An Informers' Friend does not make many decisions and does not see the need to consider alternatives or introduce a radical innovation. The advice of others – family, friends, business acquaintances – seems to be sufficient to make them confident enough to make a decision. Perhaps for this reason, Informers' Friends do not perceive risks.

5. *Busy Bees* Compared to this type of entrepreneur, the others seem to be standing still. Busy Bees make an above-average number of decisions and are juggling many ideas for future strategic changes at any point in time. Just like Informers' Friends, they do not hesitate to throw these ideas back and forth with others. Moreover, they are also involved in radical innovations, introducing new ideas to industry products and services. Quite often, the investments involved in these efforts are rather large.

More-detailed descriptions of these five entrepreneurial types can be found in Chapter 6, in which it is explained in more detail how the different entrepreneurs think. In addition, Chapters 6 and 7 empirically examine the relation between these types of entrepreneurs and cognitive styles (Chapter 6) and explore the relation between the type of entrepreneur and the use of biases and heuristics (Chapter 7). It should be noted that the entrepreneurial types are defined on the basis of their most dominant features and the degree to which they score on certain variables. These are not absolute categories. Although Lone Rangers, for example, seem to dislike asking for advice or assistance in decision-making, the results from Gibcus et al. (2008) do not imply that Lone Rangers never ask for advice. Similarly, Informers' Friends are likely to ask other people for advice, yet they may not always do this.

The Functions of the Entrepreneur

Besides emphasizing differences between types of entrepreneurs, economists have frequently reported on who an entrepreneur is and what functions he/she performs in the economy. Different authors have suggested different answers to these questions. The entrepreneur was typically viewed as:

1. *Mediator*   Jean-Baptiste Say (1845) describes the entrepreneur as a 'combiner and coordinator of productive resources'. Based on his own practical experience, Say provided empirical descriptions of what entrepreneurs actually did. He viewed the entrepreneur as the 'principal agent of production' and the universal mediator between various classes of producers, and between producers and consumers (Hébert and Link, 1982). Say placed great emphasis on risk-taking entrepreneurs and even included them as the 'fourth' factor of production in his analysis (Casson, 1982).
2. *Arbitrageur*   The entrepreneur as arbitrageur comes from Israel Kirzner (1973). He points out that an entrepreneur is someone with the ability to perceive profit opportunities and act upon them. The 'pure' entrepreneur observes the opportunity to sell something at a price higher than that at which he/she can buy it. The entrepreneur recognizes and acts upon market opportunities. For Kirzner, 'the adjustment of price is the main role of the entrepreneur. If the wrong price prevails in the market then an opportunity for profit is created' (Casson, 1982: 369). In contrast to Schumpeter's (1934) viewpoint (see below), the entrepreneur moves the market towards equilibrium.
3. *Innovator*   Joseph Schumpeter (1934) believed that the market system has an inherent tendency towards change and that the dynamic attributes of capitalism were its most useful characteristics. The entrepreneur is a first mover whose function is to innovate. As such, the entrepreneur moves the market away from its equilibrium. According to Schumpeter, innovation is an outcome of new combinations. These new combinations are broad, including the introduction of new goods, new methods of production, the opening of new markets, or new organizations that define economic development. Similarly to Schumpeter, Drucker (1985) defines entrepreneurship as an act of innovation that involves adding a new wealth-producing capacity to existing resources.

4.   *Uncertainty bearer*   The uncertainty bearer is divided into two sub-groups. The first is that of a speculator. Richard Cantillon (1755 [1964]) was the first to introduce the term, 'entrepreneur' to economics (Casson, 1982). Cantillon's entrepreneur is a speculator, but he is more than a mere arbitrageur (buying low and selling high) because of the presence of uncertainty. According to Cantillon, entrepreneurs, in conducting their transactions, buy at a certain price and sell at an uncertain one. Cantillon's entrepreneur is 'someone who has the foresight and willingness to assume risk and takes the action requisite to making a profit (or loss)' (Hébert and Link, 1982: 17).

The second subgroup is of particular interest because it is that of the decision-maker. Frank H. Knight (1921) states that, in uncertain conditions, the decision-making function forecasts demand and estimates the factors' marginal productiveness. Entrepreneurs attempt to predict and act upon change within markets. Thus, according to Knight, entrepreneurs are more than a manager or actual productive service. They are entrepreneurs by virtue of their willingness to accept the results of a particular endeavour. Consequently, in their entrepreneurial decision, entrepreneurs do not know the potential economic outcome but experimentally try different combinations. Knight argues that entrepreneurs are 'recipients of pure profit', which is the 'reward to the entrepreneur for bearing the costs of uncertainty' (Casson, 1982: 370).

Shapero and Sokol (1982) summarize all of the above by suggesting that an entrepreneur is every economic agent who undertakes an 'entrepreneurial event'. This includes the performing of initiative taking (seizing a market opportunity), consolidation of resources (uses the existing resources new production combinations), management (of the organization and the organizational assets to the best of the venture), relative autonomy (resources are disposed of and distributed with relative freedom), and risk taking (the venture's success or failure is assumed by the entrepreneur). Casson also proposes an overall definition of entrepreneurship. For him there is no difference between the manager in a company and the entrepreneur. He claims that the key trait and differentiating criterion of entrepreneurship is judgement in decision-making. Judgement is a capacity for making a successful decision when no obviously correct model or decision rule is available or when relevant data are unreliable or incomplete. The entrepreneur described by Cantillon needs judgement to speculate on future price movements, while Knight's (1921) entrepreneur requires judgement because he/she deals in situations that are unprecedented and unique. Schumpeter's (1934) entrepreneur needs judgement to deal with the novel situations connected with innovation. The insights of

these economists can be synthesized into the following statement: entrepreneurs are specialists who use judgement to deal with novel and complex
problems (Casson, 1982).

Psychological Traits of Entrepreneurs

According to Brouthers et al. (1998) the personal characteristics of the
decision-maker influence the decisions taken. Hence, in small firms rationality is expected to decrease due to the strong personal influence of the
entrepreneur. Moreover, besides the entrepreneur's economic role, it is
important to study the psychological facets of the entrepreneurial personality in order to comprehend SDM in small and medium-sized enterprises
(SMEs).

Empirical surveys found it hard to prove that entrepreneurs possess psychological or any other type of statistically significant differences compared
with non-entrepreneurs (McClelland, 1961; Brockhaus, 1980; Schere 1982;
Low and MacMillan, 1988). Especially when examining risk propensity,
researchers found contradicting conclusions and were not able to show convincing support of whether entrepreneurs are risk takers or as risk averse as
other people. Nevertheless, there are some widespread beliefs about the
entrepreneurial psychology, which merit mention here in order to gain more
insight into how small-business managers meet strategic decisions.

The need for achievement
A significant psychological explanation of entrepreneurial acts is the need
for achievement. Shapero and Sokol (1982) talk about 'negative and positive' factors to start a business. Negative or 'push' factors include unem-
ployment and frustration. Among the positive or 'pull' factors, the need to
achieve or innovate, plus the desire to gain control over one's destiny are the
most important factors. Moreover, Brockhaus (1980) found empirical
support that the entrepreneurs who were initially driven by 'push' factors
have a higher failure rate. Furthermore, Shaver and Scott (1991) consider
the achievement motivation. From this perspective the main characteristic
of the business initiator is the high need for achievement, which they define
following McClelland (1961) as a preference for challenge, acceptance of
personal responsibility for outcomes and innovativeness. Papadakis et al.
(1998) also underline that the two core aspects of entrepreneurship are the
need for achievement and the attitude to risk.

Desire to be independent and to have control over situations
Much of the literature examining entrepreneurship appears to be guided by
the assumption that, like crime, entrepreneurial acts represent deviant

social behaviour (Campbell, 1992). But jumping into risky ventures could easily be explained by the need to be independent and to possess autonomy over one's work. Hornaday and Aboud (1971) reported that in comparison with men in general, entrepreneurs had stronger needs for achievement and a higher degree of desire for independence. McGrath et al. (1992) found that entrepreneurs agreed to a much larger extent than did career professionals on the statement: 'Success is owning your own company'.

Individualism

Further to the desire of independence, Sexton and Bowman (1985) state that entrepreneurs need autonomy and dominance and are not strongly influenced by needs for support from others or conformity to the norms of others. According to McGrath et al. (1992) entrepreneurs are rugged individualists. Their research confirmed the idea that entrepreneurs favour independent action and separation from groups and clans. This finding is consistent with Hofstede's results (1980), in which high individualism is associated with an emphasis on individual initiative and achievement. However, this does depend on the type of entrepreneur.

Locus of control

The concept of locus of control refers to a generalized belief that a person can or cannot control his or her own destiny. People can be classified along a continuum from very internal to very external (Rotter, 1966). Those who ascribe control of events to themselves are said to have an internal locus of control and are referred to as 'internals'. People who attribute control to outside forces are said to have an external locus of control and are termed 'externals' (Spector, 1992; Nwachukwu, 1995; Carver, 1997). Gilad (1982) notes that almost three decades of research consistently shows that internals are alert, discover opportunities and scrutinize their environment to find information needed to formulate the optimal approach to developing those opportunities.

Ability to focus and pursue a goal

In an empirical study on the predispositional cognitive abilities that are characteristic of entrepreneurs, Levander and Raccuia (2001) found support for the hypothesis that entrepreneurs possess different cognitive and executive abilities from non-entrepreneurs. Their level of attention deficit hyperactivity disorder (ADHD), that is, hyperactivity, was observed to be higher than 4 per cent (the average of an unselected population). ADHD individuals were found to be highly over-represented among the entrepreneurs (12 out of 32), thus, explaining entrepreneurs' innovation and creativity abilities. The results show that entrepreneurs differ cognitively from

the general population by a striking difference in the capacity to focus attention on a single task. Attention is defined as the individual reception to
environmental stimuli and the ability to process information (ibid.). Thus,
the survey concludes that it is the environmental stimuli and ADHD that
lead some individuals to react and to become entrepreneurs, motivating
them for higher performance.

Optimism
Entrepreneurial insight is seeing something about an industry or a market
that others miss or fail to understand (McGrath et al., 1992). But is it a true
opportunity that entrepreneurs see or do they simply inflate their 'gut
feeling' and sense of rightness to the point where they overlook critical elements and discount uncertainties? Palich and Bagby (1995) suggest that
entrepreneurs operate by a unique set of cognitive processes, thereby supporting their optimism. Furthermore, the literature on entrepreneurial
behaviour suggests that entrepreneurs are likely to be optimistic and that
they frequently make judgements based on subjective factors (Cooper et
al., 1988; Timmons, 1990; McCarthy et al., 1993). Excessive optimism
might lead to ignoring risks, which may lead to serious damage to the business and even to its complete failure.

Other findings on entrepreneurial personality
Lyon et al. (2000) consider that entrepreneurial behaviour can be described
as aggressive, innovative, proactive, risk taking, and autonomy seeking.
Stokes (1998) suggests that owner–managers tend to concentrate on the
day-to-day operations at the expense of the long-term strategy. Levander
and Raccuia (2001) warn that typical entrepreneurial features may negatively affect the process of strategic decision-making. These include the
entrepreneur's:

- impulsive character, that is, speed is preferred to accuracy (uncalcu-
  lated risk and carelessness);
- inability to change problem-solving strategies (low degree of
  flexibility); and
- inability to learn from mistakes (risk of vicious circle trap).

In addition to the above, Bazerman (1999) recognizes common behavioural traits and identifies 10 'important money mistakes' when making
decisions about money (or anything else). That is, entrepreneurs tend to be:

- *overconfident* when making decisions, trusting in established routines
  when they ought to be more wary of the efficacy of those routines;

- *unprepared* when making decisions, assuming that decisions fully reflect their knowledge and competence;
- *ignorant* of others' decision-making and motives, assuming that others share the same dispositions and attitudes;
- *exclusive*, assuming that their decisions are theirs alone, often failing to anticipate the interaction effects between themselves and others;
- *competitive*, wanting to win while believing that their decisions will mean that others' welfare will be somehow less as a consequence;
- *focused on the short term*, thereby discounting the long term in favour of immediate 'impulses';
- *focused upon immediate reference points* of value, ignoring the wider implications of any decision for their total well-being;
- *recursive* in the sense that one decision is the prelude for another decision and so on (decisions escalate);
- *ignorant of the alternatives*, while emphasizing what is immediately relevant and known from previous decisions; and
- *easily influenced* by 'big' events rather than by the causal structure of economic and financial processes that produce those events.

2.4   THE ENVIRONMENT

Successful decision-making requires an accurate understanding of the environment in which that decision will be played out. Without that understanding, it is impossible to assess the probable consequences and choose thoughtfully among them (Messick and Bazerman, 1996). SMEs act in a certain environment in which different stakeholders and forces are present (such as competitors, governmental agencies, customers, suppliers, investors and so on). Each of them has a more or less significant impact on SME performance by presenting opportunities and imposing threats on its activities. Hence, each firm has to decide about how to act in its environment and to somehow align its activities with surrounding actors. The decision environment is defined as the collection of information, alternatives, values and preferences available at the time of the decision (Harris, 1998). Ideal decision environments include accurate and all possible information sources, and every possible alternative. However, information and alternatives are always limited due to time and effort constraints to gain information or identify alternatives. The time constraint refers to the fact that decisions must be made at a certain time or the opportunity may have expired; the effort constraint reflects the limits of manpower, money and priorities (ibid.).

As it is almost impossible to have all the information needed to make a decision with certainty, most decisions involve an undeniable amount of risk. Many firms face an unstable business environment with high levels of uncertainty present (Dess et al., 1997). Improvements in information processing and telecommunications have led to major changes in most industries. Along with this, improvements in transportation and the growth of foreign economies (for example, in South-East Asia) have created a global marketplace and redefined certain industries. In addition, as consumers are exposed to more choices, loyalty has become less important than it once was: a slightly better deal elsewhere can easily result in loss of customers (Eisenhardt, 1989). Also, competitors can change rapidly, with new ones appearing from the other side of the world facilitated by globalization processes.

For those who remained self-employed, the rules of the game have also changed: everything has to be done yesterday. In the past, managers were acting under the general motto 'efficiency through stability'; in the contemporary environment it is transformed into 'survival through change' (Duncan, 1989). Turbulent developments cause rapid changes in the modern business reality and it is hard to find a reliable point of reference. Uncertainty, the inevitable element in entrepreneurial activities, is higher than ever and change is constant in the new economic landscape. According to Hamel (2000), the environment has changed radically: it no longer moves in a straight line; rather it is discontinuous, abrupt and seditious. Thus, firms have to constantly adjust their decisions to rapid developments.

Entrepreneurial Approaches to Overcome Uncertainty

In such extremely complex circumstances the use of cognitive biases in decision-making (see Chapter 3) may be justified: they may not only be the easier, but also the only possible way to deal with the turbulent environment. Busenitz and Barney (1997) claim that using biases and heuristics as simplifying mechanisms for dealing with these multiple problems may be crucial. More specifically, overconfidence may be particularly beneficial in implementing a specific decision and persuading others to be enthusiastic about it as well. There are two dominant notions about how decision-makers cope with uncertainty and hostile environments:

1. Environmental heterogeneity affects the strategic decision process characteristics such as rationality, and leads to greater use of cognitive simplification processes (Schwenk and Shrader, 1993). Hence, this hypothesis claims that in order to deal with the external pressure and

complexity, entrepreneurs seek to minimize their cognitive effort by creating 'short cuts' in their thinking (such as relying on intuition or routine). Another element of the same hypothesis is suggested by Loasby (1998). He argues that collecting information about all possible outcomes is too expensive, which leads decision-makers to reduce their costs by postponing decisions and then simplifying the postponed decisions. Consequently, this results in various forms of error.

2. Fredrickson and Iaquinto (1989) claim that planning is most likely to lead to increased performance in stable industries, but can be harmful in turbulent ones. Through several empirical studies the researchers prove that comprehensiveness (that is, rationality) exhibited a positive relationship with organizational performance in a stable environment and a negative relationship with performance in an unstable environment (see also Frese et al., 2000). Dean and Scharfman (1996) also reported results showing the positive impact on planning in stable industries. In their survey, Papadakis et al. (1998) found no convincing support for any of the theses.

To predict how decision-making is influenced by environmental developments, it is critical to understand how individual entrepreneurs process and interpret these developments. With respect to their environment, a central issue in analysing entrepreneurs' behaviour is their ability to process information and their risk propensity. Although these issues are explained in much more detail in the next chapter, we introduce them here to cover the environmental context of entrepreneurial strategic decision-making.

Entrepreneurial risk propensity

Psychologically, people prefer a reasonably deterministic world in which there are known explanations for things that happen (Messick and Bazerman, 1996). In decision-making, however, there is always some degree of uncertainty in any choice. In this context, Knight (1921) claims that every effective exercise of judgement is coupled with a corresponding degree of uncertainty bearing, of taking the responsibility for the selected course of action. According to him, the very essence of free enterprise is the concentration of responsibility in its two aspects of making decisions and taking the consequences of decisions when put into effect.

Very few studies have shown statistically significant differences between entrepreneurs and non-entrepreneurs in their risk-taking propensity (Brockhaus 1980; Low and MacMillan, 1988). Nevertheless, this individual psychological trait continues to be discussed as an important variable for understanding entrepreneurial behaviour. Palich and Bagby (1995) defend the idea that entrepreneurs do not differ from other people in respect to their risk propensity. Rather, they react differently to environmental stimuli, especially when the data are equivocal. Entrepreneurs are more capable of processing and storing ambiguous data, thus perceiving equivocal business scenarios more positively than others. Hence, it is not their risk propensity, but their different cognitive processes that make entrepreneurs more optimistic about certain business ventures. Furthermore, Palich and Bagby found empirical support for the theses that when presented with identical situations, entrepreneurs will categorize them as having more strengths, opportunities and potential for gain than non-entrepreneurs. Most importantly, their study provides evidence that entrepreneurs simply tend to associate business situations with cognitive categories that suggest more favourable attributes when the environmental data are equivocal, that is, exactly as in the case of the contemporary high turbulent business environment with its high degree of uncertainty.

Forlani and Mullins (2000) also studied the risks incarnated in entrepreneurial ventures but their thesis is slightly different. According to them, risk propensity appears to directly impact on venture choice behaviour, rather than indirectly affecting behaviour through the perceptual process. The researchers found empirical support for the following hypotheses:

- the greater the variability in predicted outcomes of a proposed new venture, the greater will be its perceived risk and the less likely it will be selected for funding;
- the greater the magnitude of a proposed new venture's largest potential loss, the greater will be its perceived risk;
- the greater the risk propensity of the entrepreneur, the less will be the perceived risk associated with a particular new venture;
- the greater the risk propensity of the entrepreneur, the more likely he or she will be to select new ventures having higher levels of risk.

Furthermore, Forlani and Mullins tried to identify the elements of the perceived venture risk by entrepreneurs, claiming that the central factors taken into account are the hazard incorporated into the venture (if things go wrong how much can be lost, the potential loss) and the variability in the anticipated outcomes of the venture (the probability of actual returns deviating from the expected return or outcome).

Entrepreneurial information processing

Entrepreneurs are faced with a rapidly changing competitive environment, which emphasizes the need for the swift interpretation of opportunities and threats in strategic decision-making (see Dess et al., 1997). At the same time, today's rapidly changing markets offer little assurance that a decision will not soon be found to be inappropriate or obsolete (Dickson, 1992). Probably the most important impact of modern environmental complexity on enterprises is the intensification of information and communication processes. Information became the most sophisticated modern weapon to defeat competition. Some authors even call it a fourth production factor (Loasby, 1976). However, the immense number of new opportunities are only one side of the coin. The process could also represent a real threat for some enterprises. Information flows are so intense and so diverse that for most companies it is hard to distinguish between relevant and irrelevant data. As much as the Internet helps businesses, it could also be a dangerous source of disinformation. The phenomenon of 'immediatization' (pressure for multitasking performance) makes the problem even more complicated (Eisenhardt, 2000). Most entrepreneurs face difficulties in selecting the correct information and making a decision in the short term.

As time passes, the decision environment continues to grow and expand. New data and new alternatives appear. Ideally, more information should enable the decision-makers to assess more precisely the probabilities on possible outcomes. However, Zacharakis and Meyer (1998) state that additional data even when relevant make the decision more complex. Even if more information is available, people usually do not analyse all of it, although they think they do (Zacharakis and Shepherd, 2001). Furthermore, the phenomenon of information overload should also be taken into consideration. People often have problems selecting and processing the needed data from the constantly intense environmental flows (Loasby, 1998). Mental fatigue occurs, which results in slower work or poor work quality. This could lead to fast, careless decision-making or even decision-paralysis – no decisions are made at all (Harris, 1998). According to Mador (2000), the process of information gathering and analysis in SMEs is often chaotic and opportunistic.

2.5 THE PROCESS OF STRATEGIC DECISION-MAKING

Decision-making is a multistage and multicriteria process (Hall and Hofer, 1993), which is non-linear and recursive. That is, most decisions are made by moving back and forth between the set of criteria (the characteristics that the final choice has to meet) and the identification of alternatives (the possible outcomes to choose from). The process of decision-making has been conceptualized in many different ways (for example, Mintzberg et al., 1976; Harrison, 1987; Nutt, 1993, 2002). What can be derived from the literature is a variety of phases that decision-makers go through. These include the collection of information, establishing a direction that indicates a desired result, a systematic search for ideas, the evaluation of these ideas in the light of the direction chosen, and implementation of preferred ideas (Nutt, 2002). Before we elaborate on the different phases in the decision-making process, we first describe some of the most influential decision-making process models.

We have selected four popular theoretic models of the decision-making process, which reflect some of the core assumptions of the decision theories reviewed earlier. Rational choice is somewhat incorporated in the 'elimination-by-aspects' (EBA) model, and bounded rationality is depicted by the satisficing model. Furthermore, the models of Mintzberg et al. (1976) and Mintzberg and Westley (2001) represent a detailed framework of the stages in making a strategic decision.

Theoretic Models of the Decision-Making Process

Tversky's EBA model

According to Tversky (1972), choice is a sequential elimination process. He illustrates his argument by presenting an alternative as a set of aspects of characteristics. At each stage in the process, one attribute is selected from those included in the available alternatives. The selection of this specific attribute automatically eliminates all the alternatives that do not have this attribute. This process continues until a single alternative remains. When a selected attribute is included in all the alternatives, a new attribute is selected. For example, when considering the purchase of a new computer, the first aspect considered important could be a minimum storage capacity of the hard disk of 1000 GB. All computers with less storage capacity would be eliminated. Given the remaining alternatives, another aspect might be the choice for a laptop over a desktop, which would eliminate all desktops. The purchaser might also set a price limit, which would further eliminate several alternatives. The process continues until one alternative remains and all other computers are eliminated. In doing so, the decision-maker gets closer and closer to the desired goal until its final achievement.

Simon's satisficing model

Simon (1979) suggests an even simpler strategy: satisficing. The 'satisfactory' decision-making rule or heuristic is a two-step rule. First, the decision-maker forms some kind of aspiration that reflects the minimal acceptable level of each relevant attribute that is to be looked for. When the decision-maker comes across the alternative that meets the minimal standards (the aspiration), the search will be ended by choosing that alternative.

The main distinction between Tversky's and Simon's models is that EBA is a negative strategy while 'satisficing' is a positive strategy. In EBA, decision-makers try to eliminate options, whereas Simon's model works under the assumption that decision-makers accept an alternative that reaches minimum levels of aspiration.

Mintzberg et al.'s model of unstructured decision processes

Indisputably, the most integrative and popular attempt to create a descriptive framework of the decision-making process in literature belongs to Mintzberg et al. (1976). In their well-known study of 25 strategic decision processes across a range of organizations, the scientists suggest that there is a basic structure underlying these 'unstructured' procedures. The theorists define the characteristics of strategic decision process as novel, complex and open ended with decisions not so much made under uncertainty, but within a continuous state of ambiguity, where almost nothing is given or easily determined. Their proposed model illustrates that while strategic decisions are immensely complex and dynamic, it is possible to give them conceptual structuring.

Mintzberg et al. argue that the structure can be described by seven elements comprising three 'central phases' (identification, development and selection), three sets of 'supporting routines' (decision control, decision communication and political) and six sets of 'dynamic factors' (interrupt, scheduling delays, timing delays and speedups, feedback delays, comprehension cycles and failure recycles). The general model describes the interrelationships among them and the decision processes studied are shown to fall into seven types of 'path configurations'. Three decision stimuli sit in a continuum, namely 'opportunities' (voluntary decisions to improve a secure position) at one end, 'crises' (decision responses to intense pressures) at the other and 'problems' in the middle, each capable of integrating or moving along the continuum.

Mintzberg and Westley's three-axis model

It is disputable whether entrepreneurs follow to the letter the pattern that Mintzberg et al. (1976) propose. Because it was created in the 1970s (that is, by its very nature based on rational assumptions) this model does not take into consideration many cognitive anomalies of rational choice. This has led Mintzberg to revise his point of view to a certain extent (Mintzberg and Westley, 2001). Without denying the rational approach, the researchers defend the thesis that the conventional rationality is no longer the only advisable way to determine the desired course of action. Good decisions are the output of careful analytical thinking combined with two other possible 'ingredients' of decision-making, namely intuition and proactive behaviour. Consequently, Mintzberg and Westley claim that there are three approaches to meeting a strategic decision:

1. *Thinking first (rational)*   When the prerequisites needed to make a decision are partly unknown or too complex, decision-makers try to structure the initial endowments and to classify them according to their previous experience and knowledge (Loasby, 1998). Hence, they adjust new circumstances to old decision situations and apply the same techniques as previously used (re-usage of knowledge). This rational way of decision-making consists of a clearly identified process: define–diagnose–design–decide. Such an approach could be extremely dangerous in the contemporary business environment where market characteristics change rapidly and require constant change. 'Relying on autopilot' may guide entrepreneurs to the 'boiled frog' situation (Bankova, 1991).

2. *Seeing first (intuitive)*   Intuition is a sophisticated form of reasoning based on 'chunking' that an expert hones over years of job-specific experience (Prietula and Simon, 1989). Eisenhardt (1989) argues that intuition is related to the continuous engagement in the details of business, and is therefore related to firm success. Eisenhardt and Zbaracki (1992) refer to intuition as the more incremental adaptations that are based on deep and intimate knowledge of a certain situation. Intuition is not emotion; it is a subconscious, complex, fleeting and unbiased state (Khatri and Ng, 2000). It is not the opposite of rationality, nor is it a random process of guessing, but rather a complementing path to come to a decision. According to Khatri and Ng, intuition is connected to experience and expertise. They propose three indicators of intuition: reliance on judgement, reliance on experience and the use of gut feeling. Mintzberg and Westley (2001) link it with deep knowledge, usually developed over years, followed by a period of incubation, during which the unconscious mind mulls over the issue; at a certain moment there is a flash of illumination. That eureka moment often comes after sleep – because in sleep, rational thinking is turned off, and the unconscious has greater freedom; the conscious mind returns later to make the logical argument. 'Seeing first' is a subconscious manner of decision-making, which requires a significant amount of prior experience. Here Mintzberg and Westley follow the Gestalt psychology developed by Graham Wallas in the 1920s, which identifies four steps in creative discovery: preparation, incubation, illumination and verification.

3. *Doing first (action-oriented)*   If rationality is helpless and strategic vision is not present, Mintzberg and Westley advise simply to 'jump

into the pool' and to undertake an action. The feedback of the action will direct the further steps. Thus, 'doing first' is a way to evaluate possible alternatives, to see which one suits the organization best and continue following it. It is strongly based on learning from experience. This approach is advisable when the situation is novel and confusing, and things need to be worked out. Mintzberg and Westley (p. 91) argue that decision-makers need to find out what works, make sense of that and then repeat successful behaviour while discarding the rest. They build on Weick's (1979) organizing model which consists of enactment, selection and retention. Enactment is the process in which individuals create an image of their environment. Selection refers to the process that leads to a choice for an alternative among many possibilities. Those choices that are most useful and successful are retained in the form of rules and routines.

Mintzberg and Westley argue that an integrative and successful decision-making process should rely on all three axes. However, there is little empirical research that supports this view. Compared to the literature on rational decision-making, there are few empirical studies on intuitive processes of SDM (Elbanna, 2006) and even fewer on action-oriented decision-making. Khatri and Ng (2000) conducted an empirical study about the role of intuition in SDM. Furthermore, in a study of entrepreneurial personality, Levander and Raccuia (2001) demonstrated that rationality has a lower priority than instinct in shaping entrepreneurs' behaviour. Most empirical studies that have included the role of intuition in decision-making processes are initial attempts to clarify the potential impact of intuition. Bourgeois and Eisenhardt (1988) and Eisenhardt (1989) demonstrated that intuition played a role in increasing the speed of strategic decisions. However, the small sample sizes and a focus on specific industries do not lend themselves to generalizing the promising results of this stream of research (see Elbanna, 2006). More research is needed in each of these areas.

Steps in the Decision-making Process

The different steps in the decision-making process have already been described. In the remainder of this chapter we shall describe each of the steps in more detail. We draw from the works of Mintzberg et al. (1976) and Noorderhaven (1995) who have described the various steps in the decision-making process. Note that some of these steps might not be directly observable in entrepreneurial decision-making (see also Chapter 5). Yet, we have chosen to elaborate on a 'complete' description of the decision-making process, giving ample attention to each of the steps.

Recognition

This first step marks the beginning of the decision-making process. Decision-makers notice certain weak signals in their environment (Noorderhaven, 1995). Here, the need to make a decision becomes visible as a difference between certain actual situations and some expected standards or goals. Thus, the entrepreneur realizes that a key moment has come and action has to be taken. Recognition depends on the way information is gathered and processed in the entrepreneurial mind and by the environmental characteristics (encouraging or restrictive). Whether decision-makers notice these signals also depends on the available time. Whereas managers in large firms might be backed up by specialized departments, entrepreneurs in SMEs normally lack these resources and are left with only their available time.

The initial interpretation of signals is important for the other steps in the decision-making process (ibid.). Decision-makers often think in terms of threats and opportunities. An entrepreneur who sees an opportunity is likely to respond differently from one who receives the same signal and identifies it as a potential threat (Smircich and Stubbart, 1985). How these signals are interpreted not only depends on the individual, but is also socially influenced. Entrepreneurs might consult with friends, family or ask the advice of consultants. They may also look at their competitors and make their own interpretation. The mere fact that a certain issue is detected does not mean, however, that it is correctly understood (Noorderhaven, 1995).

Formulation

While recognizing that a strategic issue or problem is important, the exact formulation of the problem is equally important and needs to be done with great care. The formulation determines what and who will be involved in the decision-making process (Nutt, 1993). In this stage, the entrepreneur seeks to comprehend the evoking stimuli and to determine the cause–effect relationships for the decision situation. Existing information channels are reviewed and new ones found in order to clarify the issues and get the necessary information into the formulation process. Determination of the scope is critical here (Noorderhaven, 1995). Issues that are formulated too broadly lack focus and fail to direct attention, whereas those that are defined too narrowly may lead to restricted search. In this way, accurate problem formulation is a means to set a direction. Either the direction can be more opportunistic and 'latch onto a ready-made idea found' in the identified problem or 'it can identify a need embedded' in the problem and offer an objective (Nutt, 2002: 43). In the case of need-based directions, decision-makers examine the rationale for action and set a specific target in terms of results required. When decision-makers are opportunistic they will opt for ready-made solutions.

Exactly how problems or strategic issues are formulated partly depends on the origin and background of the person who identified them in the first place. Firms tend to categorize problems in terms of their internal structure (Noorderhaven, 1995). This implies that problems will be formulated differently depending on whether they were recognized first by, for example, marketing, legal or product development departments. People differ in the way they perceive information and interpret situations. In their classic book on organizations, March and Simon (1958) claimed that specialization affects the information people receive. When organizational members conduct a specific task it is likely that this will affect their frame of reference and the perceptions on their environment. As Vennix states: 'a production manager "sees" different problems than a financial manager, and a RandD manager "sees" different problems than a personnel manager' (1996: 15). People interpret situations in their own way, depending on their mental models or interpretative schemes. These models or schemes are developed over a long period and are influenced by a person's background (social and educational) and the direct environment of the individual (see, for instance, Daft and Weick, 1984; Dougherty, 1992). These schemes are the knowledge bases by which individuals interpret information and frame problems.

Search

This stage is devoted to finding solutions, that is, to identify the available alternatives. This is a hierarchical, stepwise process of alternative seeking. Cyert and March (1963) hypothesize that search begins in immediately accessible areas, with familiar sources. Initial failure in search also leads to the use of more active search procedures in more remote areas (Mintzberg et al., 1976). The nature of the search process largely depends on the nature of the problem. Some problems call for simple-minded search processes, whereas others need considerably more resources and a search that resembles a more active process of finding new and better solutions (Noorderhaven, 1995). If ready-made solutions cannot be found, the decision-maker is likely to engage in design activities that will lead to custom-made solutions (Mintzberg et al., 1976). Here the decision-makers either modify available alternatives or create alternatives that do not yet exist. According to the approach used in this stage, the final decisions are classified as: ready-made (adopted from an existing alternative in the environment); modified (when a ready-made solution is developed to fit the particular situation); or custom-made (when a solution is invented especially in order to meet the decision criteria).

Evaluate

Thus, from the previous steps the decision-maker has derived a set of alternatives. In order to be able to evaluate the various options, the decision-maker has to set criteria that the ideal decision should meet and eliminate the infeasible solutions (ibid.). The decision-maker considers the negative (cost, consequences, problems created, time needed and so on) and the positive (money won, time saved, added creativity, or happiness to customers and so on) characteristics of each alternative. A great number of factors have to be observed, most of them 'soft' or non-quantitative. This is how elements of bounded rationality intervene in the decision-making process. Being the most powerful and often the only decision-maker, the entrepreneur often transfers his/her cognitive biases into the decision-making process at this stage. Thus, the information collected about each alternative should include costs, benefits, risks and acceptance in order to judge the full merits of each one (Nutt, 2002). Due to time and cost limitations, the evaluation process tends to have a more sequential nature, meaning that first a single option is developed and considered before other options are taken into account. When the first option is rejected, the process will continue to evaluate other options.

Noorderhaven (1995: 31–2) presents two evaluation models that are concerned with evaluating ideas on more than one criterion: compensatory and non-compensatory. In compensatory models, the scores on the various attributes are combined into an overall score. A low score on one criterion can be compensated by a high score on another. In non-compensatory models, there is no attempt to combine scores on different criteria. A variety of non-compensatory models exist, such as conjunctive models (the decision-maker sets a minimum score for each criterion and one by one each option is evaluated on all criteria) and the lexicographic model (criteria are arranged in order of importance and all alternatives are evaluated against the most important one). Whatever mode of evaluation is chosen, it is possible that decision-makers use any one of these automatically, without being aware of the limitations. The choice for an evaluation model can, however, also be a strategic means to manipulate the outcome of the decision process (Noorderhaven, 1995).

Choice

There are different routines for choosing an alternative. Mintzberg et al. (1976: 258) distinguish three different modes: judgement, bargaining and analysis. In judgement, a decision-maker makes a choice in his/her own mind with procedures that he/she does or cannot explain. Bargaining refers to a selection process made by a group of decision-makers with conflicting goals. In the analysis mode, there is a factual evaluation, followed by managerial choice by judgement or bargaining. According to Mintzberg et al., judgement is the most favoured mode of choosing an alternative, perhaps because it is fast, convenient and least stressful. The actual choice of an alternative depends on many different factors, some hard, some soft.

The somewhat artificial distinction between evaluation and choice (Mintzberg et al. combine these in an evaluation–choice routine) results from the fact that the most optimal alternative is not always selected. There may be political reasons for not choosing the best alternative. In organizations this frequently happens (Noorderhaven, 1995). However, it is also possible that the best alternative is rejected because it does not 'feel good' (Janis, 1989: 72). Whatever choice is being made, it indicates a clear commitment to action. The final step in the decision-making process is the actual implementation of the decision.

Implementation

When a decision for a specific alternative has been made, it is the actual implementation of that choice that probably has the largest impact on an organization in terms of resources, time and energy (Harrison, 1987). There are various ways of implementing decisions. Stakeholders should be involved somewhere in the process to increase acceptance of the decision. Involvement seduces stakeholders to go along with the decision (Nutt, 2002). Other ways of implementing decisions successfully are by using persuasive arguments to 'sell the decision to others by dramatizing its alleged benefits' (ibid.: 44). Decision-makers need to choose when to 'start' the implementation of their decision. It can be initiated in an early stage by using participation in order to increase acceptance. When decision-makers choose to follow a persuasion tactic, it is likely that implementation will be started as a final step in the decision-making process.

There are several potential caveats in the implementation stage (Noorderhaven, 1995). First, there may be resistance to the implementation of the decision. Decisions that have a strong impact on an organization are especially likely to be resisted by some groups. The decision-maker should be aware of potential resisters in order to avoid the risk of failure. Second, it can take a long time between the decision and the actual implementation. In today's dynamic and complex environments, it is necessary to act swiftly. The decision might no longer fit the current situation if too much time has elapsed. Third, especially in larger firms, decisions should be backed by senior management. There is a risk that they might lose interest in the issue at hand. When top managers have a strong preference to focus on new issues at the expense of old problems, their decisions will have limited impact on the organization (ibid.: 34).

2.6   SOME EMPIRICAL INSIGHTS

Unfortunately, there are not many existing surveys conducted on entrepreneurial decision-making in a later stage of the business. Most of the
research is concentrated on the 'entrepreneurial act', hence, on the motivation of founding a business (start-up decision-making). Nevertheless, these
results could be considered as applicable to the current research because
SDM at a later stage of the business development is somewhat similar to
new venture creation. Strategic decisions, which lead to a turning-point in
the development of small firms, such as entering a new market or introducing a new product, usually involve high levels of uncertainty comparable to those of establishing a firm in the first place. Thus, it is reasonable to
assume that starting entrepreneurs are susceptible to the same pressures as
entrepreneurs who already have certain experience.

Are Entrepreneurs Rational in Their Decision-making?

The strategy process focuses on the formulation and implementation of the
strategic decision, and is connected to formal planning (detailed business
plan elaboration). In an empirical study, Olson and Bokor (1995) observed
that half of the examined small, fast-growing enterprises did not develop
an initial formal plan. Moreover, Levander and Raccuia (2001) found that
entrepreneurs often deal with a situation without planning in advance,
which decreases firm performance when they are confronted with more-
complex problems. Busenitz and Barney (1997) argue that entrepreneurs
simply do not have the time to conduct a thorough, rational decision-
making process. They also claim that more extensive use of heuristics in
SDM may be a great advantage during the start-up years. Papadakis et al.
(1998) observed that strategic decisions for new business investments and
marketing activities seem to be subject to a less-comprehensive analysis
than strategic decisions on capital investment and internal reorganization.
Furthermore, Frese et al. (2000) found proof that an opportunistic strategy
might be a useful approach to deal with uncertainty until the decision-
makers become familiar with the industry and the specifics of the market,
hence in the beginning of the business history.

Van Gelderen et al. (2001) observed that complexity of the environment
will lead to increased use of complete planning, but changeability of the
environment will lead to less frequent use of rationality. Furthermore,
changeability of the environment will lead to the increased use of an opportunistic strategy, and a lack of munificence in the environment will lead to
an extensive use of reactive strategies. Nevertheless, it is more advisable to
use a planning strategy when the firm becomes larger and when the owner

has a better grasp of the operative business conditions (Frese et al., 2000). Moreover, Frese et al.'s survey shows that small-business owners in the Netherlands have a high uncertainty avoidance (hence preference for detailed planning) score, similar to that in Germany. Finally, Brouthers et al. (1998) claim that larger small firms, in terms of both sales and number of employees, are significantly more rational than the smaller small firms. According to their empirical findings, small firms tend to gravitate around the average rates of rationality. However, their results also demonstrate that personal characteristics play a role in decreasing rationality.

Most Common Factors Influencing the Entrepreneurial Strategic Decision

It is difficult to identify the factors that influence human decision-making in general, as this is an individual cognitive process that is hard to track while it occurs. Thus, researchers have to rely on post hoc analysis of the strategic decision (typically interviews with the decision-makers). This is not necessarily a reliable strategy because people tend to overstate the information they relied upon and use far less information (typically five to seven factors) to make a decision than they actually think they use (Zacharakis and Meyer, 1998). Ex post facto data could be biased by inaccuracies in the recall ability of the entrepreneurs (Hall and Hofer, 1993).

Nonetheless, a significant amount of research is dedicated to identifying what firm-based factors lead small-business owners to take their first steps towards developing and expanding their business. According to Wells (1974), the entrepreneur's abilities and the abilities of the entrepreneurial team are decisive in the SDM process: their background, previous experience and level of commitment. Tyebjee and Bruno (1984) claim that the size of the investment, cash-out potential, geographic location and product differentiation are most influential for the strategic choice. According to Papadakis et al. (1998), the decision-specific characteristics influence the decision-making process more than any other environmental, organizational, or managerial factor.

Furthermore, Mullins (1996) claims that prior performance and firm competency are among the significant decision criteria that direct the strategic course of action. He argues that under conditions of better prior performance and a higher level of firm competency, direct market responses are less likely to occur. Consequently, under conditions of poorer prior performance and a higher level of firm competency, direct market responses are more likely to occur.

Frese et al. (2000) argue that entrepreneurs use the approach of concentrating on the most difficult, most unclear, and most important issues first. Only after solving this first critical point are further steps planned.

Furthermore, following a very rational approach, Campbell (1992) claims that the entrepreneurs elaborate very formal cost–benefit analysis of the potential benefits and compare them with the alternative costs, and if the expected net present benefits are positive, the strategic decision would be implemented.

2.7 CONCLUSION

This chapter has provided an overview of the literature on decision-making in general and entrepreneurial decision-making in particular. We first introduced the notion of rationality and general decision theory. We discussed classical rationality, bounded rationality and neoclassical rationality models of decision-making. Next, we presented an analytic framework of SDM in SMEs. This framework consisted of three elements: the entrepreneur, the environment and the strategic decision process. Each of these elements was subsequently examined on the basis of a literature review. Finally, we presented some empirical findings on entrepreneurial strategic decision-making as discussed in the extant literature.

In this chapter we have tried to focus on entrepreneurs as much as possible. It should be noted, however, that less attention has been paid to individual entrepreneurs in much of the decision-making literature. For example, most of the process descriptions are derived from studies in which managers (in large firms) and policy makers are the unit of analysis. Exactly how these processes discover entrepreneurs, while it is often acknowledged that they are somewhat different from managers, has not been clarified in the literature. In Chapter 5, Gibcus and van Hoesel try to fill that gap by closely studying the decision-making process of entrepreneurs.

3. The psychology of entrepreneurial strategic decisions

Petru L. Curşeu, Patrick A.M. Vermeulen and René M. Bakker

3.1 INTRODUCTION

We make choices every day. Some of them are trivial (for example, choosing between wearing the black or the brown shoes), while others bear major consequences for ourselves or for others around us (for example, deciding to relocate a business). For some of our decisions we can estimate with relative certainty the probability of the outcomes associated with all the alternatives we consider, whereas for others it is impossible to do so. In some of our choices we use already existing strategies or heuristics, while in others we search for additional information and even create new alternatives by combining that which we already know. Some choices are based on routines triggered by repetitive stimuli, whereas others we label 'strategic'; those which often involve the planning of actions in an uncertain and unpredictable future. The question that arises is, what renders a decision strategic? Is it the importance of its consequences, the amount of knowledge required to make a choice, the procedures used to decide, or all of them together? In principle, the literature on strategic decision-making (SDM) agrees that strategic decisions involve a commitment of large amounts of organizational resources in order to attain organizational goals through appropriate means. Although the SDM process has been extensively studied in large companies, in small and medium-sized enterprises (SMEs) little to no attention has been shown to how entrepreneurs decide in high-stake situations. The main aim of this chapter is to shed light on the specificities of entrepreneurial strategic decision processes.

Strategic decision-makers in SMEs (the entrepreneurs) bear the ultimate responsibility for their strategic choices (thus labelled: entrepreneurial strategic decision-making – ESDM) and are often the only agents involved in the decision process. This personal involvement and responsibility increases the relevance of the factors related to the decision-maker for the decision-making process. A consistent body of literature has explored the personal attributes and characteristics that impact on decision-making effectiveness, and several attitudinal (for example, risk taking), motivational (for example, self-esteem), emotional (for example, anticipated affect, post-decision affect) and cognitive (for example, cognitive styles, heuristics and biases) factors have been demonstrated to impact on the way people decide. A consistent body of literature argues that these traits are also distinctive features of entrepreneurs, increasing their relevance for ESDM. Moreover, strategic decisions due to the high complexity involved are a particular form of decisions, in which decision-makers tend to focus on alternatives with high emotional relevance, are more sensitive to heuristics and biases in estimating probabilities of events and are more likely to focus on established social norms. Therefore, we argue that there are two major arguments for exploring entrepreneurial decisions as a particular form of decisions: (i) the specific characteristics of the decision-makers involved in ESDM and (ii) the constraints imposed by the high level of complexity of the decision situation.

This chapter is structured as follows. First, we briefly explore the mainstream literature on ESDM, and describe the specific task characteristics involved in strategic choices and entrepreneurs as a group of decision-makers sharing a set of stable attributes. Next, we give a detailed account of the most relevant studies that have addressed both the personal attributes as well as the task characteristics of strategic decisions. Finally, the chapter concludes with an integrative discussion of all these factors. We use a dual-processing approach and argue that the interplay between controlled and automatic information processing as well as the task representations created in the working memory (WM) space explain the distinctive features of ESDM.

3.2   ENTREPRENEURIAL STRATEGIC DECISION-MAKING

As we have argued in Chapter 1, SDM is an intentional and goal-directed cognitive process of selecting an alternative from several available, when only incomplete information on the alternatives and their possible outcomes is available and the facts, variables and contingencies involved in the decision situation are highly complex. Therefore, in general psychological terms, strategic decisions are a particular form of high-stake decisions that involve a high degree of uncertainty and complexity. According to Kunreuther et al. (2002), several factors impact on the way people decide in these situations. In high-stake decisions, very often the decision-makers' behaviour deviates from what normative theories predict. Available probabilistic information is undervalued and decision-makers fail to differentiate between probabilities. Often, high-stake decisions involve considerable risks and decision-makers fail to consider or assign a realistic probability to all the risks involved. In high-stake situations, decision-makers often think: 'bad things will not happen to me'. Therefore, they treat the probability of certain adverse events as zero, when in fact it is not. In high-stake decisions, foreseen consequences (both in terms of gains and losses) are often associated with strong emotional reactions. It is therefore a risk to focus too heavily on affective cues. Choices are often made by focusing on the informational cues with the strongest emotional significance. Moreover, high-stake decisions are often made under stress, either due to time pressure, or due to the high uncertainty and complexity of the decision situation. Under stress, decision-makers tend to focus on a rather reduced set of cues and oversimplify the information at hand. Due to this selective information processing, the quality of high-stake decisions tends to decrease markedly. A further key characteristic of high-stake decisions is the novelty of the situation. Individuals usually have little to no experience with similar decision situations and tend to rely heavily on established social norms, that is, adopting decision strategies used by others. Finally, in high-stake decisions, people tend to prefer the status quo (they do not make any decision at all and preserve the existing situation) and they fail to learn (ibid.).

Entrepreneurs are often involved in making strategic choices, and starting a new venture is arguably one of the most important ones. However, we shall not (conceptually) limit the scope of strategic choices to the starting of a new venture and rather will define ESDM in a broader sense, as any major decisions with important consequences for the small business. In this respect the decision-maker can be either the entrepreneur or the small-business owner. Therefore, ESDM has all the characteristics of the SDM, with the difference that the decision-maker is either an entrepreneur or a small-business owner.

An especially salient subject in entrepreneurship research is how entrepreneurs differ from managers or non-entrepreneurs (Busenitz and Barney, 1997; Chen et al., 1998; Tan, 2001; Stewart and Roth, 2001). The factors described in the literature are highly relevant since they reflect distinctive elements in the SDM style of entrepreneurs. In contrast to managers, entrepreneurs have been described as being risk seekers, less likely to adhere to established norms of behaviours, and less predictable in their decision-making (Busenitz and Barney, 1997: 10). Moreover, there has been a growing interest in the cognitive component underlying entrepreneurial actions (for example, Calori et al., 1994; Busenitz and Barney, 1997; Chen et al., 1998; Busenitz, 1999; Tan, 2001; Stewart and Roth, 2001; Norton and Moore, 2002; Forbes, 2005). In fact, many of the aforementioned studies hypothesize that the differences between entrepreneurs and managers can be traced back to differences in the way they process information.

To summarize, we have thus far argued: (i) that strategic decisions are highly complex and, due to the high stakes involved, the SDM process is very susceptible to biases in information processing (Kunreuther et al., 2002); and (ii) that entrepreneurs are a special category of decision-makers and several traits (for example, cognitive, motivational and emotional) distinguish them from other categories (Busenitz and Barney, 1997; Chen et al., 1998; Busenitz, 1999). Basing our analysis on these two arguments, we shall discuss the most important psychological factors involved in ESDM, from attitudinal and motivational factors (risk propensity, entrepreneurial motivation) to cognitive heuristics and emotions. We shall start our discussion with probably the most debated factor of all, namely the attitude towards risk. It is debated because it is a common-sense observation that taking risks is the very core nature of entrepreneurship, yet scientific empirical evidence testing this common-sense assumption is mixed and inconclusive.

3.3 RISK PROPENSITY IN ESDM

As stated earlier in this book, one of the four concepts inherent to SDM in general is *uncertainty*. Furthermore, decision-making under conditions of risk and uncertainty is at the heart of entrepreneurship. Hence, risk *propensity* is extremely relevant in dealing with uncertainty and therefore relevant to ESDM. Risk propensity is an attitudinal component referring to an individual's tendency to take risks in his/her actions that varies across distinct decision contexts. ESDM situations involve a considerable amount of risk and as a consequence, these 'risky decisions are not based exclusively on rational calculations but are also affected by individual predispositions towards risk' (Stewart and Roth, 2001: 145). Some individuals will be more likely to take risks than others. Following Stewart and Roth (2001), two theoretical positions concerning the difference between entrepreneurs and managers can be discerned in the current body of literature on risk propensity.

The first, most frequently used theoretical argument asserts that entrepreneurs have higher risk propensity than managers. According to this theoretical trend, entrepreneurs and managers both have to take risks; however, entrepreneurs will have a slightly higher tendency to take risks in making decisions, because they have to cope with less-structured decision situations and bear the ultimate responsibility for their actions (ibid.). Indeed, an entrepreneurial venture does seem an extra risky operation, with failure estimates of newly started businesses within the first five years of existence ranging from 50 to 80 per cent (Busenitz, 1999). Very often, entrepreneurs have to make decisions fast and with only partial information available about a highly unstructured decisional situation. Therefore, in order to make successful decisions, entrepreneurs should have a higher risk propensity than managers. This would then adequately fit what is sometimes deemed the entrepreneur's 'gambler-like reputation' (ibid.).

Running counter to this first theory on risk propensity in ESDM research, the second, less frequently visited theoretical position holds that differences in risk propensity between entrepreneurs and managers should be small or non-existent. One of the theories for this assertion (although other explanations have also been advanced) is classic motivation theory (Atkinson et al., 1960) with a focus on achievement motivation (Stewart and Roth, 2001). Individuals with a high need for achievement set demanding goals, take responsibility for their decisions, and take higher risks than individuals low in need for achievement. Since managers and entrepreneurs would both have high achievement motivation, motivation theory predicts that they should have the same predisposition towards risk, and thus similar risk propensity (ibid.).

Although risk propensity is one of the dominant themes in entrepreneurship literature, agreement on the subject is far from unanimous. Busenitz (1999) asserts that there has been little empirical evidence for the first theory's claim that entrepreneurs should have higher risk propensity than managers. An especially salient discussion on the subject, unfolding in subsequent publications in the *Journal of Applied Psychology* (Stewart and Roth, 2001; Miner and Raju, 2004), clearly illustrates this lack of agreement, where the results of a meta-analysis indicating a difference in risk propensity between managers and entrepreneurs (Stewart and Roth, 2001), was later questioned by Miner and Raju. Rather, they argue that the role of risk propensity in entrepreneurship remains unresolved. To resolve the debate, all the above mentioned authors argue that several contingent factors may account for these differences.

One recent stream of research that may shed some more light on this issue refers to contextual theories of risk taking and asserts that there are different *types* of risk that might be responsible for this moderator effect. Weber et al. (2002), for instance, introduce a scale that assesses risk taking in different content domains, and show that risk taking is indeed content specific. In short, it shows that individuals can differ widely in their risk-taking propensity in, say, financial decisions from their risk propensity in social decisions. An entrepreneur, for instance, assumed to have high risk propensity in financial decisions, might be very conservative in health, recreational, or ethical decisions. This lack of testing for domain-specific risk propensity might be responsible for confounding results in the aforementioned empirical studies of aggregated differences in risk propensity between managers and entrepreneurs.

Another possible moderating factor is discussed by Norton and Moore (2002). They argue that we should focus not on risk propensity to explain the differences between entrepreneurs and managers, but rather on the *alertness perspective*. According to this perspective, entrepreneurs have a different view of the future as compared to managers, which permits them to discover opportunities that are overlooked by others (ibid.). The main argument here is that 'entrepreneurs do not necessarily possess character traits which predispose them to engage in behavior with widely-variable outcomes, but rather that entrepreneurs *assess* opportunities and threats differently than non-entrepreneurs' (ibid.: 281, original italics). Although this theory, to the best of our knowledge, has not yet been empirically tested, the argument seems to have potential in explaining risk propensity differences between managers and entrepreneurs. In addition, the logic that we should not focus on risk propensity itself but rather on how managers *perceive* risk also underlies another way out of the risk propensity dilemma, namely the different use of biases and heuristics by entrepreneurs versus managers (for example, Busenitz and Barney, 1997).

Finally, another factor that can explain the mixed results concerning the differences in risk taking between entrepreneurs and managers refers to company type and size. In an empirical study investigating the differences between managers and entrepreneurs in Romania, Curşeu and Boroş (2004) reported higher levels of risk taking in managers as compared to entrepreneurs. The explanation advanced by the authors was that the entrepreneurs selected in the sample owned small businesses with a small number of employees and a rather low financial turnover, while managers were operating in larger companies with substantially higher turnovers. In addition, a medium positive correlation between the financial turnover of the company and the entrepreneur's risk propensity was found. These results suggest that only entrepreneurs who own large companies have a higher risk propensity, while the owners of SMEs will have a rather low risk propensity.

To return to the meta-analyses on risk propensity, we conclude that, besides the upshot that replicating research *can* thus yield interesting findings, little is yet known about risk propensity and its relation to entrepreneurs versus managers. The intuitive appeal of entrepreneurs being somehow different in the area of risk taking as compared to managers, inspired scholars to look for alternative causes to explain the relation, besides the three theoretical positions described above. Some of these alternative arguments will be briefly discussed below in association with motivational and emotional determinants of ESDM effectiveness.

3.4 ENTREPRENEURIAL MOTIVATION

Human behaviour, including decision-making, is determined by the interplay between cognitive, motivational and emotional factors (Reed, 2006) Therefore, motivational factors play an important role both in the decision to start a new venture as well as in other strategic choices once the new business is operating. In general, motivation refers to the factors through which goal-directed behaviour is initiated, energized and maintained (Huczynski and Buchanan, 2007). For ESDM, three such factors received considerable attention in the literature: self-efficacy, cognitive motivation and tolerance for ambiguity.

The construct of *entrepreneurial self-efficacy* (ESE), initially developed by Chen et al. (1998), is one of the more significant new concepts that have in recent years emerged from entrepreneurship research (Forbes, 2005). ESE was originally proposed as a key individual difference between entrepreneurs and non-entrepreneurs (ibid.). It is an extension of general *self-efficacy*, a concept that has been extensively applied in clinical and social psychology and it is defined as a set of individual beliefs concerning an individual's capability to mobilize and use cognitive and motivational resources in order to increase the sense of control over different life events (Bandura, 1977). Previous research on general self-efficacy showed that this individual difference is one of the best predictors of individual performance in a wide variety of tasks (ibid., Bandura, 1986; Wood and Bandura, 1989). The relation between self-efficacy and performance seems more complex, however, because high levels of performance also lead to increased self-efficacy (Chen et al., 1998). Therefore we can describe this particular relation as 'bidirectional causality'.

Concerning entrepreneurs, in relation to the four basic concepts inherent to SDM that were introduced at the beginning of this book, self-efficacy is closely related to control as a key component of SDM situations. People are inclined to look for situations in which they anticipate high personal control, but avoid situations in which they anticipate low levels of control (ibid.), that is, persons will be drawn towards tasks about which they have high self-efficacy, and will tend to avoid tasks in which they have low self-efficacy (Forbes, 2005). When we state that entrepreneurs, in order to become so, at the very least have to make the decision to start and manage their own business, ESE is one of the individual differences that explain why some individuals make this decision while others do not. In conclusion, ESE 'refers to the strength of an individual's belief that he or she is capable of successfully performing the roles and tasks of an entrepreneur' (Chen et al., 1998: 301). As a consequence, the baseline proposition of ESE research is that, *ceteris paribus*, individuals with high ESE will tend to become entrepreneurs and persons with low ESE will be inclined to avoid becoming an entrepreneur.[1]

Note that ESE is not the same as another well-known cognitive construct having to do with control, namely locus of control. The two obviously have similarities (they both are individual factors and related to control), but the two concepts draw from two distinct streams of literature. Whereas self-efficacy draws from the individual differences, personal attributes and motivation literature, locus of control draws from attribution theories. Although it is beyond the scope of this chapter to review the differences between these two concepts, it should be noted that individuals with high levels of self-efficacy are most likely to have a tendency to attribute their success to internal causes, and their failures to external factors. In attribution theory terms this is known as 'fundamental attribution bias', and it has been argued that entrepreneurs have a stronger tendency towards this fundamental attribution bias than non-entrepreneurs (Hewstone et al., 1996). To the best of our knowledge this theoretical proposition has been subjected to an empirical test in only one study (Curşeu and Boroş, 2004), which showed that compared to managers, entrepreneurs do indeed have a stronger tendency to attribute their successes to internal factors (81 per cent of the factors used to explain success were internal for entrepreneurs, while only 71 per cent were for managers) and their failures to external factors (94 per cent of the factors used to explain failure were external for entrepreneurs, while only 78 per cent were for managers). This fundamental attribution bias has a strong motivational role for increasing self-esteem which is essential for task involvement and performance. Based on this discussion, one could hypothesize that an entrepreneur with high ESE would also score high on internal locus of control when it comes to financial successes (that is, ascribing these to his/her skills or intelligence), and high external locus of control for financial débâcles (that is, attributing these to general misfortune). To the best of our knowledge, until now no empirical test of the positive association between ESE and the fundamental attribution bias in entrepreneurship has been published in the general academic literature.

Cognitive motivation is another relevant motivational factor that influences ESDM effectiveness. Need for cognition is a central concept for cognitive motivation (Cacioppo et al., 1996). Individuals high in need for cognition tend to seek, acquire, think about and reflect on relevant information when solving cognitive tasks, while those low in need for cognition tend to rely on cognitive heuristics, social comparison or others' expertise (Cacioppo and Petty, 1982; Cacioppo et al., 1996). In a comprehensive review, Cacioppo et al. analysed the empirical relationships of need for cognition with other personality traits, cognitive attributes and performance outcomes. When compared to individuals low in need for cognition, people high in need for cognition possess high intrinsic motivation to engage and enjoy effortful cognitive activities; they are able to recall more relevant information about the task, to analyse accurately the quality of arguments, and to generate more alternative solutions to problems; they are less uncertain when estimating the cause-and-effect relationships; and they possess more knowledge, have better logical reasoning abilities, and have a higher performance in cognitive tasks (ibid.). Moreover, people high in need for cognition have been shown to have a lower uncertainty regarding cause-and-effect relations (Weary and Edwards, 1994) and also to have a higher tendency to maximize information gain (Sorrentino et al., 1988) as compared to people low in need for cognition. In addition, Sarmány-Schuller (1998) showed that need for cognition has a negative and significant relation with the self-esteem of the decision-maker. To conclude, people high in need for cognition tend to seek information in order to reduce uncertainty (Cacioppo et al., 1996), they have lower levels of self-esteem (Sarmány-Schuller, 1999), they experience lower levels of uncertainty (indecisiveness) in decision-making situations, and are less sensitive to decision-making heuristics and biases (Curşeu, 2006). These premises lead to the conclusion that people high in need for cognition are more analytical in their thinking strategies and closer to the rationality ideal in decision-making as described in the previous chapter. In a study on a sample of Romanian entrepreneurs, Curşeu and Boroş (2004) showed that entrepreneurs score significantly lower on need for cognition than both middle-level managers and top managers. Differences in need for cognition are therefore possible explanatory variables for the differences in decision-making effectiveness and are in line with the results describing entrepreneurs as intuitive decision-makers.

Tolerance for ambiguity is yet another motivational trait that was explored in relation to ESDM. A core argument in the entrepreneurial cognition literature is that because the decision situations faced by entrepreneurs are ambiguous in general (for example, novel, complex and sometimes even intractable), the entrepreneurs' ability to tolerate these situations is a key factor for decision effectiveness. Tolerance for ambiguity (TA) is defined as the tendency to perceive ambiguous situations as desirable rather than threatening (Budner, 1962). In a review of four studies that explored the differences in TA between entrepreneurs and managers, Sexton and Bowman (1986) argued that managers have a significantly lower tendency to tolerate ambiguous situations as compared with new venture founders. Nevertheless, several other authors argue that TA does not differentiate entrepreneurs from managers (Shane et al., 2003). In a study of top Fortune 500 start-up companies, Bhide (2000) argues that the most successful entrepreneurs are those capable of operating with incomplete information and still making informed decisions. In Bhide's view, tolerance for ambiguity refers to making informed choices in conditions in which it is known that relevant information is missing.

To summarize, with respect to motivation, entrepreneurs: (i) have a high sense of self-efficacy and in particular they have a strong set of beliefs that they can control the success of a business; (ii) have a strong tendency to maintain a high level of self-efficacy by a fundamental attribution bias; (iii) have a relatively low (as compared to managers) cognitive motivation, defined as a tendency to engage in and enjoy effortful cognitive activities; and (iv) have, as compared with other categories of decision-makers, a high tolerance for ambiguity. Next, we shall address the sensitivity to cognitive biases and heuristics, a set of cognitive factors highly relevant for ESDM effectiveness.

3.5   SENSITIVITY TO COGNITIVE BIASES AND HEURISTICS IN ESDM

SDM is often not a rational process (Busenitz and Barney, 1997). As Simon (1957) stated, people intend to act in a rational way, but they succeed only to a very limited extent, therefore people are, by nature, limited in their rationality (which Herbert Simon deemed 'bounded rationality') which makes a purely rational decision-making process difficult, if not impossible. Starting with Simon's work in the 1960s and Tversky and Kahneman's work in the 1970s, a large body of empirical evidence disconfirmed these 'rationality assumptions' behind human decision-making behaviour. Because of the limited possibilities of knowledge representation in the cognitive system and limited computational resources, decision-makers do not analyse the available information rationally and extensively in order to make a decision (Gingerenzer et al., 1999; Shafir and LeBoeuf, 2002). Apart from limited rationality, other reasons associated with the organizational context account for the lack of purely rational decision-making processes (Busenitz and Barney, 1997). Such reasons include the high costs associated with extensive information gathering and information processing as well as differences in decision-making procedures adopted by managers, or differences in the values of decision-makers.

A number of biases and heuristics influence the information processing in decisional situations. Some of the most important are: availability, anchoring, representativeness heuristics (Tversky and Kahneman, 1974, 1982), the framing effect (Tversky and Kahneman, 1974, 1981), the

Ellsberg paradox (Ellsberg, 1961), the Allais paradox (Allais and Hagen, 1979), overconfidence (Bazerman, 1986) and counterfactual thinking (Roese, 1997). These heuristics, biases and paradoxes are rules and cognitive mechanisms or short cuts that assist decision-makers in the process of making choices (Busenitz and Barney, 1997), and are therefore instances in which human decision-making behaviour deviates from the norms of rationality (Curşeu, 2006).

Biases and heuristics help decision-makers to derive simplified models when dealing with complex problems (Simon, 1957). For instance, biases and heuristics have been found in executives' cognitive maps of their industries (Calori et al., 1994). Although it might seem that these simplifications of reality would hardly enhance decision-making effectiveness, frequently these 'short cuts' yield acceptable solutions for people in situations where they face uncertainty and complexity (Busenitz and Barney, 1997; Gingerenzer et al., 1999) – which we now know is the case in SDM. Moreover, these simplifications help decision-makers in overcoming the risk of becoming overwhelmed by the complexity and uncertainty of their environment (Calori et al., 1994).

An important premiss in research that incorporates the use of biases and heuristics holds that individuals may not be subject to the use of biases and heuristics to the same extent (Busenitz and Barney, 1997; Busenitz, 1999; Curşeu, 2006). In this respect, entrepreneurs are a group of decision-makers that seems very sensitive to some of the cognitive heuristics and biases. As mentioned before, the use of biases and heuristics can also be linked to the risk propensity dilemma. Scholars studying the use of biases and heuristics assert that entrepreneurs do indeed seem to take more risks than do non-entrepreneurs, but then point out the ambiguous empirical evidence concerning risk propensity differences between managers and entrepreneurs. These scholars argue that the differences between entrepreneurs and non-entrepreneurs can be traced back to their different use of biases and heuristics rather than to their risk propensity. More specifically, these authors assume that entrepreneurs use biases and heuristics that lead to simplified problem domains to a greater extent than do non-entrepreneurs, and this explains the main difference in the way entrepreneurs and managers *perceive* risk (Busenitz, 1999). Very often in entrepreneurship, decisions involve high levels of complexity, with a high degree of uncertainty, and choices have to be made quickly, thus the decision situations have a set of characteristics that foster the use of simplifying mechanisms (for example, some heuristics and biases). In other words, proponents of the biases and heuristics view argue that 'entrepreneurial activities simply become too overwhelming to those who are less willing to generalize through the use of biases and heuristics' (Busenitz and Barney,

1997: 14). In the entrepreneurship and SDM literature, three heuristics have received considerable attention: overconfidence, representativeness and counterfactual thinking.

Overconfidence is a bias that refers to an individual tendency to overestimate one's capabilities, knowledge and skills as well as to be overly optimistic about one's future (Bazerman, 1986; Busenitz, 1999; Camerer and Lovallo, 2000; Juslin et al., 2000). More than 80 per cent of drivers who were asked to rate themselves based on their driving skills, placed themselves in the top 30 per cent of the best drivers out there (Svenson, 1981). Moreover, the confidence in the correctness of an answer to a general knowledge test is much higher than the percentage of the correct answers to the test. When people were asked: 'Which country has the larger population? (a) Finland or (b) Zambia', the average confidence in the answer was generally higher than the percentage of the correct answers (for example, only 80 per cent answered correctly in the sample of respondents who reported 100 per cent confidence in their answers) (Juslin et al., 2000).

The overconfidence bias can be traced back to two different approaches (Benos, 1998), which we shall discuss here as they are related to the SDM context. In the first line of reasoning, decision-makers who lack important pieces of information try to forecast the missing pieces. Given the inherent complexity of SDM and decision-makers' bounded rationality, these estimates will rarely be entirely correct. However, the more they infer about the situation, the more likely they are to treat their judgements as being better than in reality they are (ibid.). For entrepreneurs this would be the case even more than for non-entrepreneurs. In the second line of reasoning, the decision-maker receives imperfect information about characteristics of the decision he or she is facing. Non-entrepreneurs might treat these signals cautiously, recognizing the noise that these signals are likely to contain. Entrepreneurs, on the other hand, might be more inclined to interpret the signals to be perfect, thereby overestimating their accuracy (ibid.). Based on these arguments, entrepreneurs seem more sensitive to the overconfidence bias. Overconfidence has been documented to exist in a wide variety of situations (for an overview, see Lichtenstein et al., 1982).

As mentioned before, it has been shown that entrepreneurs can be more overconfident than non-entrepreneurs (Busenitz and Barney, 1997; Busenitz, 1999) because of the higher levels of uncertainty they face in their decision-making. This serves multiple purposes. First, it helps entrepreneurs to successfully face the multiple hurdles associated with starting and running a business. Moreover, if entrepreneurs were not overconfident, many new ventures would never be launched (Tan, 2001). In addition, entrepreneurial overconfidence also serves to encourage and persuade other potential stakeholders (for example, investors) to invest in the idea

(Busenitz and Barney, 1997). As a final purpose, overconfidence encourages the entrepreneur to take action before it makes complete sense from a rational point of view (ibid.), enabling the entrepreneur to grasp opportunities and jump on the bandwagon before competitors move in.

However, overconfidence is one way to explain why many SMEs disappear from the market in the first 10 years. Camerer and Lovallo (2000) advanced three explanations for this negative impact of overconfidence on business success. The first is that new entrepreneurs have only few opportunities to make money and overconfidence can lead to negative decisional outcomes; the financial resources of the new entrepreneurs will be exhausted very quickly. The second explanation resides in the fact that taking high risks entails the possibility of obtaining high profits and although the expected profit is in reality low, due to their high overconfidence, entrepreneurs will most likely take these risks anyway. Finally, SMEs tend to fail due to suboptimal SDM because given their overconfidence, entrepreneurs do not estimate correctly how many competitors they really have. To summarize, overconfidence as a means to simplify an overly complex decision situation has both positive and negative implications for ESDM.

Representativeness was one of the most important heuristics described in a series of studies by Tversky and Kahneman that focused on probabilistic judgements on uncertain events (Kahneman et al., 1982; Tversky and Kahneman, 1982; Laibson and Zeckhauser, 1998). The subjective probability of an event is determined by the degree to which it (i) reflects the salient features of the process by which it is generated, (ii) reflects previous experience with a particular event or combination of events and (iii) is similar in essential characteristics to its parent population (Tversky and Kahneman, 1982).

One aspect of the representativeness heuristic refers to the general tendency of judging the probability of an event based on how representative that event is for a class or category or events. In this case, representativeness is related to the prototypicality of the alternatives and to stereotyping, because usually only a few attributes are generalized in order to make a judgement about the probability of a certain event or phenomenon. This form of representativeness is also labelled 'conjunction fallacy' because it reflects people's tendency to consider specific scenarios more likely than general ones. In an illustrative example of this fallacy (Tversky and Kahneman, 1983), respondents (decision-makers) are asked to estimate on a 1 (not probable at all) to 8 (very probable) Likert scale the likelihood of eight options attached to the following scenario: Linda is 31 years old, single, outspoken and very bright. She majored in philosophy. As a student, she was deeply concerned with issues of discrimination and social justice, and also participated in anti-war demonstrations.

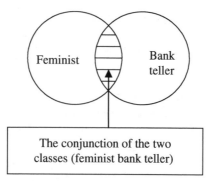

Figure 3.1   A graphical illustration of the conjunction fallacy

1.   Linda is a teacher in a elementary school;
2.   Linda works in a book store and takes Yoga classes;
3.   Linda is active in the feminist movement;
4.   Linda is a psychiatric social worker;
5.   Linda is a member of Women Voters;
6.   Linda is a bank teller (cashier);
7.   Linda is an insurance salesperson;
8.   Linda is a bank teller (cashier) and is active in the feminist movement.

More than 85 per cent of the respondents rated alternative 8 as more probable than 6 and 3. In probabilistic terms, alternative 8 has a lower probability than alternatives 6 and 3 (the probability of an isolated event is always higher than the probability of the same event in conjunction with another) (ibid.). This type of problem is very similar to a general class inclusion problem, in which a set of elements are included in a more general class. Similarly, 'feminist bank tellers' is a subset of elements included in both classes: feminists and bank tellers. For a different representational framework, see Figure 3.1.

Another particular form of representativeness that is studied in entrepreneurship literature is the willingness of decision-makers to make generalizations based on small and non-random samples of events (Busenitz and Barney, 1997) or what is also deemed the 'law of small numbers' (Laibson and Zeckhauser, 1998: 10). The ultimate example of when individuals use small, non-random samples as a basis for observation is, obviously, when they rely on personal experience to make choices or judgements (Kahneman et al., 1982). A classic example of reliance on personal experience when making probabilistic judgements is the assumption that chance is self-correcting. Imagine that someone flips a coin and for five consecutive throws it is tails (T). The majority of respondents asked to estimate the next event, answered that after the next throw it would most likely be heads (H). Moreover, respondents consider that the sequence H, T, H, T, H, T, is more likely to occur than H, H, H, T, T, T. Therefore, when people are asked to estimate the probability of an independent event, they often assume that the probability of that event is dependent upon previous events.

Since entrepreneurs, as argued before, in general have access to less information than do managers, it makes sense to assume that in order to make any decisions at all, they would have to use the heuristic of representativeness more than do managers. Large, non-random datasets are scarce in entrepreneurial settings, especially because large-scale research might prematurely give away the entrepreneur's innovative idea to competitors. Given these circumstances, entrepreneurs might have to rely more on personal experience, than do managers in organizations. In fact, some empirical evidence for the hypothesis that entrepreneurs use the representativeness heuristic more than do managers has been found (Busenitz and Barney, 1997).

Counterfactual thinking is a set of evaluative cognitions referring to past events or decisions, in which alternative courses of actions are considered and imagined as opposed to, or compared to, the real facts that took place. In other words, counterfactual thinking refers to evaluations as: 'if only that would have happened . . .', 'what might have been if . . .' or 'if only I would have . . .' (Roese, 1997; Baron, 1999). Research has argued that counterfactual thinking leads to both positive and negative emotions, and on the other hand it has positive as well as negative effects on judgements and choice (Roese, 1997). Counterfactual thinking is an important way of sense making and it has affective as well as cognitive consequences (Baron, 1999).

Two mechanisms explain the emotional and cognitive consequences of counterfactual thinking: causal inferences effects and contrast effects (Roese, 1997). Often, engaging in counterfactual thinking leads to (implicit) causal associations among facts or events. As argued by cognitive dissonance theory (Festinger, 1957) people strive for a cognitive equilibrium/balance and in order to do so, often make causal attributions and causal associations between events (Kelley, 1973). Although not all causal attributions originate from it, counterfactual thinking is an important way to establish causal inferences and thus maintain the sense of cognitive coherence of the decision-maker. For example, an entrepreneur may be convinced that if he/she had not relocated the company, he/she would still be in business today, meaning that the entrepreneur establishes in an implicit way an association between relocation and bankruptcy. The opposite counterfactual reasoning is also possible. Another entrepreneur may think that if he/she had not relocated the company, he/she would have been out of business, meaning that in this case an implicit association is made between relocation and success. This example is also illustrative of the second mechanism for the consequences of counterfactual thinking, namely the contrast effects. The contrast effects refer to the fact that a particular outcome (relocation) is judged worse if a more desirable alternative outcome is salient (not being bankrupt), and judged better if a less desirable outcome is salient (not being successful). Moreover, the direction in which the comparison is made is also relevant for the salience of the valued/undesirable outcome. In an athletic competition, bronze medallists are often more satisfied with their achievement than silver medallists. For the former, the rationalization is often 'I have made it to the podium' (downward comparison), while for the latter the rationalization is 'I could have made it to first place' (upward comparison) (Roese, 1997).

Because of the association with a general need for cognitive balance/equilibrium (or sense making in other approaches – see Weick, 1979 for more details), counterfactual thinking has important emotional consequences. If the comparison is made upward (a better outcome is imagined), it is very likely that engaging in counterfactual thinking is associated with negative emotional reactions, while if the comparison is made downward (a worse outcome is imagined) the emotional reaction is positive. It should be noted, however, that counterfactual thinking is very often triggered by negative emotions, thus it is more likely for a decision-maker to engage in counterfactual thinking when he/she experiences negative emotions. Therefore, it is very likely that counterfactual thinking is associated with upward comparisons, because it is triggered by negative emotions and thus through the contrast effects it also leads to negative emotions. Nevertheless, because it contributes to the re-establishment of cognitive equilibrium (sense making) it leads to positive emotional outcomes. Going back to our previous example, the bankrupt entrepreneur will most probably feel bad because of the failed business (which could have been successful), but at the same time will experience a sense of cognitive coherence and will be untroubled because there is a plausible explanation for the failure. According to Roese (1997) this combination of effects has positive implications for future actions and decisions because it heightens the desire to learn and it fosters behavioural intentions associated with improvement in performance.

Concerning the incidence of counterfactual thinking for entrepreneurs, Baron (1999) shows that in general, entrepreneurs are less likely than non-entrepreneurs to engage in counterfactual thinking and to think about how things might have turned out in different conditions. These results lead to the conclusion that on the one hand, entrepreneurs protect themselves from experiencing negative emotions associated with failures, but at the same time engaging in less counterfactual thinking also prevents them from learning because analysing alternative actions may lead to the development of better strategies and improve performance (ibid.).

To summarize, on the one hand, entrepreneurs are sensitive to cognitive heuristics and biases that lead to a simplification of complex decision situations, but on the other, they are less susceptible to biases that are associated with negative emotions and regret. This has major implications for the outcomes of ESDM. The arguments linked to higher sensitivity seem to suggest that by using biases and heuristics, entrepreneurs simplify an overly complex and unpredictable environment. The immediate consequence of using heuristics and biases in decision-making is the development of a less-complex representation about the decisional situation. Moreover, by being less susceptible to counterfactual thinking, entrepreneurs are less likely to experience regret and other negative emotions in their decisions, and thus persist in their decisions and maintain optimism and other positive emotions (ibid.). In cognitive terms, this pattern boils down to the amount of risk and uncertainty perceived in a decision situation. It is very likely that in strategic choices (or high-stake decisions) due to the oversimplification mechanisms and to the maintained positive emotional state, entrepreneurs perceive less uncertainty as compared to other categories of decision-makers.

3.6 EMOTIONS IN ESDM

As mentioned by Kunreuther et al. (2002), because of the high stakes involved, strategic decisions are often associated with emotional reactions. A considerable amount of literature explores the general role of emotions in decision-making (Schwarz, 2000). In a timeline perspective, emotions may impact on ESDM outcomes in three ways: emotions experienced in the moment of a decision (ad hoc emotions), anticipated emotions of a particular choice (anticipated affect) and emotions associated with the evaluation of a past decision (post-decision affect). Three theoretical approaches are especially relevant in explaining the ways in which emotions influence the outcomes of ESDM: the affective events theory (Weiss and Cropanzano, 1996), the affect infusion model (Forgas, 1995) and the affect theory of social exchange (Lawler, 2001). The aim of this section is to summarize these theoretical accounts for the ways in which emotional reactions impact on the outcomes of ESDM.

The *affective events theory* (AET) (Weiss and Cropanzano, 1996) argues that events and facts related to the work environment and work content induce various emotional experiences, which in turn influence subsequent judgements and behavioural reactions. Over time, repeated emotional experiences associated with work-related events may accumulate and generate a general and stable set of emotional states associated with the work environment. This stable emotional state will most probably exert a consistent impact on problem solving and decision-making in organizations. AET explains the impact of emotional states at the time of decision-making. In other words, the stable emotional state generated by work-related events has an impact on the very moment in which the decision is made. For example, entrepreneurs, who are in general satisfied with their work and with the way the company is performing, will experience an impact of these general positive emotions on decision-making processes, while entrepreneurs who are unsatisfied with their work will experience an impact of the negative mood states on decision-making. Most researchers agree that positive mood states are associated with higher creativity and higher cognitive flexibility, but at the same time they will increase the likelihood of using a heuristic type of reasoning (as opposed to an analytical one) and to an unrealistic optimism in decision-making (Schwarz, 2000; Goss, 2007). Moreover, a general positive mood is not necessarily associated with a higher work performance. Negative mood states are associated with a general tendency to process information in a more systematic and analytic way (Schwarz, 2000; Goss, 2007) and people experiencing negative emotions are often more realistic and accurate in their perceptions and judgements than people experiencing general positive emotional states (Alloy and Abramson, 1982).

The reliance on heuristic reasoning when positive emotional states are experienced and on analytic reasoning when negative emotional states are experienced has a motivational explanation. People in a general positive mood are motivated to preserve this state and they are less likely to get involved in effortful cognitive activities (for example, extensive information search), while people in a general negative mood have a tendency to escape it and therefore they will get involved in various goal-directed activities (for example, effortful information processing). Also, in a more evolutionary perspective, experiencing negative emotions is a strong signal that things are not right or problematic and they have to be properly analysed in order to change the status quo, while positive emotions usually signal a stable and peaceful environment, therefore information processing will be based on routines and simple heuristics developed in time (Schwarz, 2000). Based on the observation that entrepreneurs as compared with non-entrepreneurs have a stronger tendency to preserve a positive mood and avoid negative emotional experiences (Baron, 1999), we can conclude that it is very likely that they are more prone to be trapped into a heuristic information processing mode than to engage in a more analytic reasoning of strategic information.

Affect infusion theory (AIT) (Forgas, 1995) argues that emotions influence judgements and decision-making through two mechanisms. First, experienced emotions have a direct influence on the way in which argument and fact evaluations are used. The most relevant argument and fact evaluations in making a judgement are the ones that are emotionally relevant. An entrepreneur making an important decision will very often think in terms of: 'My feeling is that . . .' or 'I don't have a good feeling about this . . .', and therefore arguments usually associated with emotional content will play a much more important role than emotionally neutral arguments or fact evaluations. In other words, decision-makers often use affect as information in reasoning processes (affect in itself is treated as information and used in the reasoning premises). Second, experienced emotions impact on the amount and type of information being processed. Decision-makers have a tendency to process more extensively the contents (for example, arguments, facts) that are congruent with the emotional state they experience and to ignore mood incongruent information. Moreover, a neutral target will be more positively evaluated when the decision-maker experiences a positive than a negative emotional state (ibid., Schwarz, 2000). Emotions have an indirect effect on judgement and decision-making, by facilitating or blocking access to relevant knowledge representations. To conclude, AIT states that using emotionally charged arguments as a main basis for reasoning and the mood congruent information processing are strong 'affective infusions' into judgement and decision-making.

AIT argues that decision-making processes are influenced by three categories of factors: (i) those associated with the task or target (for example, degree of familiarity, typicality or complexity of the task), (ii) those associated with the decision-maker (for example, personal relevance of the issue, the affective states, cognitive capacity, personality traits, motivational goals) and (iii) features of the situation (for example, demands, publicity, availability of criteria). Forgas also describes four information processing strategies in decision-making: (i) the direct access strategy in which a pre-existing answer or choice is selected from the long-term memory (LTM); (ii) the motivated strategy is used when motivational pressures are exerted on attaining specific goals and then the aim of information processing is either positive mood maintenance or negative mood avoidance; (iii) heuristic processing is likely to occur when the problem or decision to be addressed is simple or typical; and (iv) substantive processing is the most demanding information processing strategy in which new information is generated based on existing representations. According to AIT, heuristic and substantive processing are the most susceptible strategies to affect infusion. In particular, complex strategic decisions that require the processing of uncertain and ambiguous information are very susceptible to affect infusion.

The impact of affect on strategic information processing takes place at three levels. First, at the attention level, emotions influence the way in which arguments, alternatives or facts are perceived (mood-congruent situational cues are perceived more accurately than mood-incongruent ones). Second, emotions influence the encoding of new information and learning strategies (targets are more positively evaluated when a positive rather than a negative mood is experienced). Third, they lead to selective retrieval of information from LTM and their use in making the strategic choice (a positive mood leads to a more heuristic type of retrieval, while a negative mood leads to a more analytical retrieval and combination of information) (ibid., Forgas and George, 2001). With respect to ESDM, based on the AIT we can argue that due to the complexity, uncertainty and ambiguity involved in strategic decisions (a task characteristic) and the stronger tendency of entrepreneurs to engage in heuristic information processing (personal attribute) and due to the high stake involved in the decision situation (situational feature), it is very likely that information processing in ESDM is susceptible to affect infusion.

The *affect theory of social exchange* (ATSE) (Lawler, 2001) is a sociological account of the ways in which emotions impact on the strength of social network ties. Because entrepreneurs are always embedded in different social networks and they are often involved in social exchanges while making strategic choices, this theory is relevant to explain ESDM and in particular strategic collaboration choices in entrepreneurship. Social exchange is defined in ATSE as a joint activity in which valued assets are swapped among actors in a social network. ATSE is based on a set of five main assumptions: (i) the social exchange is a source of structural interdependencies materialized in interpersonal interactions that will ultimately trigger general emotional reactions; (ii) these general emotional states have a reinforcing or punishing value for the social actors; (iii) as a consequence, through social exchanges, actors in a network tend to preserve positive emotional states and to avoid negative emotional states; (iv) the global emotions resulting from social exchanges trigger cognitive evaluations that will lead to more specific and nuanced emotions; and (v) while involved in social exchanges, actors have a tendency to explain their emotional states by referring to relevant social units (ibid.). The immediate consequence of the fifth theoretical assumption is that when positive emotions are attributed to social actors (for example, individuals or groups) the strength of ties with these actors increases and as a consequence solidarity increases too. The experience of negative emotions attributed to social units has the opposite effects, it weakens the ties and it decreases the solidarity. Lawler argues that the most notable behavioural manifestations of solidarity in social networks are: the expanding areas of collaboration, remaining in a collaborative relation despite similar or better opportunities elsewhere, accepting a higher degree of ambiguity in contractual arrangements and forgiving costly or opportunistic behaviours (ibid.: 329). In entrepreneurship, collaborative exchange is often a key predictor of venture success. Successful ventures are often started by groups of entrepreneurs and not by single individuals (Goss, 2007) and because of the high likelihood of success they trigger positive emotional states. Being involved in rewarding social exchanges may actually satisfy entrepreneurs' desire for autonomy, because it involves the possibility of initiating and maintaining (thus controlling) emotionally rewarding social ties as opposed to being involved in predefined and more restrictive social exchanges (for example, with a direct supervisor). In short, new venture formation is explained by the ATSE as a tendency to control social ties in a way that increases the likelihood of positive as opposed to negative emotional states (ibid.).

The main theoretical arguments concerning the impact of emotions on ESDM can be summarized as follows: (i) due to the high stakes involved and to the fact that they rely heavily on substantive information processing, entrepreneurial strategic decisions are susceptible to affect infusion; (ii) in general, when deciding, entrepreneurs have a strong tendency to preserve a positive emotional mood and avoid negative emotional states; (iii) the experience of positive emotions will impact on information processing in the attention stage (the arguments and facts associated with a positive emotional state will be selected and extensively processed), the encoding stage (positive outcomes or arguments will be more valued, often leading to an unrealistic optimism in decision-making) and the retrieval stage (heuristic and intuitive information processing strategies will be reinforced as opposed to systematic and analytic strategies); and (iv) entrepreneurs will seek highly rewarding collaborations and social exchanges with a high probability.

Thus far, we have reviewed the most relevant ESDM-related factors discussed in extant literature. Besides the high variety of factors and the multiple ways in which they relate to ESDM, the inconclusive results concerning their direct impact on ESDM effectiveness make integration difficult. It is therefore not unreasonable to argue that cognitive, motivational and emotional factors influence ESDM not in a direct way, but indirectly through information processing mechanisms, which are underlying, or mediating factors. This argument is not new to the entrepreneurial cognition literature (see, for example, Baron, 2004; Baron and Ward, 2004), yet no systematic attempt has been made to use systemic information processing models as integrative frameworks. Decision theorists (Smith and DeCoster, 2000; Stanovich and West, 2000; Dane and Pratt, 2007) have argued that dual-process models are central in understanding decision-making in management and entrepreneurship. We shall thus integrate the distinctive features of ESDM into a unitary information processing model, based on a dual-process view on human cognition.

3.7   A GENERIC COGNITIVE MODEL OF ESDM

The human cognitive system receives information from the environment through sensory and perceptual processes, and selects parts of it using (limited) attentional resources. The selected information is then subjected to further processing and eventually encoded as cognitive representations in the LTM. These representations will then be retrieved or activated in the WM space and used to address specific tasks such as decision-making and reasoning. In principle, LTM is a repository of both explicit representations (which can be voluntarily accessed) and implicit ones (which are inaccessible to introspection and are impossible to express through language), while WM refers to activated representations (both implicit as well as explicit) that are used to tackle a particular task. The so-called two process theories of cognition argue that between the perception stage and the WM space, knowledge is transformed through two interdependent processes: automatic and controlled processing (also known as intuitive versus rational or experiential versus rational thinking styles) (Stanovich and West, 2000; Dane and Pratt, 2007).

The automatic processing (also called System 1) is, in evolutionary terms, developed earlier; it involves a heuristic way of processing information and it does not impose computational constraints on the cognitive system because it relies on already existing heuristics stored in the LTM space. These heuristics are acquired through experience and are a form of implicit inferences, highly contextual and personalized. System 1 is activated automatically and it processes information quickly on the basis of holistic activation of these LTM heuristic structures, very often associated with emotional content. The controlled processing (System 2) is developed later in evolution and is based on analytical processing and explicit thought processes (ibid.). The speed of information processing in System 2 is slower and it puts high demands on the computational capacities of the cognitive system. While for the operation of System 1 only the outcome is conscious, the processing steps undertaken when System 2 operates are often with conscious awareness (Stanovich and West, 2000). Nevertheless, the two processes are not independent. Although the functioning of System 1 is influenced by slow and incremental learning processes, while the functioning of System 2 involves general abstractions and is influenced by short or sometimes non-repetitive learning episodes, the two systems work hand in hand in generating any outcome for a goal-directed decision (Hastie, 2001). Some external conditions (for example, presence of positive mood) or stable individual differences (for example, differences in cognitive styles) lead to the activation of System 1-related processes. The activation of these processes is not necessary detrimental to the decision outcomes. Unless it leads to oversimplified cognitive representations in the WM space the functioning of System 1 can be beneficial for the quality of decisions (Dane and Pratt, 2007). The activation of System 2 reduces the probability of developing such oversimplified cognitive representations. Direct feedback on the negative consequences of the heuristic information processing may strengthen the impact of System 2 on the functioning of System 1. Moreover, a deliberate practice involving the repetition of control strategies exerted on the detrimental influences of System 1 on reasoning and decision-making, lead to an increase in effectiveness in decision-making (Hastie, 2001; Dane and Pratt, 2007). To conclude, the outcomes of cognitive tasks result from the interaction and interplay between these two systems (for more details on the operation of the two systems, see Smith and DeCoster, 2000; Stanovich and West, 2000; Dane and Pratt, 2007). The specificities of ESDM can also be explained by the interaction between these two systems. An integrative model of the factors associated with ESDM is presented in Figure 3.2.

Strategic decisions are cognitive tasks that demand substantive information processing, meaning that they cannot be addressed by simply activating pre-existing knowledge structures from the LTM. Therefore, available information needs to be carefully evaluated, new information needs to be gathered and eventually new task-specific knowledge representations need to be created. This process heavily relies on controlled information processing (System 2). System 1 is also activated, but the heuristic processing associated with this system is rather limited by the functioning of System 2. In the specific case of entrepreneurs, however, the impact of automatic information processing in strategic decision is higher, since this particular type of decision-makers have been shown to have a higher sensitivity to a heuristic type of processing. Entrepreneurial decision-making has sometimes been deemed an 'enactment process', meaning that acting precedes thinking (Weick, 1979; Busenitz and Barney, 1997). The higher impact of System 1 in ESDM works as a two-edged sword. It has a negative impact on decisional outcomes to the extent to which entrepreneurs use oversimplification mechanisms and biased estimations of probabilities, while it may be beneficial when entrepreneurs use heuristics developed through experience to make sense of a highly unstructured strategic situation. Therefore, the specific characteristics of decision situations faced by entrepreneurs may also impact on the activation of System 1 in ESDM.

Proponents of the biases and heuristics cognitive component in entrepreneurship literature assert that entrepreneurs in their SDM face more uncertainty than do managers in large organizations (Busenitz and Barney, 1997; Busenitz, 1999; Tan, 2001). The logic underlying this argument is similar to that of why entrepreneurs might face higher levels of complexity

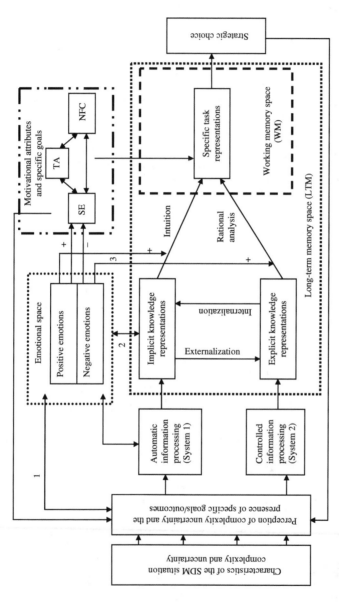

Note: SE – self-efficacy, TA – tolerance for ambiguity, NFC – need for cognition. The numbered arrows refer to ways in which emotions influence information processing stages, 1 – attention stage (emotions' impact on selective attention and perception), 2 – encoding stage (emotions' impact on encoding and learning new information) and 3 – retrieval stage (emotions' influence on selective retrieval and knowledge activation).

Figure 3.2   A dual-process model of entrepreneurial strategic decision-making

in their decision-making, which was argued earlier in this book. Entrepreneurs often have to make decisions with less information available to them than do managers. For instance, they often do not have access to historical trends or previous levels of performance, and have little specific market information – material that is often available to managers (Busenitz and Barney, 1997). Moreover, entrepreneurship's very nature demands quick decision-making and grasping of opportunities with incomplete information (Tan, 2001). Quick decisions are certainly associated with the functioning of System 1. In addition to the individual tendencies of entrepreneurs, heuristic information processing is also a potential result of the situational demands in entrepreneurial decision-making.

Private businesses ran by entrepreneurs are often too small to optimally confront complex issues and they lack the level of sophistication of large enterprises (ibid.). Furthermore, managers in organizations rely on all kinds of decision-making routines, and are accountable only for their 'piece of the pie', a luxury entrepreneurs cannot afford. The bottom line therefore, is that the predominant view in entrepreneurship literature is that entrepreneurs face higher levels of complexity and uncertainty than do managers. Intuition is often the way they tackle this high complexity and the outcomes of using intuition are twofold. If general heuristics and biases are used (usually associated with biased probabilistic judgements), the effectiveness of strategic decisions will be lower, while if highly context-specific heuristics are used (usually developed through experience by dealing with similar unstructured decisional situations), the effectiveness of strategic decisions will be higher.

Because (i) entrepreneurs are more prone than other types of decision-makers to use heuristic information processing in strategic issues and (ii) the situational characteristics faced by entrepreneurs in their work are very likely to trigger automatic information processing, the impact of System 1 on ESDM is expected to be substantial. In order to increase the amount of control of System 2 on the functioning of System 1, entrepreneurs have first to identify the instances in which their decisions are susceptible to the heuristic type of information processing. Decisions associated with strong emotional reactions (for example, the evaluation of alternatives triggers positive emotions) or decisions in which remembered similar cases are used as benchmarks, are very likely to be influenced by intuition rather than systematic analytical thinking. The use of pre-existing case representations stored in LTM is not necessarily flawed. It may simply be an enactment of expertise. It should be noted, though, that expertise needs time to develop and the accuracy of judging the similarity between several decisional situations emerges after years of business experience (Dane and Pratt, 2007).

Emotions are another set of factors that impact on ESDM. Several cognitive theories acknowledge that emotion and cognition are linked into a single interdependent representational system (Forgas, 1995) and the outcomes of information processing depend on the interplay between cognition and emotions. In particular, the functioning of System 1 is strongly associated with emotional content. The holistic associations activated by automatic information processing result in affectively charged judgements (Dane and Pratt, 2007) and thus there is a strong association between the emotional space and the functioning of System 1. Moreover, implicit knowledge representations are usually developed from emotionally relevant life experiences and thus often they are associated with a more specific or general emotional state. Another aspect of the impact of emotions on information processing refers to the retrieval of specific contents from LTM. In principle, positive emotional states strengthen judgements based on intuition, while negative emotions strengthen rational and analytical processes. Experiencing a general positive mood may be interpreted as a sign of success in making the choice, and thus having a good intuition, while experiencing a negative mood will lead the decision-maker to question the effectiveness of intuition and be more analytical in the decision processes. For the specific case of ESDM, the role of emotions is particularly important because entrepreneurs are very keen on maintaining a general positive mood, and therefore the intuitive judgements will be strengthened as opposed to the rational and analytical ones. To conclude, in addition to the general tendency to use a heuristic type of information processing, entrepreneurs will be more inclined to rely on intuitive judgements when making strategic choices because they like to maintain a positive mood.

A distinct impact of emotions is on the motivational attributes and goal setting. Negative emotions decrease, while positive emotions increase the sense of self-efficacy. When an entrepreneur is successful in previous decisions – and likely to experience a positive mood – he/she may put more trust in his/her ability to tackle strategic issues, while when previous decisions are flawed – negative emotions are experienced – it is very likely that the self-esteem of the entrepreneur will be lowered. Also, as mentioned in our discussion earlier, the experienced emotions have a strong effect on goal setting. When positive emotions are experienced, the general goal will be to maintain these emotions, while when negative emotions are experienced, the general goal will be to correct and escape from these states. Through the perceptual processes, these specific goals will in turn influence the information processing in the cognitive system.

The core element of the model presented in Figure 3.2 and the main outcome of the interplay between Systems 1 and 2 is the specific task representation activated in the WM space. This activated representation drives the selection of a particular course of action. Previous research in cognitive sciences has repeatedly shown that performance in problem solving and the decision-making effectiveness depends not on the information available, but on the cognitive representations activated in the WM space. This representation refers to the combined set of implicit knowledge representations and explicit knowledge representations activated from the LTM under the influence of both emotional and motivational factors. The characteristics of this representation are always reflected in the strategic choices made by entrepreneurs. In strategic situations, due to the high complexity and uncertainty involved, the specific task representations are supposed to result primarily from controlled information processing. Nevertheless, in the specific case of ESDM, the content of the WM representations is also influenced by the automatic information processing as well as by motivational factors (for example, tolerance for ambiguity, self-efficacy, need for cognition). As we shall argue further in Chapter 4, the impact of motivational factors on decision effectiveness is mediated by the complexity of the representation developed in the WM space.

The specific task representations are therefore intermediary factors between the decision situation (information environment) and decisional outcomes. In line with previous managerial cognition arguments (Calori et al., 1994; Walsh, 1995) we argue here that a requirement of success in ESDM is that the complexity of the knowledge representation concerning a particular strategic issue should at least match the complexity of the information environment in which the decision-maker operates (see also Dane and Pratt, 2007). Therefore, in order to be effective in their strategic choices, entrepreneurs have to develop complex representations about the strategic decision situation. The more-specific aspects related to the complexity of the WM representations are discussed in Chapter 4.

NOTE

1. Let us note here, perhaps superfluously, that obviously many other variables – both contextual and individual – in the life course may affect this decision.

4. The role of cognitive complexity in entrepreneurial strategic decision-making

Petru L. Curşeu

4.1 INTRODUCTION

Good decision-making is essential for organizational success. Imagine the owner of a small IT company who decides to diversify the products portfolio. The way in which this decision is implemented may lead to a rapid development of the company and a substantial increase in profit, or (as unrelated diversification) to complete failure and bankruptcy. Both the turbulent environment in which the company operates and the fact that most of the information available has a certain degree of uncertainty, create a high degree of complexity for this decision. The entrepreneur will most probably try to make sense of all the information available and then make an informed decision. In the end, the strategic decision of how to diversify the product portfolio will reflect the entrepreneur's efficacy in processing the information at hand. Therefore, the quality of a strategic decision does not depend on the available information, but rather on how well the decision-maker understands this information. In other words, if the entrepreneur has a complex and comprehensive understanding of the available information, the quality of the decision will substantially increase. This example illustrates the role of cognition and in particular the role of cognitive representations in decision-making effectiveness. The aim of this chapter is to explore the role of cognitive complexity as a key cognitive factor for strategic choices in entrepreneurship.

In the last decades, the role of entrepreneurial cognitions in decision-making received considerable attention. In 2002, the journal *Entrepreneurship Theory and Practice* devoted a special issue to information processing and entrepreneurial cognition. In this special issue, Mitchell et al. (2002) define entrepreneurial cognition as the 'knowledge structures that people use to make assessments, judgments, or decisions involving opportunity evaluation, venture creation and growth' (p. 97). However, there is no systematic attempt to explore the characteristics of these knowledge structures in relation to decision-making effectiveness. This chapter focuses on the complexity of cognitive representations as a core component of effective decision-making. The main arguments are that: (i) cognitive representations developed by entrepreneurs concerning the decision situation are mediating factors between individual differences (for example, entrepreneurial self-efficacy, risk taking, need for cognition) and decisional outcomes, (ii) the complexity of these representations reflects the interaction between controlled and automatic information processing, and (iii) more complex representations are beneficial for decision quality.

4.2   COGNITION AND DECISION-MAKING IN ORGANIZATIONS

Cognition plays an important role in shaping human behaviour in a variety of situations from social interactions (Cannon-Bowers et al., 1993; Mathieu et al., 2000; Dunn et al., 2002) to decision-making and problem solving (Lang et al., 1978; Lord and Maher, 1990). Modern cognitive theories contributed heavily to the understanding of human behaviour in organizations. Applied to organization studies, cognitive theories explain the way in which people and groups in organizations use the information at hand to come to a decision, solution or action. Cognitive theories and models are used to explain decision-making (Brief and Downey, 1983; Dutton and Jackson, 1987), problem solving (Lang et al., 1978), organizational socialization and intergroup conflict (Ashfort and Mael, 1989), career success (O'Reilly and Chatman, 1994), or power (Krackhardt, 1990). Problem solving and decision-making are central organizational areas of application for cognitive theoretical models. Rational, limited capacity, expert and cybernetic information processing models are equally used to explain problem solving and strategic decision-making (SDM) (Lord and Maher, 1990). Problem solving is an essential process for managerial effectiveness and cognitive models have been used to understand the unstructured aspect of strategic planning and decision-making.

The most influential cognitive models used to explain the effectiveness of decision-making within organizations are those stressing the impact of activated cognitive representations on the decisional outcome. Interpretative as well as concrete and unambiguous cognitive representations are more effective in producing superior decisional outcomes and increasing the quality of decision as compared to more general cognitive representations (Boland et al., 2001). Cognitive representations are ways of reducing environmental complexity and help the decision-makers to

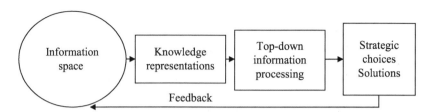

Figure 4.1   A framework for top-down information processing in SDM

impose order in volatile and uncertain environments (Wood and Bandura, 1989; Porac and Thomas, 1990) and they influence decision-making process and outcomes (Boland et al., 2001). In a more general context, cognitive representations are conceptualized as mediators in the relation between the situational cues (knowledge) and behaviour (Davis and Luthans, 1980; Gioia and Manz, 1985; Wood and Bandura, 1989).

The cognitive literature refers to information processing affected by activated cognitive representations as 'top-down' information processing. Therefore there is a basic distinction between knowledge representations and the processes through which these representations are transformed and/or combined in order to make a decision or to solve a problem. In top-down information processing, cognitions (cognitive schema or more generally knowledge representations) developed in previous experience influence the subsequent cognitive processes (for example, decision-making or problem solving). Activated knowledge representations can have a positive influence (for example, the effect of previous experiences and expertise) as well as a negative impact (for example, the impact of cognitive frames and cognitive biases) on information processing (Walsh, 1995). A framework of the role of knowledge representations on information processing is presented in Figure 4.1.

The information environment depicted in Figure 4.1 is a characteristic of the external world that it is mirrored (represented) in the cognitive system of the decision-maker. According to the law of requisite variety (Ashby, 1965), in order for the cognitive system of the decision-maker to adapt successfully to the environment, the complexity of the knowledge representation should at least match the complexity of the information environment (for more details, see Walsh, 1995; Dane and Pratt, 2007). Previous studies showed that managers' cognitive complexity (the complexity of the cognitive representations developed and used by managers) and their cognitive abilities (ability to efficiently process complex information) are accurate predictors of their career success, and good predictors of the effective handling of complex, uncertain and unstable environmental conditions (Wood and Bandura, 1989; Ginsberg, 1990; Calori et al., 1994; O'Reilly and Chatman, 1994).

Therefore complex decision situations (in particular, strategic decisions), require complex cognitive representations. The complexity of the knowledge representation is a critical element for successful strategic decisions.

4.3 COGNITIVE COMPLEXITY

As argued in several instances in this book, SDM is inherently complex (for example, Simon, 1972; Mintzberg et al., 1976; Calori et al., 1994; Noorderhaven, 1995). The most effective decision-makers in these complex situations are the ones able to create complex cognitive representations in their working memory (WM) (for details, see Chapter 3). Cognitively complex individuals are able to tackle a decision situation using a variety of angles and strategies and thus are more effective than cognitively simple individuals. The concept of 'cognitive complexity' refers to the 'structural complexity of an individual's cognitive system' (Kelly, 1955). It was initially introduced by Bieri (1955) as a personality trait, but over the years has been redefined as being a feature of information processing in cognitive systems (Curşeu and Rus, 2005).

Cognitive complexity results from two interrelated cognitive processes: differentiation and integration. Calori et al. (1994: 439) assert that, according to complexity theory, 'the complexity of an individual conceptual system is determined by two interdependent aspects: the number of parts or dimensions of the system and the nature and extent of rules for integrating these parts'. This approach to cognitive complexity is in line with Streufert and Swezey's (1986) definition of cognitive complexity as the ability to differentiate alternative perspectives and to integrate these perspectives into an informed decision (Curşeu and Rus, 2005). This quality to simultaneously differentiate and integrate knowledge was explored both as a personal characteristic of the decision-maker (correlated to other cognitive and motivational attributes) and a situation-specific factor. On the one hand, previous research (Stanovich and West, 2000) argues that cognitive complexity is closely related to general cognitive abilities (for example, general intelligence) and therefore some individuals are in general able to form more-complex cognitive representations about specific decision situations than others. On the other hand, cognitive complexity is often defined in relation to a problem domain, meaning that a particular decision-maker is able to form complex representations for a particular category of problems (for example, business administration) and not for others (for example, chess play). Starting from these two lines of reasoning, this chapter conceptualizes cognitive complexity as a two-faceted concept.

A first way to look at cognitive complexity is as an attribute of a cognitive system. According to this approach, cognitive complexity differs across individuals and in general, some individuals develop and use more complex cognitive representations than others. It can be argued that individuals high on general cognitive abilities are able to develop more-complex cognitive representations (Stanovich and West, 2000). Individuals with high cognitive complexity are able to *differentiate* a system in many distinct elements, and then discover patterns and relations among these elements to *integrate* these elements into a coherent action. In addition, the more an event can be differentiated and several aspects of it considered in novel relationships, the more refined the response and successful the solution (Curşeu and Rus, 2005). Individuals with high cognitive complexity are thus more successful in applying several complementary perspectives to the understanding of their environment than others, and are, therefore, multidimensional in their thinking. This makes cognitively complex individuals more flexible in their thinking strategies, they have a higher performance in cognitive tasks and in particular they are more efficient in problem solving than cognitively simple individuals (Calori et al., 1994; Curşeu and Rus, 2005). In short, the conceptual structure of a cognitively complex person is highly differentiated (having many distinct dimensions or ideas), finely articulated (having each continuum capable of discriminating the magnitude of a number of stimuli), and flexibly integrated (that is, having dimensions which can be interrelated in many ways and are amenable to alternative functions of schemata) (ibid.).

A second view on cognitive complexity holds that it may differ across specific domains – one can be cognitively complex in one domain (say finances), but relatively simple in another (say history of art) (Streufert and Swezey, 1986). It is generally accepted that in order to be able to develop and use complex representations in a particular field, a substantial amount of experience in that field is needed. The contextual character of cognitive complexity means that certain decision-makers are cognitively complex in some areas, but simple in others. Some people are able to develop complex and accurate representations about maths problems or financial issues, but on the other hand they have a rather simple understanding of how to run a business. In other words, being an expert in finances will not necessarily make you an expert entrepreneur. In order to be successful, an entrepreneur needs to be able to understand a variety of situational cues and thus develop complex representations in a large number of domains. A successful entrepreneur needs a good understanding of business administration, the market and market dynamics as well as specific knowledge related to the object of the business. Not all this knowledge is always needed at the same time. However, strategic choices are certainly instances in which the cognitive complexity plays an important role, and relevant knowledge from several domains needs to be integrated into a comprehensive set of representations.

In this chapter, cognitive complexity is defined in relation to the concept of knowledge representations (or cognitive representations). In this way the dual facets of cognitive complexity (as an individual difference or a context-dependent attribute) can be related to the characteristics of knowledge representations developed in relation to a decision situation. In other words, cognitive complexity reflects the structural complexity of the knowledge representations developed in the WM space of a decision-maker. The complexity of these representations depends on the general cognitive abilities of the decision-maker (individuals high on general cognitive abilities are capable of forming more-complex representations) and in the same time is context dependent (depends on the field of expertise of the decision-maker). To conclude, cognitive complexity refers to 'the complexity of the knowledge structures in a cognitive system, and it describes the sophistication of those cognitive structures that are used for organizing and storing cognitive contents' (Curşeu et al., 2007: 188).

Although knowledge representations have received considerable attention in the entrepreneurial literature in recent years, in most of the studies the knowledge representations have not been directly identified. Generally, their presence and nature was inferred from proxies (for example, demographics, type and level of expertise and experience). Therefore, there is a need to put forward methods for evaluating the structure and in particular the complexity of the knowledge representations. In cognitive sciences, several methods from cognitive mapping to process tracing are used to elicit and represent the cognitive structures associated with a specific situation. Cognitive mapping is certainly one of the most popular methods used so far as a knowledge elicitation and representation tool (Hodgkinson and Clarkson, 2005). The next section provides an illustration of how an ideographic variant of cognitive mapping can be used to evaluate cognitive complexity in entrepreneurial strategic decision-making (ESDM).

4.4   THE EVALUATION OF COGNITIVE COMPLEXITY

As argued before, a feasible way to elicit cognitive representations and to evaluate the cognitive complexity is by 'cognitive mapping' (see Calori et al., 1994; Curşeu and Rus, 2005), in which the configuration of a cognitive map gives a direct view on the level of complexity of the knowledge representation of the decision-maker (Calori et al., 1994). Cognitive maps are graphical representations reflecting both the cognitive contents and the structure and relations between these contents. The term 'cognitive map' has several meanings. In cognitive psychology it mostly refers to the way people represent geographical locations (Downs and Stea, 1977), while in management and organization studies the term refers to more general types of cognitive representations that consist of sets of concepts and the relationships among them (Hodgkinson and Clarkson, 2005). In the last stream of research other terms have been used to refer to the same concept: mental models, mental (cognitive) frames, causal maps, cognitive networks and conceptual networks (Carley, 1993).

Although the important role of a cognitive approach in understanding ESDM is generally accepted, cognitive mapping was not extensively used as an elicitation and representation technique. Forbes (1999) reviewed 34 studies in the field of entrepreneurship research. Twenty-five of these studies were empirical. Of these 25, 18 were survey-based studies, six encompassed a qualitative design, with one study using cognitive mapping. Cognitive mapping is certainly a method that could very well contribute to the exploration of entrepreneurial cognition in ESDM because it allows the evaluation of cognitive structures inaccessible to direct observation (Huff, 1990; Calori et al., 1994; Carley, 1997; Klein and Cooper, 1982; Hodgkinson et al., 2004).

The diversity of terms used in the literature (for example, cognitive maps, mental maps, frames of reference, mindsets, cognitive base, beliefs, and cognitive structures) as well as the diversity of mapping approaches (for example, ideographic or nomothetic approaches), both explain why this technique is underused in entrepreneurial research. Several attempts have been made in recent years to develop a common terminology as well as a clear taxonomy of mapping approaches (Calori et al., 1994; Hodgkinson and Clarkson, 2005). Hodgkinson and Clarkson distinguish between ideographic and nomothetic cognitive mapping techniques as well as between cognitive maps in general and cause maps in particular. Ideographic mapping techniques are based on the assumption that the knowledge representations are both domain and person specific. In other words, each person, in contact with particular situational cues (a knowledge domain), will develop a set of representations that are distinctive from the ones developed by other persons. Ideographic cognitive mapping process aims at eliciting the whole conceptual richness of a particular decision-maker or problem solver in the exact way in which the thoughts are expressed in the natural language. Nomothetic cognitive mapping is based on the assumption that different categories of decision-makers or problem solvers share similarities in their cognitive maps and a set of standard concepts or variables are used by the researcher in the mapping process. Respondents are asked to organize these concepts in a meaningful way or to estimate the similarities among the concepts based on a pair-wise comparison. The matrices resulting from these comparisons are subjected to statistical analyses, and in this way cognitive maps can also be compared in a quantitative way (ibid.). Based on ideographic and nomothetic approaches, several types of cognitive maps can be elicited through cognitive mapping. In line with Huff (1990), in this chapter we use the term 'cognitive map' to describe the structure of knowledge representation, and 'cognitive mapping' as the technique or the process through which a cognitive map is created.

Cognitive Maps

In essence, a cognitive map is a 'representation of the perceptions and beliefs of an individual about his own subjective world' (Klein and Cooper, 1982: 63). A cause map is a particular form of cognitive map in which all the relations established among the contents contained in the map are causal (Hodgkinson and Clarkson, 2005). Cognitive maps illustrate the ways in which individuals make sense of their social world (Carley, 1997). There are two views on the degree to which individuals are aware of, or have pre-constructed, their cognitive maps (ibid.). Some consider cognitive maps as tacit, that is, 'in the mind', and therefore by definition unobservable. Proponents of this view assert that researchers can study only a representation of the cognitive map that exists in the mind of the participant. On the other hand, others treat the cognitive map as an emergent structure that only comes into being ('emerges') when a participant articulates it (ibid.) and is thus by definition observable. A practical consequence of this key difference between these two views is thus whether a cognitive map refers to the tacit construct that exists in the mind of individuals, or to the outcome of an individual articulating this map (for example, a drawing of the concepts and relations). Whether directly observable or indirectly represented, all scholars agree that cognitive maps, at the very least, consist of concepts and relations.

Concepts, in this context, are the building blocks of cognitive maps and are illustrative of the way in which human beings think (Gómez et al., 2000). In this sense they are mental representations of objects, persons or experiences that can be, for instance, concrete, abstract, fictitious or real. Therefore in theory, the number of concepts in the world is infinite. Since human beings in general, and decision-makers in particular, want to economize on the number of concepts they take into account (remember bounded rationality and biases and heuristics that were discussed in earlier chapters), concepts serve the purpose of generalizing (that is, they make it possible to overlook irrelevant differences between objects) (ibid.). A basic issue in cognitive mapping is how many central concepts should be used. Thus far, no single overarching set of concept types has emerged that is valid through all research questions. However, to facilitate automated coding and analysis of the maps, it is usually advisable to try to restrict the number of key concepts to as few as possible (ideally one) within the boundaries of the substantive questions the researcher is interested in (Carley, 1993).

Relations are the connections between concepts in a cognitive map. For a large part, they constitute the meaning of the concepts they link, that is, 'a concept is such only by virtue of the way in which it is linked and connected to other things' (Gómez et al., 2000: 173). Thus, a relation is 'an interconnection between concepts in a universe of discourse' (ibid.). Relations can have different characteristics. Some scholars (see, for instance, Carley and Palmquist, 1992) assert that there are four basic dimensions in which relations differ, namely: strength, sign, direction and meaning. Other scholars (see, for instance, Gómez et al., 2000: 174) rather come up with a more elaborate list of possible relation types, for instance: equivalence, taxonomic, structural, dependent, topological, causal, functional, chronological, similarity, conditional and purpose. Whichever taxonomy of relations a researcher wishes to adhere to, the choice should always be guided by the substantive questions the researcher is interested in, meaning that he or she should preserve the information about a relationship when it makes sense from his or her theoretical point of view (Carley, 1993).

Cognitive Mapping

According to Hodgkinson and Clarkson (2005), the process of cognitive mapping consists of four steps: (i) knowledge elicitation, (ii) construction of the cognitive map, (iii) analysis of the cognitive map and (iv) aggregation and/or comparison of the cognitive maps.

First, in the knowledge elicitation stage, ideographic cognitive mapping focuses on written material. Therefore, relevant methods of identifying the contents (that is, specific knowledge) to be organized in cognitive maps are interviewing the respondents (for example, decision-makers or problem solvers) or using other types of written documents in which the decision situation is clearly and extensively described. Any material expressed in a textual form can be further subjected to cognitive mapping (Axelrod, 1976; Swan, 1995).

Second, in the map construction stage, most of the ideographic cognitive mapping techniques that use written protocols consist of three steps: concept elicitation, conceptual refinement and relationships identification. First, the main concepts in the text are identified (we shall refer to these as 'first-order' concepts). The first-order concepts encapsulate the whole meaning of the text. Second, based on similarity between them, the concepts will be grouped into categories. However, not every first-order concept needs to be placed in a category. The aim of the categorization is just to organize the contents of the map and create a meaningful structure. Finally, the next step is the elicitation of second-order constructs in order to identify the way in which conceptual categories and concepts are interconnected. Based on these second-order concepts, the nature of the relationships among the concepts will be established (ibid.; Hodgkinson and Clarkson, 2005).

To illustrate the ideographic cognitive mapping, let us consider a short fragment of an interview transcript with an entrepreneur describing a strategic decision (selected from the sample described in Iederan et al., 2007):

> My company was initially focused on selling IT components and providing computer service, and two years ago I decided to extend our activities to software development. I thought it was a good opportunity to start software development in Romania, because several companies from Western Europe and the USA outsourced the development for some of their products to Romanian companies due to their lower prices as compared to Western companies. Also, the market for our custom-made computers decreased because the offer of ready-assembled computers, in a variety of configurations, has increased substantially over the last years and several large retailers now offer a variety of IT products. However, to start with, the new software development was not easy. First, finding employees with good software development skills and knowledge was not easy. The applicants demanded high wages and during the last years there was a scarcity of good software developers on the market. Moreover, there were a few big software development companies out there and it was difficult to get big contracts due to this harsh competition. Also, they were offering better salaries for their software developers. To get contracts, we advertised via the Internet, but the first contracts we had were with our bigger customers for whom we used to carry out IT hardware service. We had to deal with all these obstacles in order to succeed. We started with a few small contracts and in time we managed to get bigger ones because we gained more experience both at the operational as well as the marketing level. At the moment we have a larger customer from Western Europe and we have already started to develop a product that will enter the larger European market. Now the profits have started to grow and we are doing better than two years ago when we started with this development.

The graphical representation of the cognitive map is presented in Figure 4.2. The core element in the transcript is the decision to extend the core activities of the company, hence it will be placed in the central position of the cognitive map. Among the first-order concepts are the causes of the decision (a high demand for software products, a decrease in profit from regular activities and a low demand on the market for disparate IT components), the obstacles (harsh competition and the scarcity of specialized

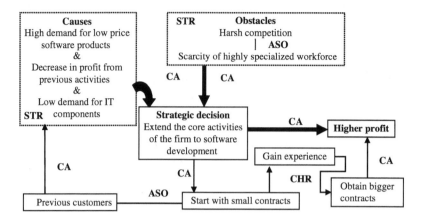

Note: CA = causal relation; ASO = association relation; CHR = chronological relation; STR = structural relation; bold arrows: first-order links; thin arrows: second-order links; concepts in bold are first-order concepts.

Figure 4.2   Example of a cognitive map (1)

workforce), and the consequences of the decision (obtaining a higher profit). All these first-order concepts are linked through first-order links. In the next step, second-order concepts that clarify the structure of the map are identified and connected through the second-order connections with the rest of the structure.

The third step of the cognitive mapping is the analysis of the cognitive map. Previous research used structural indicators inspired from social network theory to analyse cognitive maps (Scott, 2000). The number of concepts used in the map, the number of conceptual categories, the number of connections among the concepts as well as the types of connections are illustrative examples. In the example depicted in Figure 4.2, several types of relationships between concepts can be identified. Based on the typology advanced by Gómez et al. (2000), the arrows depict causal relationships (for example, causes leading to a strategic choice), the straight line depicts association (starting with small contracts associated with previous customers), the dotted boxes depict structural relationships (clusters of causes or obstacles for the decision) and a chronological sequence is depicted as a series of arrows among events (start with small contracts, gain experience and in time obtain bigger contracts) in the low right of Figure 4.2. Therefore, this map consists of 11 concepts, interconnected by 10 connections of four different types (causal, association, structural and chronological).

Based on Gómez et al.'s taxonomy, several types of connections among the concepts in a map can be distinguished: a causal relation (CA) describes how a given action or phenomenon induces (determines) another state, action or event (for example, A is the cause of B, A needs B, A fires B, if A than B) or describes the conditions or actions followed by consequences or reactions (for example, A enables B, A needs B); association (ASO) describes how two or more concepts are correlated (for example, A is related or associated with B, A is connected to B, A is in contact with B) or describes a combination of concepts (for example, A and B are combined with . . .); equivalence (EQ) establishes the equality between two or more apparently different concepts, including similarity (establishes which concepts are similar or analogous and to what extent) (for example, $A = B + C$, A is similar to B); a topological (TOP) relation describes the spatial distribution of concepts representing physical items (for example, A is above B, A is to the right of B, A is inside B); a structural (STR) relation describes how a concept or a group of concepts can be decomposed into parts (also inclusion/exclusion relations, A is a part of B, A and B are parts of C), or how several concepts share a common trait or are united by a common element (A, B and C share common elements); a chronological (CHR) relation describes the way in which two or more concepts are related in a time sequence (for example, A occurs before B, A and B occur simultaneously, A occurs during B, A starts before B ends); a hierarchical (HIE) relation describes the categorical relation between concepts (one or several elements are subordinated to one or several others) (for example, A is subordinated to B, A, B and C are subordinated to D), or taxonomic relations (for example, A can be classified as B, C and D) (see also Curşeu et al., 2007).

In the last stage of the cognitive mapping, aggregation and/or comparison, several structural indicators can be computed. A central structural indicator is cognitive complexity. Three basic scores are discussed here as essential for computing the complexity of a cognitive map: map connectivity, map diversity and the comprehensiveness of the map. Cognitive map connectivity (for the example presented in Figure 4.2, CMC = 10) is the most frequently cited indicator for comparing cognitive maps (Bougon, 1992; Cossette and Audet, 1992; Eden et al., 1992; Langfield-Smith, 1992; Calori et al., 1994) and it refers to the total number of connections established between concepts. Cognitive map diversity (for the example presented in Figure 4.2, CMD = 4) refers to the number of distinct relations (types of relations) established between the concepts on the map. Cognitive map comprehensiveness (for the example presented in Figure 4.2, NoC = 11) refers to the number of concepts used to define a particular conceptual domain and is computed simply by counting the non-repetitive concepts used in the cognitive map. These three indicators can be used to compute different forms of cognitive complexity.

Absolute cognitive map complexity (ACMCo) reflects cognitive complexity by taking into account the number of distinct concepts used to define a particular conceptual domain, the number of connections established among these concepts as well as the diversity of the relations among them. The ACMCo is computed by simply multiplying the three basic indicators described earlier (ACMCo = NoC × CMC × CMD, therefore for the example presented in Figure 4.2, ACMCo = 440). A high value for ACMCo, indicates that the group uses many concepts, richly interconnected in different ways to define a particular conceptual domain.

Relative cognitive map complexity (RCMCo) refers to the complexity of the cognitive map in relation to the number of concepts used to define a conceptual domain. RCMCo can be computed using the formula: CMCo = (CMC × CMD)/NoC (for the example presented in Figure 4.2, CMCo = 3.63). This formula for computing cognitive complexity is derived from the definition provided by Calori et al. (1994: 439): 'the complexity of an individual conceptual system is determined by two interdependent aspects: the number of parts or dimensions of the system and the nature and the extent of rules for integrating these parts'. A high value for RCMCo indicates that the group map is richly interconnected and diverse in relation to the number of concepts used in the map (for another coding example, see Curşeu et al., 2007). In theory, these two cognitive complexity indices have no fixed range and in order to be able to compare across maps, other indices with a fixed range (0 to 1) inspired from social network analysis can be used (for example, cognitive map density, for details, see Scott, 2000).

What makes cognitive mapping relevant for ESDM research is that it allows the researcher to explore the way in which entrepreneurs represent knowledge relevant for a particular decisional situation (Klein and Cooper, 1982). Therefore, cognitive mapping offers the researcher insight into an unseen space, namely the WM space of the decision-maker (for more details, see Figure 3.2 in Chapter 3). In addition, cognitive maps allow the map maker to focus on action and explore, for example, how previous events influence current events and what is expected in the future (Huff, 1990). In addition, as Klein and Cooper (1982: 70) put it: 'a cognitive map can be viewed as an external model of a decision process, a model which can present the complex ideas and interrelationships perceived by a decision-maker in a concise, tangible and manageable form'. Also, maps allow for holistic synthesis of the knowledge used in a strategic decision (Calori et al., 1994). Carley (1993) describes the technical advantages of map analysis, among others the possibility of exploring the micro-level differences in people's cognitive maps, the ability to examine hierarchies of meanings, the possibility of staying close to the text[1] but also to move beyond it, and exploring the implicit cognitions associated with the decision-making process. Therefore, cognitive mapping allows the researcher to gain insights into both explicit and implicit decision-making processes.

4.5 COGNITIVE COMPLEXITY AND ESDM

The aim of this section is to create an integrative framework of cognitive complexity and its role in ESDM. The main concepts presented so far in this chapter as well as the concepts discussed in Chapter 3 are integrated into a set of theoretical propositions concerning the role of cognitive complexity. This framework will by no means be exhaustive with respect to the factors that influence ESDM. However, it contributes to the ESDM literature by emphasizing the role of cognitive complexity in ESDM as well as its interplay with the other factors in determining the ESDM outcomes.

Calori et al. (1994) argue that the relation between a CEO's cognitive complexity and firm performance is moderated by the complexity of the environment. More specifically, Calori et al. argue that the CEO's cognitive complexity should match the level of complexity of his or her environment, in order to have a positive effect on decision outcomes. In other words, the cognitive complexity of the decision-maker needs to 'fit' the complexity of the environment in which the decision is being made (Curşeu and Rus, 2005). This argument is in line with the law of requisite variety (Ashby, 1965), stating that the success of adaptation for a complex system depends on the extent to which its internal complexity fits the degree of complexity existing in the environment in which the complex system is embedded. In cognitive terms, in order to be effective, a decision-maker needs to form cognitive representations that fit the complexity of the environment in which the decision-maker operates.

The highly flexible, dynamic and complex environments in which most of the small and medium-sized enterprises (SMEs) operate, create high demands for cognitive complexity on entrepreneurs. The organizational environment exerts a much higher pressure on entrepreneurs of SMEs than on managers of large companies. First, because many institutions in large organizations are created as means to reduce environmental complexity for managers having to make strategic decisions at the highest levels of the organization (Chandler, 1962; Calori et al., 1994). For instance, decision-making 'routines' are simplifying mechanisms and are heavily emphasized in large organizations (Busenitz and Barney, 1997). Second, large organizations clearly differentiate responsibility and often create specific units responsible for strategic decisions and strategic planning. This also helps in reducing the environmental complexity that a manager has to face in SDM. Entrepreneurs have fewer assisting institutions in reducing the complexity of their environment and less task differentiation than do managers of large companies. Therefore entrepreneurs face more complexity pressures in SDM than do managers of large companies and thus high cognitive complexity is a requisite for success in ESDM. Because, as argued in Chapters 2 and 3, SDM is inherently complex and SMEs often operate in complex and dynamic environments, the cognitive complexity of entrepreneurs needs to fit these environment characteristics in order to lead to positive ESDM outcomes. Therefore the first theoretical proposition is:

Proposition 1: Cognitive complexity is beneficial for ESDM effectiveness.

As argued before, cognitive mapping is a way to elicit cognitive representations developed in relation to a particular knowledge domain. Over the years, cognitive mapping has been applied in a wide variety of settings, for instance to measure cognitive complexity, both at the individual (Calori et al., 1994) and the group (Curşeu and Rus, 2005; Curşeu et al., 2007) levels, tendencies in voting behaviour (Carley, 1986), and managers' perception of competitive positioning of the firm (Reger, 1990). One of the fields for which cognitive mapping is especially suitable is ESDM research. Hodgkinson et al. (2004) argue that cognitive mapping is one of the most popular methods for studying people's cognitive representations in SDM. A distinction is often made between explicit and implicit cognitive representations. Explicit representations are accessible through introspection and can be expressed through language, while implicit representations are unconscious and their existence is often inferred from specific behaviour or specific cognitive performances (in decision-making or problem-solving tasks). Cognitive mapping is a particularly relevant method for elicitation and representation because it allows the elicitation of both types of representations. Although they are usually derived from transcripts of other written materials, in the coding stage it is possible to depict specific implicit associations in a cognitive map.

Proposition 2: The existing cognitive complexity in relation to a knowledge domain (for example, specific decision situation) can be evaluated using the structural features of a cognitive map depicted through textual analysis of written documents that accurately describe the decision situation.

The integrative ESDM framework presented in Chapter 3 argues that the most proximal factor to decisional outcome is the cognitive representation developed in the WM space (see Figure 3.2). This cognitive representation is the result of the interplay between the functioning of System 1 (automatic information processing) and System 2 (controlled information processing). Moreover, individual differences (for example, risk propensity), motivational attributes (for example, self-efficacy, tolerance for ambiguity or need for cognition) and emotional states play an important role in shaping the structure of these cognitive representations. As argued in this chapter, cognitive complexity refers to the richness of these cognitive representations formed in the WM space.

The role of automatic and controlled information processing in ESDM is extensively discussed in Chapter 3. The main argument is that the functioning of System 2 is associated with analytical reasoning and extensive information search; the functioning of System 1 is based on the activation of highly contextual (pre-existing) schemas from the long-term memory (LTM). System 2 puts high demands on the computational resources of the human cognitive system, while System 1 is rather automatic and it does not require many computational resources. In line with these general observations, it can be argued that the functioning of System 2 results in the formation of more complex representations in the WM space, while the functioning of System 1 leads to simplified representations. The heuristics information processing specific to the activation of System 1, simplifies the overly complex and unpredictable decisional situations. The very first consequence of the use of cognitive heuristics and biases (especially overconfidence and representativeness heuristics) is a less-complex representation of the decisional situation. Therefore, through the lever of cognitive complexity, general heuristics and biases are expected to have a negative influence on the outcomes of ESDM.

It should be noted, however, that the functioning of System 1 may also generate complex representations. Implicit knowledge representations developed through experience (thus reflecting expertise) and stored in the LTM can be activated and used automatically when situational constraints match the profile of existing representations. Although automatic and heuristic, this type of information processing may lead to complex representations and thus positively impact on ESDM effectiveness. Consider, for instance, experienced physicians. When examining a patient, often these experts are able, based on only a few quick tests and two or three careful questions, to rule out many serious conditions without ordering expensive and time-consuming lab tests or carrying out exhaustive examinations of all contingencies. Generally, these specialists prove to be right in their initial analysis. Thus, for experts, the use of cognitive heuristics can in fact yield satisfactory results (for more insights on the use of expert heuristics in decision-making, see also Christensen-Szalanski et al., 1983 and Smith and Kida, 1991). Therefore this particular category of heuristics is certainly *not* detrimental to the ESDM outcomes because it does not reduce the complexity of the representations developed in the WM space. Nevertheless, because the implicit schemas stored in LTM are highly contextual (they are developed in relation to recurring specific events or cases) they should be used in situations with a high degree of similarity. Using these schemas in more general situations has the opposite effect and decreases the effectiveness of ESDM.

To conclude, the activation of System 2 is expected to increase ESDM effectiveness because it leads to highly complex representations formed in the WM space, while the activation of System 1 is expected to increase the cognitive complexity and thus be beneficial for ESDM only when (i) the activated schemas are developed through extensive experience and (ii) they match the situational constraints. The above discussion is summarized in the following theoretical proposition:

Proposition 3: The relationship between the activation of Systems 1 and 2 and the outcomes of ESDM is mediated by the complexity of the representations formed in the WM space (cognitive complexity).

Risk propensity is a key concept discussed in Chapter 3 in relation to ESDM and a high risk propensity refers to an individual's tendency to take risks in decision-making. It is an essential factor in the dynamics of an SME and it has positive as well as negative influences. Any economic activity involves a certain amount of risk, and founding a new enterprise is certainly no exception. Therefore risk propensity is essential for the initiation of a new business. However, high risk propensity also brings a tendency to act without careful consideration of all the aspects of the decision. In this sense, it is expected that risk propensity will lead to negative outcomes in ESDM due to the fact that it decreases the complexity of the knowledge representation in a particular strategic issue.

Proposition 4: The relationship between risk propensity and the outcomes of ESDM is mediated by cognitive complexity.

However, risk taking is a much more complex concept with far-reaching implications for ESDM. These implications cannot be encapsulated in a simple linear relation with cognitive complexity as a mediating factor. It is not unreasonable to assume that the two variables interact in determining the ESDM outcomes (risk propensity has a positive impact on the outcomes of the ESDM only to the extent to which it is associated with a high cognitive complexity). Further research is therefore needed in order to elucidate the relationship between the entrepreneurs' risk propensity and the outcomes of ESDM.

Another promising research direction concerns the impact of different types of risk propensity (for example, financial, social) for cognitive complexity.

The second set of concepts discussed in Chapter 3 are the motivational attributes: self-efficacy, need for cognition and tolerance for ambiguity. Self-efficacy refers to the beliefs of the entrepreneurs that they can mobilize their cognitive and motivational resources in order to control the decisional situations. If entrepreneurs have a high self-efficacy and a high sense of control, they will engage in more extensive information search, develop a better understanding of all the ESDM facets and master the complexity associated with it in a more effective way. Need for cognition is a central concept for cognitive motivation (Cacioppo et al., 1996) and individuals high in need of cognition enjoy being involved in effortful cognitive activities. In relation to decision-making and especially with rationality in decision-making, Curşeu (2006) showed that need for cognition is positively associated with rationality in decision-making (operationalized as lack of sensitivity to general cognitive heuristics and biases). Therefore it is very likely that individuals high in need of cognition will develop more-complex cognitive representations in their WM. Tolerance for ambiguity refers to the decision-makers' ability to confidently make choices when relevant information is missing. Entrepreneurs who feel comfortable in making decisions when it is known that information is missing, will most probably develop less-complex cognitive representations in their WM space. In conclusion, the cognitive lever through which motivational attributes influence ESDM outcomes is cognitive complexity.

Proposition 5: The relationship between motivational attributes (self-efficacy, need for cognition and tolerance for ambiguity) and the outcomes of ESDM is mediated by cognitive complexity.

4.6   SUMMARY AND CONCLUSIONS

This chapter has examined the role of cognitive representations formed in the WM space in ESDM. The complexity of these representations is the key factor explored as an antecedent of ESDM. Cognitive complexity is defined as the richness of a cognitive map and operationalized as the degree of differentiation and integration present in the map. An ideographic cognitive mapping was presented and two indicators of cognitive complexity were discussed. Based on the analysis of ESDM presented in earlier chapters, a set of theoretical propositions was put forward to explain the role of cognitive complexity in ESDM. It has been argued that because ESDM involves high degrees of complexity, a highly complex set of representations formed in the WM space is beneficial for the outcomes of ESDM. The key contribution of this chapter is the argument that cognitive complexity has a mediating role in the relationship between several motivational attributes and information processing modes on the one hand, and decisional outcomes on the other. Although the theoretical propositions advanced here shed light on the role of cognitive factors in ESDM, empirical research is needed in several directions.

Further research should also take into account different types of entrepreneurs. Until recently, there have been few attempts to study empirically the existence of different types of entrepreneurs. Carland et al. (1984) make a distinction between two categories of entrepreneurs, namely growth-oriented and income-oriented entrepreneurs (which Carland et al. deemed small-business owners). The difference is that the former starts a business with the primary focus on profit and growth, and the latter with a primary focus on family income (Stewart and Roth, 2001). However, the first empirical venture to formulate a stable, empirically funded taxonomy of different types of entrepreneurs has recently been proposed by Gibcus et al. (2008). A cluster analysis performed on data collected from a sample of 646 Dutch entrepreneurs in small firms (that is, with no more than 100 employees), revealed five types of entrepreneurial decision-makers: Daredevils, Lone Rangers, Doubtful Minds, Informers' Friends and Busy Bees. Many of the variables on which the taxonomy was based involve direct or indirect links to the cognitive factors also mentioned in this chapter; the propositions articulated above may work differently for different types of entrepreneurs. Therefore there is a need for empirical exploration of this specific issue.

An important claim of the chapter is that cognitive complexity mediates the impact of several motivation attributes on ESDM outcomes. This proposition certainly covers the cognitive mechanisms through which motivational attributes influence the outcomes of the ESDM. However, the cognitive component of the motivation accounts for only half of the story. The role of emotional factors that help entrepreneurs deal with lack of structure and uncertainty should also be explored in further empirical studies. Therefore, in addition to the cognitive component of motivation, another relevant issue to be further explored is the interaction between emotional and motivational factors in ESDM.

NOTE

1. It should be noted here that 'text' refers to its broadest meaning, and thus includes 'any symbolic data that is concept based either written or verbal' (Carley, 1997: 534). Thus, for instance, television shows, interviews, dialogues, books and correspondences can all ultimately be considered as text (see Carley, 1997).

PART II

Empirical studies

5. Strategic decision-making processes in SMEs: an exploratory study

Petra Gibcus and Peter van Hoesel

5.1 INTRODUCTION

Small and medium-sized enterprises (SMEs) play a key role in the modern market economy. Strategic decisions made by small and medium-sized business entrepreneurs form the heart of entrepreneurship and can therefore be considered as essential for the dynamics in the economy. While there is an abundant literature concerning strategic decision-making in large firms, surprisingly little is known about the decision-making process within SMEs. Brouthers et al. (1998) state that past strategic decision-making research focuses mostly on the 'procedural rationality' of decisions in large multinational firms. However, many researchers have argued (for example, ibid.; Papadakis et al., 1998; Beattie, 1999; Gilmore and Carson, 2000; Cummins et al., 2001) that independent entrepreneurs (owners/directors of SMEs) and managers of large firms differ when it comes to decision-making. For example, Busenitz and Barney (1997) assert that entrepreneurs are more susceptible to the use of decision-making biases and heuristics than are managers in large organizations. Brouthers et al. (1998) claim that intuition plays a much larger role in small firms.

In 2002, EIM Business and Policy Research started a research programme that investigated the decision-making process of small and medium-sized business entrepreneurs in the Netherlands. The objective of this programme is to map the decision-making process of entrepreneurs in SMEs. The following central question was formulated: what are the stages and crucial moments in the decision-making process of entrepreneurs in SMEs? In 2002, researchers from EIM interviewed 10 entrepreneurs about the crucial factors and moments in their decision-making process, because this process largely takes place inside the head of the entrepreneur. We looked for strategic decisions resulting in a clear discontinuity in the evolution of the organization. This study provided us with many insights into the decision-making process of SMEs, and it helped us to perceive the crucial stages and moments in the process.

The results from this first pilot study, although provisional, show that the decision-making process consists of three stages (emergence of the idea, elaborating the idea and implementation of the decision) and two crucial moments (trigger and informal decision, and formal decision). Some aspects of the decision-making process of entrepreneurs needed to be clarified in more detail. There were some gaps that needed to be filled, especially when it came to the emergence of an idea. Hence, a set of hypotheses was developed (in a second pilot study) to examine whether a new set of cases would confirm the stages and moments found in the first pilot study. The results of both studies are described in this chapter. The combined results of both studies helped us to describe more precisely the decision-making process of entrepreneurs in SMEs.

The structure of this chapter is as follows. First, we briefly discuss the research methods used in the pilot studies. Next, the provisional results of the first pilot study are discussed. In the following section we examine four hypotheses and support or reject them using the results of the second pilot study. We accumulated much information from both pilot studies to give an accurate description of the entrepreneurial decision-making process.

Furthermore, this inductive study offered some insights into three concepts (opportunity recognition, information processing and entrepreneurial risk propensity) that are important for understanding decision-making in a complex environment. Therefore we discuss some of our findings by looking back at these theoretical concepts (which were discussed at length in Chapters 2 and 3) and provide suggestions for further research.

5.2   RESEARCH METHOD

A few years ago EIM carried out two pilot studies on the SME decision-making process. The first had a very exploratory character. As a literature search was performed parallel to the pilot studies, we were barely influenced by decision-making models described in the literature in our analysis. The only influential article was that of Mintzberg et al. (1976), but it did not affect our analysis to any great extent. We let the entrepreneurs 'talk' and listened to their stories as represented in the interviews. The results of the first pilot study resulted in a different approach in the second study, which was more of a confirmatory exercise – we wanted to expand and hypothesize our findings from the first study.

For the first pilot study, entrepreneurs from the EIM SME Panel were selected. This panel was set up and is controlled by EIM. Its major objective is to collect information about the knowledge, attitudes and opinions of entrepreneurs with respect to various (government) policy-related issues. In each round, about 2000 companies were interviewed by means of computer-assisted telephone interviewing (CATI). The entrepreneur or the general manager of the company provided the answers. The EIM SME Panel consists of Dutch companies with fewer than 100 employees, distributed equally across three size classes (0–9, 10–49 and 50–99 employees) and eight sectors. The eight sectors distinguished are construction, manufacturing, trade, hotel and catering, transport, financial services, business services and personal services.

During the second measurement in 2002, the panel included four questions about decision-making: (i) 'Did you make one or more strategic decisions in the last three years?'; (ii) 'If yes: could you give a short description of your last strategic decision?'; (iii) 'Did this decision work out positively or negatively?'; and (iv) 'Are you satisfied with the result of your decision?'. In these interviews the focus was on strategic decisions that had resulted in a clear discontinuity in the course of the organization. From the EIM SME Panel, 10 entrepreneurs were selected who were willing to disclose more about their strategic decision-making during an in-depth interview. For practical reasons the selected SMEs were not distributed across the whole country; they belonged to several sectors and the decisions concerned various matters.

The set-up of the second pilot study was somewhat different from that of the first. It was decided not to interview the same members of the EIM SME Panel about their decision-making process, but instead a new panel was created to select the case studies by using a telephone survey. The sample consisted of 200 completed telephone interviews. All 200 SMEs have a minimum of one and a maximum of 99 employees. The persons spoken to were always the directors/owners, that is, those who were making the important decisions. The survey was distributed equally across the following sectors: construction, manufacturing, trade, hotel and catering, transport, financial services, business services and personal services. Forty-nine entrepreneurs agreed to have a discussion (face-to-face interview) with one of the researchers about their decision-making process. Of these 49, 12 were selected for an in-depth interview. The selection consisted of six entrepreneurs with a 'go' decision, two with a 'no-go' decision and four with ideas or plans that possibly will result in a strategic decision. During the interviews the entrepreneurs were asked about relevant facts and motives that finally resulted or will result in the decision.

5.3   A PROVISIONAL DESCRIPTION OF THE DECISION-MAKING PROCESS

From the results of the 10 cases of the first pilot study we discovered that an entrepreneur goes through three distinct stages and distinguishes two crucial moments in the decision-making process. These (provisional) stages and crucial moments are as follows:

- stage 1: emergence of an idea;
- moment 1: trigger and informal decision;
- stage 2: elaborating the idea;
- moment 2: formal decision; and
- stage 3: implementation of the decision.

We shall describe each of these below.

Stage 1: Emergence of an Idea

Entrepreneurs are always thinking about the future of their firm and are constantly on the look-out for opportunities and threats. They regularly take stock of their environment – their competitors, their customers, their suppliers or their sector in general. The entrepreneurs also examine the internal organization of the firm, for example, what is the state of the production process, how do the employees perform under the current conditions and how profitable is the firm? In addition, they gather information from, for example, trade and management journals, meetings, courses or the Internet. In eight out of 10 cases it was not possible for us to pinpoint one particular moment when the idea first arose. In none of the cases could we trace one single event that led to a 'eureka' moment. Rather, the entrepreneurs talked about a maturing process. The idea slowly penetrates the consciousness of the entrepreneur, who considers him-/herself as the creator of the idea. These entrepreneurs are almost constantly aware of their idea. In two cases we were able to indicate the precise moment when the idea appeared; it arose completely by chance, and coincided with the moment we call the 'trigger' (see Box 5.1).

The entrepreneurs thought very carefully about the rational argumentation of their idea. At the same time, intuition and emotion play an important role in their argumentation, as the entrepreneurs frankly admit. It is quite possible that at first emotions are dominant and that subsequently the idea is carefully thought through in a more rational way. In seven cases it was hard to recognize any emotional dominance, because the entrepreneurs were obviously reasoning in retrospect. Three entrepreneurs acknowledged the dominance of emotional arguments such as 'I'm very proud of my company' or 'it's nice doing this too'. These emotional arguments were complemented with rational arguments. Because entrepreneurs think a lot about their arguments we suspect that they weigh up the alternatives in their mind. As a consequence, the argumentation of the idea becomes more rational. It is remarkable that none of the entrepreneurs wanted to abandon his/her idea at any moment during the process. Apparently they find potential alternatives unattractive. Sometimes this is understandable because the entrepreneurs are under pressure to solve a problem or to reduce an area of tension. But even in cases where the entrepreneur is not under any pressure, the possibility of abandonment does not arise.

Despite the strength and maturity of the idea, its elaboration rarely comes automatically. In nine cases the entrepreneur indicated that something extra was needed: a trigger. The period between idea and trigger differs from case to case. Some entrepreneurs need only a couple of weeks, whereas others need a year or even longer. As mentioned previously, in two case studies the idea emerged at the same moment that the trigger occurred. This means that the elaboration of the idea began immediately and the entrepreneurs did not require any time to allow their idea to mature.

Moment 1: Trigger and Informal Decision

The trigger is the direct stimulus for the entrepreneurs to take action and elaborate on their idea. In one case study the entrepreneur stated that he could not remember anything that worked as a trigger. In the other nine, we did perceive a trigger. In seven case studies the trigger came from outside the organization. The trigger can be direct or indirect. If the idea is immature, a strong direct trigger is necessary before the entrepreneur takes any action. A relatively mature idea needs only a rather indirect trigger. In this case there is no obvious continuation of the mental process until then. It concerns an indirect, temporary and unique event (see Box 5.1 for examples).

We found it quite surprising that entrepreneurs experience such a decisive moment as a trigger as relatively unimportant compared to the major thread in their thoughts. When we asked the entrepreneurs about the crucial moments in their thought process they could not indicate such a moment. The entrepreneurs talked about a period in which the idea slowly gained strength. The trigger leads to immediate action. The action taken by the entrepreneur after the trigger occurs shows us that the entrepreneur made an informal decision. It is hard for the entrepreneur to let go of the idea after this particular moment even if obstacles have to be overcome. The moment the trigger occurs, the entrepreneur takes some direct action that eventually leads to the final decision. The informal decision is not put in writing. It is an intention in the entrepreneur's mind or a verbal agreement between associates.

BOX 5.1   EXAMPLES OF DIRECT AND INDIRECT TRIGGERS

The wife of a sound engineer arrived home with a film that had to be edited. This seriously encouraged the sound engineer to research the possibility of doing some film editing.

The entrepreneur of an installation company heard that some of his employees wanted to do some other work in addition to their normal work. This triggered the entrepreneur to fulfil his idea of starting up an additional firm.

A research agency and a communication firm had the idea of cooperating through a joint venture. Although the idea had existed for a long time, nothing had been done. A candidate who applied for a job at the communication agency had previously worked for a research agency. This candidate was the perfect person to manage a joint venture between the communication agency and the research agency. Her application triggered both agencies to act.

Source: EIM (2004).

Stage 2: Elaborating the Idea

After making the informal decision, the entrepreneurs elaborate their idea. They look at alternatives and consult advisers and banks. The entrepreneurs also bear in mind that there are risks. All this makes the elaboration of the idea a complex matter and, as a consequence, entrepreneurs often have to overcome obstacles. Others who operate in the vicinity of the entrepreneur gain more influence in this stage of the decision-making process. Usually advisers compile alternative solutions (within the boundaries of the idea). Some entrepreneurs admit that they depend very much on these advisers to consider the alternatives and for the specific input related to their profession. Otherwise we have the distinct impression that entrepreneurs are not very interested in the details provided by the advisers. All they want is for the advisers to help them to implement their idea.

The impact of risk awareness on the final decision appeared to be very low. Seven entrepreneurs had little or no doubt about their strategic decision. Those who found their idea very attractive from the start had the fewest doubts about their decision. Three others had considerable doubts, because of the high risk involved. Nevertheless, these risks did not play an important part in their final decision. Entrepreneurs are able to keep track of all the risks even if they are large. They balance the risks against the benefits that the decision brings before making a final decision.

It seems that the entrepreneur is the only person who really matters during the elaboration process. When there are one or more associates these also have substantial influence, but there is one leader who spurs on the others. All other parties involved have minor influence. Employees do not participate in the decision-making process although sometimes they are informed at this stage and know what is going on. In one case, the influence of the employees was clearly noticeable, because they formed the trigger for the entrepreneur to develop the idea. It is possible that in some cases the employees had more influence than the entrepreneur admitted. The influence of customers is also almost unnoticeable. In one case study the customers appeared to be the trigger. In others, the entrepreneurs did not explicitly take into account the probable reaction of the customers to their decision.

There appeared to be no direct influence by policy makers or public authorities on the decision-making process, for example through subsidies, tax benefits or educational programmes. Entrepreneurs dislike the administrative burdens that accompany the application for subsidies or tax benefits. In several of our cases it was evident that entrepreneurs would welcome some stimulating policy on certain aspects such as reduction of entry barriers, removing unfair competition or a good infrastructure.

Moment 2: Formal Decision

At a certain moment the entrepreneurs set up a formal agreement concerning their decision or take the first step towards executing it. We regarded the point at which the entrepreneur takes one of these two actions as the moment when the the formal decision is made, after which there is no turning back. Eight entrepreneurs have their decision in writing. In these cases agreements of a legal and/or financial nature are involved.

In all cases there was a single motive that was very dominant and was finally decisive in the decision to go ahead. For seven SMEs the motive came from inside the firm; for the other three, it came from outside the SME. The decisive moment has, in all cases, an obvious economic principle. In most cases we could also recognize some non-economic elements, such as being proud of the SME or the need for a new challenge.

The strategic decisions of the entrepreneurs have different natures that stress their diversity. These decisions were divided into two categories: those concerning a change in the organization of the SME and those relating to investments in products and processes. In short, in seven out of the 10 case studies we talked to entrepreneurs who had made changes in their organization; the other three involved the strategic decision to invest in products or processes.

Stage 3: Implementation of the Decision

After the entrepreneurs had made a formal decision, they were able to implement it. The implementation was not easy for four entrepreneurs. At the time of the implementation, difficulties arose which were more serious than previously thought, and which resulted in financial difficulties. Eventually these problems were resolved, although for most firms the consequences were unpleasant. In all other cases the implementation of the decision went quite smoothly, although three entrepreneurs did admit that the implementation was not as fast as they had expected.

All the entrepreneurs are satisfied about their decision. They admit that they at least tried to make the best of it. If they had not made their decision they certainly would have had some regrets later on, because an opportunity would have been lost. This was also the case for entrepreneurs whose decision had less favourable results. Because enough time has passed since the formal decision was made, it was possible for the entrepreneurs we interviewed to judge the results of their decision: five were found to be very pleased; three are content with the decision, but have some marginal misgivings; two openly state that the decision did not have the result that they expected although they are still convinced that their idea is good and will not give up easily. These last entrepreneurs are trying to correct their mistakes. They have no doubts about the idea, but consider the way in which the decision was implemented to be responsible for mistakes.

5.4   SECOND PILOT STUDY: HYPOTHESES

In the previous section we described a first impression of the decision-making process within SMEs. However, some aspects remained unanswered or needed to be investigated more thoroughly. As such, four hypotheses were formulated. To carry out a preliminary test of these hypotheses, another sample of entrepreneurs was interviewed in a second pilot study.

Alternative Ideas

After the first pilot study we assumed that the entrepreneurs did not consider any alternative ideas. We were also aware that we had not paid special attention to this issue and therefore we wanted to explore this further. Hence, Hypothesis 1 is formulated as follows:

Hypothesis 1: Entrepreneurs do not consider alternative ideas in their decision-making process.

Entrepreneurs in the second pilot study were asked whether alternative ideas played a role in the decision-making process, and we found such ideas in more cases than we expected. The results show that entrepreneurs do not focus exclusively on just one idea. In fact, they are aware of other competitive ideas and seriously consider them. In the cases where we do not know whether the entrepreneurs had alternative ideas, it is possible that there were some, but the entrepreneurs could not remember what these ideas were. In fact, probably all the entrepreneurs had alternative ideas but these were written off at an early stage or totally crowded out. We saw in the first pilot study that it was hard to distinguish the idea-generating process of the entrepreneurs and how they evaluate alternative ideas. In the second pilot study, extra attention was paid to the idea underlying the decision-making process.

In seven out of the 12 cases, the entrepreneurs said that the idea came by chance. In these cases the idea itself came from someone else (external factor). The entrepreneurs reacted very quickly to this idea and almost immediately after it emerged they recognized the opportunity. Intuition, but also emotion, plays an important part in dealing with such ideas, and these emotions are dominant in the beginning. The 'gut-feeling' has to be good, otherwise the idea is rejected immediately. Other entrepreneurs argued that the idea arose because they had to solve a problem. These entrepreneurs are more conscious about the idea. Once the entrepreneur has conceived the idea, it gradually matures in the mind of the entrepreneur until an opportunity arises. After alternative ideas have been discarded, the idea that remains gains strength. The entrepreneurs are gradually convinced that this idea needs to be implemented just as we experienced in the first pilot study. Eventually the idea develops into a strong motive (or a set of motives), which requires action. The results from our second pilot study lead us to reject our first hypothesis. Entrepreneurs do consider alternative ideas. However, they discard most of these at a very early stage in the decision-making process.

Relation between the Trigger and the Informal Decision

Usually the elaboration of the idea does not come automatically. In the first pilot study it was discovered that something additional was needed. That something was called a trigger. In the first pilot study, two types of triggers were distinguished: direct and indirect. When an idea is relatively weak there has to be a strong direct trigger that spurs the entrepreneur into action, but a relatively strong idea needs only a weak indirect trigger. In order to investigate the role of these triggers, a second hypothesis was formulated:

Hypothesis 2: An informal decision is made after some kind of event (the trigger). If the idea of the entrepreneur is comparatively mature, an indirect or weak trigger will lead to the informal decision. If the idea is comparatively immature, the informal decision is made after a strong trigger that has a strong relation with the idea.

In each case such a trigger could be distinguished, although the entrepreneurs pay little attention to these triggers. Indeed, it was hard for two entrepreneurs to recall any such trigger. Only when the idea and the trigger occur simultaneously is the entrepreneur aware of the trigger. Just as in the first pilot study, we noticed in the second one that the period between the idea and the trigger differed in each case study.

In two cases the idea and the trigger occurred simultaneously. Once entrepreneurs are aware of this trigger it is hard for them to let go of their idea. Sometimes some obstacles have to be removed but the entrepreneurs are convinced that these can be overcome. All the time the idea remains very powerful. The entrepreneurs do not let go of their idea after the trigger, and start elaborating it from that moment on. We consider the moment of the trigger as the moment when the informal decision is made. Hypothesis 2 surely holds for the cases in which the idea and the trigger occur simultaneously. If entrepreneurs did not have any thoughts about the idea then the trigger has to be very powerful before they react to it. The external idea is the trigger in these cases. We found that the trigger was so strong that it ultimately led to an important strategic decision being made by the entrepreneur. Other ideas are more mature and these are the result of a process in which the idea gradually matures inside the mind of the entrepreneur. In these cases only a weak trigger is necessary to galvanize these entrepreneurs into action. Hypothesis 2 also holds for more mature ideas.

Influence of Other Persons

After the informal decision has been made the entrepreneurs take action. They work out their idea, consider alternatives and risks, and overcome obstacles. Once everything has been worked out the entrepreneurs make their final decision. In the first pilot study we discovered that the entrepreneur is the only person who really matters in the decision-making process. This was investigated more thoroughly in the second pilot study and results in Hypothesis 3:

Hypothesis 3: In SMEs with an owner–manager (or owner–managers) the decision-making process is rarely influenced by other persons.

One entrepreneur was very direct in giving his answer to the question whether the decision-making process was influenced by other persons. When he was asked about the impact of others on the decision-making process he answered: 'I hardly ever consult "outsiders" if it concerns drastic decisions'. In firms with several co-owners it is always the case that all the owners are informed about the decision that is going to be made. They are all involved in the process. Just as in the first pilot study, we found that one entrepreneur takes the lead in this case.

Entrepreneurs often talk to their family about their business and their decisions, because they feel understood by their family members. However, eventually entrepreneurs go their own way and make their own decision. Most entrepreneurs do not actively involve their (non-business) partners in their decision-making processes. These partners often have their own opinion about the situation, but they do not stand in the way of the entrepreneur's decision.

The role of employees is usually negligible. In some cases the entrepreneur informs the employees about the decision or asks them for advice, but according to the entrepreneur the employees have no influence on the decision-making process. In one case the entrepreneur talked a lot with the IT manager, because the entrepreneur knew little about data warehouses. But ultimately it was the entrepreneur who decided that it was time to implement the data warehouse. External advisers, such as accountants, tax consultants or notaries help the entrepreneur to elaborate the idea. On the basis of both pilot studies, the third hypothesis is confirmed. Entrepreneurs are hardly influenced by others, except for direct associates. They will inform their family and their employees, some of who may also be asked for advice, but the entrepreneur is always responsible for the final decision.

Informal versus Formal Decisions

In the previous section we described the formal decision as the point of no return. However, we found that there is almost no way back even when the trigger occurs and the informal decision is made. We wanted to investigate, based upon a new set of cases, whether the informal and formal decisions differed, and formulated Hypothesis 4:

Hypothesis 4: The moment of the informal decision is the decisive moment in the strategic decision-making process. The formal decision is therefore not markedly different from the informal decision.

The new cases offered us better insight into the way the entrepreneur makes the formal decision. After the informal decision has been made, all entrepreneurs have their own way of elaborating the idea and dealing with possible obstacles. At some point there is a decisive moment when they are persuaded to make the formal decision. These decisive moments vary across the cases, from being dissatisfied about the current job, to lack of confidence in the current situation, and recognizing the opportunity for further growth. In all cases, one idea is dominant and the entrepreneur is convinced that this idea will be a success. For this reason it is very hard for entrepreneurs to let go of their idea. The entrepreneur works out the informal decision in such a way that the idea will be implemented in the end, even though sometimes it can be very difficult. In the long run the informal and formal decisions do not differ from each other, which means that our cases seem to support Hypothesis 4.

Although we did not hypothesize explicitly about the external environment, we did encounter its importance on various occasions when analysing the interviews. For example, the trigger for the decision often emerged from outside the organization, and most ideas are generated in close interaction with the external environment. To predict how decision-making is influenced by environmental developments, it is critical to understand how the individual entrepreneur cognitively processes and interprets these developments. Although these issues were not explicitly included in the pilot studies, the inductive nature of this study did offer some insights into each of these issues.

5.5   DECISION-MAKING IN A COMPLEX ENVIRONMENT

Entrepreneurs make decisions in an environment in which various actors and forces are present (such as: competitors, government regulations, customers with their specific demands, suppliers, tax authorities, investors and so on). Each of these plays a more or less significant role in the performance of the firm by presenting opportunities and imperilling its activities. Successful decision-making requires an accurate understanding of the environment in which that decision will be played out. Without that understanding it is impossible to assess the potential consequences and make a well-informed choice (Messick and Bazerman, 1996). In the case of SMEs, it is especially important to include the broader environment for at least three reasons. First, it is argued that these firms often face a hostile or uncertain environment in their decision-making activities (Hambrick and Crozier, 1985; Covin and Slevin, 1989). Unlike managers in large firms, for instance, they do not have access to extensive information sources. Managers of large firms tend to be backed up by staff members who continuously scan the environment and gather information (Busenitz and Barney, 1997). Second, the environment of small firms is dynamic and complex (Covin and Slevin, 1991). As a result, entrepreneurs tend to make decisions on the basis of biases and heuristics (Busenitz and Barney, 1997). Furthermore, in a more dynamic and complex environment it is believed that the comprehensiveness (or rationality) of strategic decision processes tends to be lower (Fredrickson, 1984; Fredrickson and Mitchell, 1984) and cognitive issues become more important (Forbes, 1999). Three concepts are crucial in analysing decision-making processes within the context of the environment: the ability to recognize opportunities, information processing and dealing with risk propensity. We briefly explain the theoretical background of each concept and subsequently indicate how these were enacted by the entrepreneurs in our pilot studies.

Opportunity Recognition

In a rapidly changing world, organizations need to continually identify new opportunities beyond existing competencies (Krueger, 2000). Opportunity recognition and information search are often considered to be the first critical steps in the entrepreneurial process (Christensen et al., 1994; Shane and Venkataraman, 2000). Opportunities are created, or built, using ideas and entrepreneurial creativity (Dellabarca, 2000). McGrath (1999) argued that entrepreneurs have access to numerous 'shadow' opportunities (that is, opportunities that have not been recognized). Shane and Venkataraman (2000) state that 'why', 'when' and 'how' certain individuals exploit opportunities appears to be a function of the joint characteristics of the opportunity and the nature of the individual. Furthermore, they highlight three main areas of difference between individuals that may help us understand why certain individuals recognize opportunities while others do not: knowledge (and information), cognitive and behavioural differences. The process of search and opportunity recognition can be influenced by the cognitive behaviour of the entrepreneur. Chandler et al. (2002) suggest three categories when it comes to opportunity recognition processes: proactive search (Drucker, 1985), reactive search (Ardichvili et al., 2003) and fortuitous discovery (Kirzner, 1979).

Our empirical results indicate that initiatives discovered through proactive search are implemented more rapidly than those discovered through reactive searches or by chance. As time passes, the advantages in implementation speed are reduced and in some cases nullified. This implies that the opportunity recognition process has an impact on the speed of implementation, and may have longer-term impacts on profits. In line with McGrath (1999) we are of the opinion that entrepreneurs have access to numerous opportunities, many of which they do not recognize. It was hard for us to detect whether knowledge, cognitive or behavioural differences had affected the recognition of the opportunity. The opportunities that arise are essential for the entrepreneur, but we found that some entrepreneurs are looking for opportunities more actively than others. We agree with Chandler et al. (2002) that opportunities recognized by a proactive search were implemented more rapidly than those that were recognized by a reactive search or accidental discovery.

Information Processing

Information search behaviour can be bounded by the decision-maker's knowledge of how to process information as well as the ability to gather an appropriate amount of information (Woo and Lochovsky, 1992). Entrepreneurs with limited experience may use simplified decision models to guide their search, while the opposite may be the case with experienced entrepreneurs (Gaglio, 1997). Cooper et al. (1995) found that novice entrepreneurs sought more information than entrepreneurs with more entrepreneurial experience, but they searched less in unfamiliar surroundings. Further, entrepreneurs with high levels of confidence sought less information. Over time, habitual entrepreneurs are likely to acquire information and contacts that provide them with a flow of information relating to opportunities. The ability of entrepreneurs to learn from previous business ownership experiences can influence the quantity and quality of information subsequently collected (Gaglio, 1997). In addition, it allows informed and experienced entrepreneurs to identify and take advantage of disequilibrium profit opportunities (Kaish and Gilad, 1991). This entrepreneurial learning process goes beyond acquiring new information, by connecting and making inferences from various pieces of information, that have not previously been connected. Some people habitually activate their mental schema for processing information and can bring this ability into play in the midst of an otherwise overwhelming amount of stimuli (Gaglio, 1997). This may explain why the pursuit of one set of ideas and opportunities invariably leads entrepreneurs to additional innovative opportunities that had not previously been recognized (Ronstadt, 1988).

The results from our pilot studies show that unconsciously entrepreneurs are always looking for information by surfing on the Internet, reading a trade journal or talking to other entrepreneurs in the business. We noticed that in decision-making, the entrepreneurs searched for the most necessary information to pursue their idea. Too much information will probably lead to delays or confusion. The entrepreneurs formulated and created an image inside their head about the way they wanted to execute the strategic decision. Other persons have no influence on the entrepreneurial idea. The entrepreneurs in our cases do not use all available information. We received the impression that the decision was always well thought out. Consequently, there was less need for information. The idea has been nourished and given a chance to develop. Once the opportunity has been identified and information relevant to the venture has been obtained, the next step for the entrepreneur (or the team of entrepreneurs) is to acquire new resources or effectively manage existing resources, in order to exploit the opportunity. Sometimes having an idea and seeing the opportunity in order to exploit the idea occurs almost simultaneously. However, in the majority of cases there is a 'time lag' between the two.

Entrepreneurial Risk Propensity

One of the major challenges of decision-making is dealing with uncertainty. In a very early study, Knight (1921) claims that every effective exercise of judgement is coupled with a corresponding degree of uncertainty, of taking the responsibility for the selected course of action. Risk-taking propensity refers to an individual's willingness to take or avoid risks in decision-making (Jackson et al., 1972). Very few studies have shown statistically significant differences between entrepreneurs and non-entrepreneurs in their risk-taking propensity (Brockhaus 1980; Low and MacMillan 1988). However, Palich and Bagby (1995) defend the idea that entrepreneurs do not differ from other people with respect to their risk propensity. Rather they react differently to environmental stimuli, especially when the data are equivocal. Entrepreneurs, through the cognitive process of categorization, are more capable of processing and storing ambiguous data, thus perceiving equivocal business scenarios more positively than others. Hence, it is not their risk propensity but their different cognitive processes that make entrepreneurs more optimistic about certain business ventures.

The entrepreneurs in our pilot studies were more risk averse than risk loving. If the entrepreneurs had to accept a small risk then this risk was not a threat to the continuity of the SME. When the entrepreneurs had to accept greater risks then it was easy for them to identify these risks clearly. But above all, the entrepreneurs knew how to deal with these risks.

5.6 CONCLUSION

In this chapter we have tried to increase our insight into how entrepreneurs make strategic decisions. It has helped us to perceive the crucial stages and moments in the decision-making process of SMEs. The results from the first pilot study, although provisional, show that the decision-making process consists of three stages (emergence of the idea, elaborating the idea and implementation of the decision) and two crucial moments (trigger and informal decision, and formal decision). Some aspects of the decision-making process of entrepreneurs needed to be clarified in more detail. There were some gaps that needed to be filled, especially when it came to the emergence of an idea. Hence, a set of hypotheses was developed (in a second pilot study) to examine whether a new set of cases would confirm the stages and moments found in the first study. The results of both studies are described in this chapter. The combined results of both studies helped us to describe more precisely the decision-making process of entrepreneurs in SMEs.

Although our pilot studies helped us to distinguish the stages and crucial moments in the decision-making process of entrepreneurs, we need more insight into the impact of the important strategic decisions on the performance of SMEs and the differences between sectors. We feel that there are some important distinctions to be made on the basis of environmental dynamics, which differs across industries. For that purpose we need quantitative data, which would provide us with information concerning the percentage of SMEs that make important decisions and how many decisions they make during a certain period. We also wish to look for differences between sectors. Do entrepreneurs in a certain sector make more decisions than those in another sector? And perhaps the decision-making process differs across sectors. In addition we need more empirical research on some of the underlying cognitive mechanisms that trigger and guide entrepreneurial decision-making. These issues are addressed in the following chapters.

6. Entrepreneurial decision styles and cognition in SMEs

Gerardus J.M. Lucas, Patrick A.M. Vermeulen and Petru L. Curşeu

6.1 INTRODUCTION

This chapter focuses on decision-making in small and medium-sized enterprises (SMEs). The success of an SME depends to a large extent on effective strategic decision-making (Robinson and Pearce, 1983). However, not much is known about the decision processes that underlie the decisions of SME entrepreneurs. In contrast to decision-making in large enterprises, decision-making procedures in SMEs involve fewer actors or just one actor and generally do not involve organizational politics. Hence, it has been argued in the literature that explaining decision-making processes in SMEs requires new models (Brouthers et al., 1998; Papadakis et al., 1998; Gilmore and Carson, 2000). Busenitz and Barney (1997) argued that entrepreneurs are more likely to fall prey to biases in decision-making and to improperly rely on heuristics compared to decision-makers in large firms. This implies that decision-making by entrepreneurs in SMEs is indeed a distinct phenomenon, with its own characteristics and peculiarities. Given that in a typical SME one or only a few individuals are involved in decision-making, we assume that the decision-making style of such an entrepreneur is bound to have an impact on the decision process, as well as on its outcomes.

Chapter 2 argued that a variety of entrepreneurial types can be distinguished. The most relevant difference in this regard is their approach to decision-making and their perception of what is important in this process. Gibcus et al. (2008) provide us with a taxonomy of entrepreneurial types to build upon. Using in-depth interviews conducted with a subset of the entrepreneurs who participated in their telephone survey, we seek to explore in detail the cognitive dimension of the decision-making process. Our goal is to demonstrate that each of the five types of entrepreneurs identified by Gibcus et al. is characterized by distinct cognitive decision content.

Our contribution to the understanding of entrepreneurial decision-making will be both conceptual as well as empirical. Conceptually, we hypothesize that different entrepreneurial decision styles are mirrored in distinct cognitions. Answering the call of Mitchell et al. (2007), we capture how entrepreneurs think when making strategic decisions. Empirically, our study serves to validate the taxonomy of Gibcus et al. (2008). In addition, by using interview data instead of survey data, we shall be able to provide a far richer, more elaborate, picture of the different entrepreneurial decision styles.

The benefits of increasing our knowledge of different types of entrepreneurial decision-makers and what cognitive processes characterize their decision-making efforts are extensive. For scholars, this allows for a greater ability to explain the variety in SME strategies. Moreover, it helps to resolve ambiguities, such as why one SME has a different response to an environmental change from another. These ambiguities can be explained using entrepreneurial type as a contingency factor. Given a specific environmental event, subsequent decisions, acts and outcomes depend on the type of entrepreneur that is responsible for the decision. The substantive explanation for this is that the entrepreneurial types will have a different interpretation of what is going on and/or a different opinion of how best to act given their assessment of the situation. This opens up interesting avenues of research. For instance, one could explore under what circumstances each of the types is most effective. Alternatively, studying whether the different types of entrepreneurs vary in their susceptibility to decision-making biases could be rewarding. For practitioners, having knowledge of the existence of these issues allows for a more informed and tailored approach when dealing with SME entrepreneurs. In addition, policy makers would be able to better gauge the impact of proposed policies and fine-tune them to achieve the desired outcomes.

In the following, we present a short overview of the theory on cognition in decision-making in which we shall argue that the cognitive content of the decision-making process of SMEs entrepreneurs has a major impact on how this process takes place. We shall then describe our methodology before proceeding to our results. In our discussion and conclusion we reflect upon what can be learned from our study, what questions remain to be answered and how future research could advance our understanding of SME entrepreneurs and their decision-making.

6.2 THEORY AND HYPOTHESIS

Cognition plays an important role in shaping human behaviour in a variety of situations, including decision-making. The most influential cognitive models used to explain the effectiveness of decision-making in organizations are those stressing the impact of activated cognitive representations on the decisional outcome (Boland et al., 2001). Cognitive representations are a reflection of the environment in the mind of the decision maker. They help the decision-maker to make sense of various environmental cues. The final decision is thus the result of the way in which the decision situation is cognitively represented (Wood and Bandura, 1989; Porac and Thomas, 1990; Chattopadhyay et al., 2006). Cognitive representations explain the way in which employees deal with complex cognitive tasks, emphasizing the fact that the complexity of the cognitive representation of the task successfully predicts task performance (Wyman and Randel, 1998; see also Chapter 4 in this book). In the particular case of managers, cognitive complexity (the complexity of the cognitive representations developed and used by managers) and cognitive abilities (their ability to efficiently process complex information) are accurate predictors for their career success, and good predictors for the effective handling of complex, uncertain and unstable environmental conditions (Wood and Bandura, 1989; Ginsberg, 1990; Calori et al., 1994; O'Reilly and Chatman, 1994; Chattopadhyay et al., 2006).

Thus, from previous research on cognition in decision-making it emerges that cognitive representations of the situation faced by the decision-maker are vital in coming to a decision. Moreover, these representations need to capture the relevant aspects involved (accuracy) and possess a sufficient degree of sophistication (complexity) in order for a proper decision to emerge. As such, these insights lead us to conclude that the cognitive content matters a great deal in decision-making. Huff and Reger (1987) argued that strategy research should focus on the content as well as on the process. Mitchell et al. (2007) argue that cognition is vital to understanding entrepreneurial behaviour, and hence decision-making. One of the main questions that needs to be studied is 'how do entrepreneurs think' (ibid.: 2) or in other words, what happens in the cognitive system of the entrepreneur, while she/he makes a decision? Our study aims to answer that question in the context of strategic decision-making in SMEs, taking into account a particularly relevant aspect of cognition, namely cognitive representations.

The characteristics of small firms make cognition in decision-making much more important than it is in large firms. Entrepreneurs, by virtue of leading smaller firms that are often engaged with novel, innovative products and services, face more hostile and uncertain environments (Hambrick and Crozier, 1985; Covin and Slevin, 1989; Brouthers et al., 1998). Moreover, entrepreneurs lack the staff and resources for environmental scanning and elaborate information processing. Brouthers et al. found that this results in a more qualitative approach to information processing. Given that this environment is quite dynamic and complex, it has a great impact on the firm. The need to deal with it, while having to do so without a lot of resources, leads to less comprehensive, more opportunistic decision behaviour, greatly influenced by biases and heuristics (Fredrickson, 1984; Fredrickson and Mitchell, 1984; Gartner et al., 1992; Busenitz and Barney, 1997; Chattopadhyay et al., 2006).

The general idea that emerges from these insights is that the decision-making process of entrepreneurs is influenced by the interplay between the attributes of the decision-maker and the specifics of the situation that he/she is facing. The portrayal of the situation that the entrepreneurs believe they are facing is influenced by what they see as important and how they think they should come to a decision. Wood and Bandura (1989) argued that the perception of a decision-maker matters a great deal for the decision behaviour and accomplishments. They showed that factors such as self-efficacy, controllability of beliefs, perception of managerial abilities and personal goals are involved (see also Bandura and Wood, 1989). Ginsberg (1990) similarly argued that cognition and perception shape strategic behaviour (see also Dutton and Jackson, 1987 and Forbes, 1999). Brouthers et al. (1998: 136) state: '[s]mall firm managers tended to choose strategies based on their personal desires and backgrounds'. Given that perception and the approach to decision-making play an important role in the process, the type of entrepreneur making the decision has an important influence on the decision-making outcome.

In essence, we argue that entrepreneurs differ in their decision-making style and the underlying differences are actually related to the content of their cognitions concerning the decision they are making. Thus, how a decision-maker's memory is structured (semantic structure) determines what information is available during the act of decision-making (Coronges et al., 2007). In turn, the available information shapes the decision that will be reached. Therefore, differences in the type of decision-making strategy one has will be mirrored in the cognitive contents associated with a particular decision. Behaviour is shaped by what concepts are included in the semantic network of a decision-maker and how these relate to one another (ibid.). Based on the documented existence of different types of entrepreneurs and to the fact that the cognitive content shapes decision-making, we hypothesize:

Hypothesis 1: Entrepreneurs of the same decision-making type will have similar cognitive content in relation to the decision-making process.

6.3   RESEARCH METHOD

We used the interview data (see Appendix) to investigate whether the different types of decision-makers are characterized by distinct cognitive processes that reflect their peculiarities. In contrast to the survey data the taxonomy was derived from, the data from these interviews are more extensive and detailed and hence very suitable to capture cognitions.

The specific approach to analyse the interviews is the following. They were content analysed and processed into cognitive maps (see Figure 6.1) which reflect the cognition involved in the decision-making process (three coders under the supervision of the third author were involved in this process). Three steps were involved in composing the cognitive maps (Carley, 1993; Gómez et al., 2000). The first step involves identifying first-order concepts and links, meaning that the most important concepts used to describe the decision-making situation and process were extracted from the interview reports. In the second step, the importance of the concepts was assessed, based on such aspects as explicit mentioning during the interview, emphasis of the interviewee, spontaneity and priority in the interview. In the last step, second-order concepts and links were identified, which help to organize and structure the concepts to be included in the map. These cognitive maps should be seen as devices that capture the semantic network of the decision-maker (Coronges et al., 2007). They capture the relevant concepts involved and how they are associated with one another, and thus the cognitions that shape decision-making behaviour.

The basic set-up of the maps coming out of the three-stage process was as follows (see Figure 6.1). The top left area was reserved for causes or motives for the decision made, which is put in the centre. The bottom left was reserved for aspects that have to do with the structure and general way of doing business of the organization. The issues involved in the decision-making process were put in the bottom right. The top right dealt with the outcome and consequences of the decision. In some cases, obstacles and/or alternatives considered were mentioned by the entrepreneur; these were most often put in the top middle area. These cognitive maps provide the material for the current analysis. Based on the categorization of decision-making types, we tried to identify similarities across cognitive maps for the same type. This part of the project was carried out by the first author who was involved in neither conducting the interviews nor analysing the interviews and coding into cognitive maps. This last analysis gives us a description of the five types based on their decision content. These descriptions are compared to the characteristics that emerged from the classification analysis of Gibcus et al. (2008). This

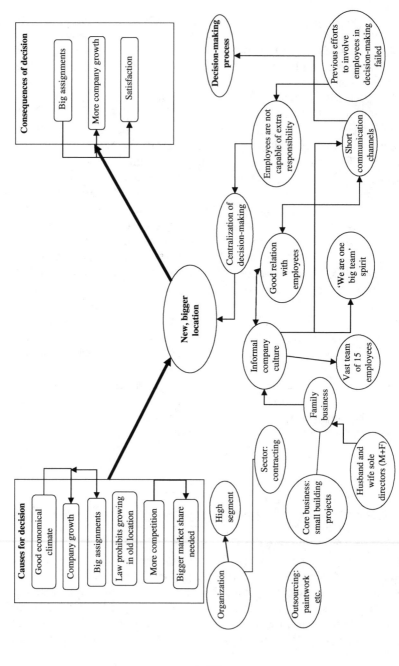

Figure 6.1 Example of a cognitive map (2)

approach allows for a far richer characterization of the five types than could be achieved based on the telephone survey. Using the cognitive map approach we can elicit thoughts, perceptions and other aspects that have to do with what the entrepreneurs were *thinking* when making the strategic decision.

Our sample includes a total of 85 entrepreneurs, among whom were 27 Daredevils, 17 Lone Rangers, 12 Doubtful Minds, 22 Informers' Friends and seven Busy Bees. Our sample includes relatively more Daredevils and Busy Bees and relatively fewer Doubtful Minds and Informers' Friends than Gibcus et al.'s sample.[1] With regard to the number of employees, our sample is somewhat biased to larger SMEs (50–100 employees).[2] The median age of our sample is 46 years (range 26–66), compared to 44 years (range 21–76) for Gibcus et al. In terms of sex, the samples are comparable (the percentage of males is 85.7 per cent compared to 88 per cent). In terms of level of education, 19 per cent of the entrepreneurs have a university education, compared to 13 per cent for Gibcus et al.

6.4 RESULTS

Tables 6.1 to 6.5 provide an overview of the most important aspects mentioned in the maps for each type. The frequency counts should be interpreted as the number of entrepreneurs of that specific type who mention a specific aspect. Alternatively, one can think of it as the number of maps for the category in question that include the aspect. The aspects mentioned are allocated to a number of categories, which correspond to some extent to the main areas of the maps described earlier.

The results for the Daredevils can be found in Table 6.1. The motives and reasons mentioned for making the decision indicate that they are driven by a strong sense of purpose. Eight out of 27 felt the need to act, to ensure the growth of their firm and keep ahead of the competition. In the words of the owner/director of a paint company: 'we need to become a bigger player on the market'. The director of a commercial services company indicates that he 'did not wait for the outcome of the market research' and went ahead with the implementation of his decision. In addition, six Daredevils perceived an opportunity. The type of decision made is quite diverse, but most often this involved a change in organizational structure or composition of the management (15/27). In the case of a financial services firm, the relationship with a valuable employee was intensified by making that employee a co-owner. Other decisions involve innovation (4/27), relocation, firing employees (both 3/27) and cooperation with other organizations (1/27). The director of a

*Table 6.1   Daredevils (*n = 27*)*

Common theme	Frequency	Common theme	Frequency
Motives		Company structure (*cont.*)	
Feeling the need to act/ grow/stay ahead	8	Decentralized decision-making	5
Seeing opportunity	6	Formal structure/ culture	2
Economic problems/ near bankrupt	5	Emotions and perceptions	
Problems with business associate	1	Risks present	6
Type of change		Freedom/flexibility	5
Changes in structure/ management	15	Confidence	3
Innovation	4	Low risks	1
Relocation	3	Decision process	
Firing employee(s)	3	Seeking advice/help	14
Cooperation	1	Search for information	8
Obstacles		Financial factors important	8
Government	7	Intuition/doing what feels right	4
Contractual hazards	1	Alternatives considered	2
Company structure		Outcome	
Flat structure/informal culture	14	Satisfaction with outcome	20
Short communication channels	8	Dissatisfaction with process	7
Employee involvement	6	Regret	1
Direct/centralized decision-making	5		

specialized cleaning services company reports involvement in an innovation platform. Eight of the Daredevils see obstacles to the success of their decision, in seven cases this is due to government regulation or unpredictability. The owner of a funeral home laments 'inconsistency' on the part of the government as a serious impediment to pushing ahead with the relocation of his business. Daredevils mostly characterize their company as follows: it has a flat organizational structure and an informal culture (14/27), where communication channels are short (8/27), decision-making decentralized (5/27) and employee involvement in what goes on (6/27). The culture can be seen as 'easygoing' as described by the owner/director of a paint company. However, in some cases the opposite is true, decision-making is said to be quite direct and centralized (5/27), while two Daredevils even mention that culture is hierarchical and formal. It seems that Daredevils do not agree on the best way to run a firm.

Some Daredevils see risks that are not insignificant (6/27). However, three of them mention that they are very confident with what they are doing, and they are convinced of the value of the products and services they offer. Another aspect that is noteworthy is that five of the Daredevils have freedom and flexibility. About half of them ask others for help or advice, while about eight out of the 27 have actively gathered information. Furthermore, some Daredevils ascribe some importance to financial factors (8/27) and make decisions based on intuition (4/27). Ultimately, a substantial majority (20/27) are satisfied with the outcome, while a small minority (7/27) are dissatisfied with the decision process. Largely this is because procedures were too slow or they were not 100 per cent in control of what happened. The owner/director of a paint company clearly shows his colours by stating that he had 'been too careful'. Only two Daredevils mention that they considered one or more alternatives.

Table 6.2 gives an overview of the most common and striking aspects found in the cognitive maps of the Lone Rangers. Their motivation seems to come from a feeling that they need to change, as some part of their business is no longer adequate (9/17). A smaller number perceive an opportunity (6/17) or are in a situation where resources are munificent (4/17). The type of decision most often involves relocation or renovating the office location. Innovation and takeover are each mentioned three times. Like the Daredevils, Lone Rangers sometimes see the government as an obstacle (2/17). However, in contrast to that group, Lone Rangers run their organization with a direct, centralized decision-making style (7/17), and employee involvement is uncommon in most SMEs (3/17). A director of a beauty parlour states: 'everyone is equal, except the director'. Lone Rangers seem rather authoritarian. This is also illustrated by the statement of a funeral home director, who indicates that a 'rigid protocol and highly specified task' is what staff are expected to abide by.

What Lone Rangers desire from their organization is that it is flexible (3/17). This attitude towards employees and management is part of a more general perception that others cannot be relied upon and a desire to be in absolute control (9/17). A director/owner of a financial services company states that 'no third parties were involved in the decision'. The director of a plumbing company indicates that he coordinates everything. Lone Rangers do not seem to be very trusting, which is also evidenced by the fact that on three occasions they have informed their personnel only once the decision has been made, actively keeping them out of the process.

Table 6.2   Lone Rangers (n = 17)

Common theme	Frequency	Common theme	Frequency
Motives		Company structure (*cont.*)	
Feeling the need to change	9	Decentralized decision-making	1
Seeing opportunity	6	Autonomy	1
Munificence of resources	4	Emotions and perceptions	
Type of change		Unable to rely on others/need to check everything	9
Relocation/renovation of building	6	Risks present	4
Innovation	3	Decision process	
Takeover	3	Internal focus	6
Expand abroad	1	Search for information	5
Create new company	1	Personnel kept out/ informed after decision	3
Cutback	1		
Obstacles		Intuition/doing what feels right	3
Government	2		
Company structure		Alternatives considered	3
Direct/centralized decision-making	7	Fast process	1
Flat structure/informal culture	4	Outcome	
		Satisfaction with outcome	14
Employee involvement	3	Dissatisfaction with process	2
Flexible organization	3		

The director of a utility installation company is clear about this: 'no communication about the decision'. The director of a beauty parlour indicates that she did the same and 'kept everything under own control'. The director of a transportation company says he has the 'need to check on personnel'. A dislike of relying on others also features in the internal focus in the decision-making process (6/17). Lone Rangers do not search for information very actively (only 5 out of 17) or consider many alternatives (3/17). Ultimately, the majority is satisfied with the outcome (14/17), while two Lone Rangers are dissatisfied with the process. Characteristically, they blame others for this.

The most noticeable and common aspect mentioned by the Doubtful Minds are listed in Table 6.3. Doubtful Minds tend to portray themselves as a sort of victim, given that they see a bad economic situation as the primary motive for their decisions (7/12). The other motives also seem to indicate that Doubtful Minds are at the very least reactive rather than

Table 6.3   Doubtful Minds (n = 12 *)*

Common theme	Frequency	Common theme	Frequency
Motives		Company structure (*cont.*)	
Bad economic circumstances	7	Open culture/short communication channels	3
Need to change	4	Informal culture	3
Past failure	2	Flexible organization	1
Internal problems	1	Hierarchy	1
Threat of takeover	1	Direct/centralized decision-making	1
Type of change		Emotions and perceptions	
Fire employees	3	Regret	6
Build new location/ renovate building/ relocate	2	Doubts	1
Takeover	2	Decision process	
Hire new director/change management	2	Long process/waited a long time before acting	10
Introduce new type of employment contract	1	Others involved	7
Create new company	1	Alternatives considered	6
Innovation	1	Search for information	3
Obstacles		Spontaneous idea	1
Government	2	Compromise	1
Not being taking seriously	1	Outcome	
Mother organization	1	Satisfaction with outcome	8
Uncertainty	1	Outcome not as expected	4
Risk	1	Satisfaction with process	2
Company structure		Dissatisfaction with process	2
Autonomy/own responsibility	4		

active. This is most clearly seen in the case of the owner/director of a hairdressing salon, who mentions the threat of being taken over. The type of decision made does not clearly distinguish the Doubtful Minds, though human resource-related issues are most prominent (6/12). Most Doubtful Minds see obstacles (5/12), of whom two see more than one obstacle. The owner/director of a hairdressing salon mentions that she does not feel that she is taken seriously, and thinks that this is gender related.

Confidence does not seem to be something that Doubtful Minds possess in great abundance. This can also be concluded from the fact that half of them report having regrets about the decision and one, the director of an engineering company, claims to have made a decision that he doubted. The director of a financial services firm feels bad because he 'should have acted sooner'. The director of a company that instals heating and cooling equipment indicates that he 'should have handled the situation differently', referring to changing the management of his company. Perhaps because of a lack of confidence, Doubtful Minds prefer that their employees work autonomously and take responsibility for themselves (4/12). They characterize the culture at their companies as informal and open (both 3/12). In the words of the director of an engineering company, there are 'few rules and hierarchy'. A further consequence of their lack of confidence is the fact that they take a long time to make a decision and often wait before mustering the courage (10/12), depend on others to make the decision (7/12) and often consider alternatives (6/12). That the process takes a long time is captured most clearly in the statement of the director of an engineering company, that they had to 'invest time and energy'. The length of the process is also illustrated by the comments of the director of a fashion design company who states that she 'had the idea for a while, but didn't have the guts to do it', referring to starting her own enterprise. Searching for information is not that important (3/12). Ultimately, most are satisfied with the outcome (8/12), but it is not always as they had expected (4/12). Two Doubtful Minds report being dissatisfied with the outcome.

Informers' Friends are characterized by the aspects summarized in Table 6.4. The rationale they offer for making a decision mostly involves a feeling that they are forced to change (12/22), largely because their current situation cannot be maintained. Some of them also feel competitive pressure (7/22), while a smaller number actually observe good market conditions which offer an opportunity (4/22). The majority of the decisions they make involve either expansion (7/22) or changes in structure and/or the management (7/22). A minority revitalize the business (4/22) or relocate (3/22). Some Informers' Friends see obstacles; most mention the government (4/22) while some indicate that they feel too inexperienced (2/22). This feeling might be because doubts (5/22) are the most common perceptions that Informers' Friends have. Furthermore, they feel that they are taking risks (4/22) and sometimes regret their decision (2/22).

The companies they lead can be characterized as having an informal culture (14/22) where decision-making is mostly centralized (10/22). A contractor describes the atmosphere at his firm as 'we are one big team spirit'. The owner/director of a hair and beauty salon stresses that 'good communication is important'. However, as the manager of a car dealership puts it, Informers' Friends like to be 'able to make a big decision

Table 6.4   Informers' Friends (n = 22)

Common theme	Frequency	Common theme	Frequency
Motives		Company structure (*cont.*)	
Need to change	12	Formal structure	3
Economic problems/ competitive pressure	7	Short communication channels	3
Good market conditions/opportunity	4	Emotions and perceptions	
		Doubts	5
Disagreements about strategy	1	Risks present	4
		Regret	2
Type of change		Confidence	1
Expansion/takeover	7	Low risks	1
Changes in structure/ management	7	Decision process	
		Seeking advice/help	17
Revitalizing the business	4	Search for information	7
Relocation	3	Intuition/doing what feels right	7
Firing employee(s)	1	No involvement of personnel	5
Obstacles			
Government	4	Rely on past experience	4
Lack of experience	2	Previous failures	2
Lack of commercial attitude in employees	1	Cooperation with others	1
		Long process	1
Need for trust	1	Alternatives considered	1
Risk of reputation damage	1	Outcome	
		Satisfaction with outcome	16
Company structure		Satisfaction with process	5
Informal culture	14		
Direct/centralized decision-making	10	Dissatisfaction with process	3
Employee involvement	4	Process could have been faster	3
Flat structure	4		
Decentralized decision-making	3	Outcome not as good as expected	1

quickly'. This is illustrative of the importance of centralized decision-making for this type of entrepreneur. True to their name, Informers' Friends very often seek out advice and assistance in the decision process (17/22), while the number that gathered information themselves is far lower (7/22).

Even though they seek advice and assistance, some Informers' Friends prefer not to consult their employees (5/22). Ultimately, some of them state that they just relied on their gut feeling and did what felt right (7/22) and did not consider alternatives (only one out of 22 indicates having done so). The owner/manager of a real estate firm stated that he used 'no systematic approach'. The director of a fast-food restaurant indicates that the decision process was not based on rationality. However, the owner of a financial services provider feels that this is a mistake because 'by not putting it on paper there's no control or learning mechanism'. Given that four Informers' Friends state that they relied on past experience, while two indicate that they experienced past failures and we have already seen that another two felt that they lacked experience, we believe that they base their confidence on experience. Most Informers' Friends report satisfaction with the outcome (16/22), and some are also satisfied with the process (5/22). Three of them are dissatisfied with the decision process because it was conducted too quickly, while curiously an equal number believe that they should have moved faster. This is expressed quite clearly by the owner of a financial consultancy firm, who says that he 'should try to be less insecure in the decision-making process in the future'.

Table 6.5 provides an overview of the common aspects found in the cognitive maps of the Busy Bees. The busy nature of these entrepreneurs does not emerge from the maps, which is due to the fact that only one specific decision instance is involved. Nevertheless, we do find that six out of seven Busy Bees characterize their decision-making and/or subsequent implementation as fast or quick. The director of a photography company states: 'Dive in and we'll see'. In addition, they believe that there is a need to change (4/7) and see opportunities and/or believe they have an understanding of the situation (4/7). The decisions they make are in general of great impact: three Busy Bees report it as a takeover/merger, one had to fire a dysfunctional director, one had to fire half of the total staff and one developed a new product. With regard to the company itself, they describe it as having an open, informal culture (6/7), where communication is informal and channels are short (2/7). According to the director of an air circulation machine company, they use 'compliments as incentives'. The director of a franchise bank characterizes the atmosphere at the establishment as 'hard work, but pleasant'. The manager of a gym states that 'employees can come up with own ideas'. All seven Busy Bees report satisfaction with the outcome of the decision they made, although three of them are somewhat dissatisfied with the process. In the words of the bank director who had to fire a dysfunctional director, he 'should have discarded alternatives sooner'.

Table 6.5   Busy Bees (n = 7)

Common theme	Frequency	Common theme	Frequency
Motives		Company structure (*cont.*)	
Feeling the need to act/grow/stay ahead	4	Informal communication/ short communication channels	2
Seeing opportunities, having insight into the situation	4	Emotions and perceptions Ambition	1
Low risks due to low costs	2	Decision process	
Type of change		Fast/quick decision-making, fast implementation	6
Develop new products	1	Considering alternatives	1
Takeover or merger	3	Outcome	
Firing people	2	Satisfaction with outcome	7
Company structure		Some dissatisfaction with decision process	3
Informal organizational culture	6		

6.5   DISCUSSION AND CONCLUSION

Our results indicate that the different entrepreneurial types indeed differ in the cognitive content in their decision-making process. While earlier research described entrepreneurs as elitists, risk takers and rugged individualists (McGrath et al., 1992), we find that this does not apply invariably. It would most clearly apply to the Lone Rangers, but certainly not to the Doubtful Minds or Informers' Friends. Nor would that description do justice to the Daredevils or the Busy Bees. Thus, entrepreneurs are not a homogeneous group but rather a heterogeneous one (see Gustafsson, 2006). When making strategic decisions, they think differently. The question 'How do entrepreneurs think?' in the context of strategic decision-making hence has different answers, depending on what kind of entrepreneur we are dealing with (Mitchell et al., 2007).

Daredevils are passionate, do not like inaction and often change the structure of their organization. They prefer to manage their company informally, without too much hierarchy. Daredevils acknowledge the risks they face but do not let themselves be put off by them, nor are they afraid to ask for advice and assistance from in- or outsiders. The occasional instance of dissatisfaction is self-directed: they feel either that they acted too slowly or that they were not on top of things. This resonates with the findings of Gibcus et al. (2008) to some extent. However, we did not find that they searched for information or considered alternatives as much.

Lone Rangers are hard to please, as they are often convinced that the state of their business is no longer adequate and requires change. Moreover, they do not generally trust people, whether they are from outside the firm or their own employees. As a result, Lone Rangers prefer a more hierarchical, do-as-you-are-told style of management. They shun the outside world as much as possible, and prefer to get things done by themselves. These results are completely consistent with the description given in Gibcus et al.

Whereas Daredevils and Lone Rangers have a confident attitude, Doubtful Minds feel rather insecure. Rather than feeling in control of the situation, the situation controls them. In a sense, they are victims of their environment. Doubtful Minds sometimes regret their actions and doubt their decisions. They prefer their employees to take responsibility for themselves and act autonomously. Decision-making is something they would rather postpone as long as possible, so that they can consider multiple alternatives and be sure once they have made their choice. Doubtful Minds are in general less satisfied with their decisions than the other four types. As argued by Gibcus et al., they have a low affinity for decision-making. Informers' Friends feel forced to change, but unlike Doubtful Minds they manage to maintain a confident outlook. Their somewhat lowered confidence compared to the other three seems to derive from their need to feel experienced. Given the stress on either using or lacking experience, confidence for Informers' Friends is to a large extent based on experience. They manage their companies in a hierarchical way, but prefer not to be too overbearing. As expected, they would seek advice and assistance from both in- and outsiders. As Gibcus et al. have already postulated, information search does not need to be extensive, nor do Informers' Friends feel the need to consider alternatives. Having obtained advice, they feel secure enough to make their own decisions. For the Busy Bees we find the least consistency with Gibcus et al. This is not surprising, since the interviews focused on only a single decision. However, we do find that Busy Bees act rather quickly, both in decision-making and in the subsequent implementation of their decisions. Just like the Daredevils, they are quite passionate and manage their company in an easygoing manner. If they are dissatisfied, they blame themselves for not acting quickly and decisively enough.

The five types also share a number of commonalities. Entrepreneurs' strategic decisions are often the result of perceiving an opportunity. In addition, they are quite attentive to the environment, evidenced by the mentioning of the economic situation in a number of instances. They see the government as the greatest obstacle to the success of their strategies. In terms of decision-making, a number of entrepreneurs acted on intuition or 'gut feeling'. Research by Khatri and Ng (2000) found that managers of large corporations benefited from intuitive decision-making in unstable environments. Consistent with other work on entrepreneurship, mostly Busy Bees and Daredevils stress the need to act quickly. This 'need for speed' can be related to the window of opportunity that stays open only for so long (Busenitz and Barney, 1997).

Our contribution to the understanding of entrepreneurial decision-making is *conceptual* as well as *empirical*. Conceptually, we hypothesized that different entrepreneurial decision styles are mirrored in distinct cognitions. Our results lend support to this assertion, and give an overview of what these cognitions include for each of the five entrepreneurial types. Empirically, our study served to validate the taxonomy of Gibcus et al. (2008). In addition, by using interview rather than survey data, we were able to provide a far richer, more elaborate, picture of the different entrepreneurial decision styles.

The main implication of our research is that type of entrepreneur matters. Each of the five types will respond differently, requiring different strategies to approach and influence them. Moreover, not all entrepreneurs of SMEs will respond in the same way to changing circumstances. This opens up interesting avenues of research into the conditions under which each of the five types performs best. One of these could be to combine the insights our research offers with the finding of Westhead et al. (2005b) that entrepreneurial cognition is also influenced by the amount of experience the entrepreneur has.

Our study does have its limitations. Our non-random subsample consists of entrepreneurs who volunteered to be interviewed. Thus, our results might be biased towards the kind of entrepreneurs who are willing to be interviewed. Second, the quantity and type of information in each interview varied. Some interview reports are twice as long as others. Even though the same questions were asked, some entrepreneurs elaborated far more than others on one aspect, while others gave more attention to another factor. However, since we had multiple entrepreneurs per category, the random error of these effects should cancel out. Nevertheless, in case there is a systematic process based on the type of entrepreneur, bias could result. Based on the consistency in the sorts of aspect mentioned, we do not believe this to be a problem. Third, we have a rather small sample ($n = 85$) from just one country. More research needs to be done to confirm these entrepreneurial types and their characterization beyond the Dutch context and our sample. In conclusion, our research provides an interesting and fruitful contribution to the question 'How do entrepreneurs think?'. It clearly brings to the fore the cognitive processes of different entrepreneurs when making a strategic decision.

NOTES

1. These figures can be obtained from the first author.
2. See previous note.

7. Entrepreneurial decision-makers and the use of biases and heuristics

Marijn J.J. de Kort and Patrick A.M. Vermeulen

7.1 INTRODUCTION

In contemporary market economies, small and medium-sized enterprises (SMEs) play a key role (Gibcus et al., 2008). To survive in the changing market economy, companies are forced to make strategic decisions (Schoemaker, 1993). Deciding on the correct course of action can mean the distinction between success and failure of an SME (Brouthers et al., 1998). In the introductory chapter, it was argued that we know much less about strategic decision-making in SMEs than in large organizations. Furthermore, it has been claimed that not enough attention is paid to the ways in which entrepreneurs make decisions (Bakker et al., 2007). This chapter aims to contribute to the understanding of entrepreneurs and the way in which they make strategic decisions.

In the cognitive stream of entrepreneurship research, it has been argued that entrepreneurs are more liable to use decision-making biases and heuristics than are managers in large organizations (Busenitz and Barney, 1997). Biases and heuristics are judgemental rules, cognitive mechanisms and subjective opinions that people use to assist in making decisions (Barnes, 1984; Schwenk, 1984; Busenitz and Barney, 1997). This helps entrepreneurs in their decision-making in a complex and uncertain environment, but can also lead to large and persistent biases with serious implications (Barnes, 1984). The representativeness heuristic and overconfidence bias are often mentioned as being critical in understanding entrepreneurial behaviour (for example, Tversky and Kahneman, 1974; Busenitz, 1999). Bakker et al. (2007) argued for more research into the overconfidence bias and representativeness heuristics. In this chapter we respond to their call.

Chapter 2 examined different types of entrepreneurs (see Woo et al., 1991; Gustafsson, 2006). However, little systematic research has been conducted to categorize different types of entrepreneurs and subsequently relate these types to variations in decision-making practices (see Forbes,

1999). We build on the work of Gibcus et al. (2008) who empirically identified a taxonomy of five different types of decision-makers in SMEs: Daredevils, Lone Rangers, Doubtful Minds, Informers' Friends and Busy Bees. We shall develop hypotheses to explore the relation between these five types of entrepreneurial decision-makers and the use of the representativeness heuristic and overconfidence bias. Our research question is stated in the following way: what is the relation between types of entrepreneurial decision-makers and the use of cognitive bias and heuristics in making strategic decisions?

The main goal of this chapter is to explore the relationship between different types of entrepreneurial decision-makers and the use of biases and heuristics; in particular the overconfidence bias and the representativeness heuristic. As such this chapter will contribute to our understanding of the ways in which different types of entrepreneurs make strategic decisions. This can be placed in the context of a growing scientific interest for a better understanding of the cognitive component underlying entrepreneurial actions (see Bakker et al., 2007).

7.2   THEORY AND HYPOTHESES

Representativeness is one of the most common of all decision-making biases and heuristics (Hogarth, 1987). Representativeness is a decision-making short cut that may be particularly common in entrepreneurial settings (Katz, 1992). Decision-makers use the representativeness heuristic when they generalize about a person or an event based on only a few attributes of that person or only a few observations of similar events. The 'insensitivity to predictability' and 'the law of small numbers' indicates that stereotype thinking prevails when entrepreneurs make a decision. Busenitz and Barney (1997) show that entrepreneurs make more use of the representativeness heuristic when compared to managers in large firms. Nevertheless there is also reason to believe that representativeness, and especially the willingness to generalize from small, non-random samples, is a decision-making short cut that may be used differently for the five types of decision-makers.

Most entrepreneurs do not have the resources to engage in systematic data collection to the same extent. In a study on the process of reasoning in entrepreneurial decision-making, Leaptrott (2006) demonstrated that entrepreneurs differ in the extent to which they use information in decision-making. Entrepreneurs who search for extensive information and take into consideration more alternatives are less susceptible to the use of the representativeness heuristics. Moreover, entrepreneurs who ask for advice are also less susceptible.

The five types of entrepreneurs described in Gibcus et al. (2008), differ in the extent to which they involve others in the decision-making process. Gibcus et al.'s analysis shows that Busy Bees and Informers' Friends are more likely to consult other people in the decision-making process than are Daredevils and Lone Rangers. The influence of people on the decision-making process could result in a better estimation of the chances, which implies that the possibility that the evidence of predictions is reliable increases. This argument is in line with Charness et al. (2007) who conducted an experiment to see whether groups influence the possibility of using non-rational decision-making in situations of risk, such as the representativeness heuristic. They argue that individual decisions that are made in a social environment will benefit from the experience and expertise of others. This underlines that such experience and expertise can help to make a better estimation of the chances regarding various aspects of a decision and thus reduce the representativeness heuristic. Cooper et al. (1988) found that entrepreneurs could decrease the use of the representativeness heuristic when they form relationships with outsiders who can provide objective assessments for the decision situations. If the reliability of prediction increases, the use of the representativeness heuristic decreases. Entrepreneurs who consult many others in making decisions (Busy Bees and Informers' Friends), will score lower on the use of the representativeness heuristic than those who tend not to seek such advice (Daredevils and Lone Rangers). This leads to our first hypothesis:

Hypothesis 1: Informers' Friends and Busy Bees make less use of the representativeness heuristic than Daredevils and Lone Rangers.

Overconfidence is a bias which occurs when decision-makers are overly optimistic in their initial solution and then are slow to incorporate additional information about a situation into their solution because of their initial confidence (Fischhoff et al., 1977). Overconfidence is divided in two types (Griffin and Varey, 1996). First, optimistic overconfidence is the tendency to overestimate the likelihood that one's favoured outcome will occur. Second, overestimation of one's own knowledge is overconfidence in the validity of the judgement even when there is no personally favoured hypothesis or outcome. It has been shown that entrepreneurs are more overconfident than non-entrepreneurs (Busenitz and Barney, 1997; Busenitz, 1999) because of the higher levels of uncertainty they face in their decision-making.

Entrepreneurs who face an uncertain and complex environment and do not search for information might suffer from an overconfidence bias. They ignore the fact that when making a strategic choice, they actually lack important information. This is often a result of the fact that they are susceptible to the belief that their judgements are better than they really are. Entrepreneurs who are involved in extensive information search are assumed to be less overconfident. Thus, a disparity between the level of information search and the environmental conditions regarding a decision leads to the use of overconfidence biases. Gibcus et al. (2008) identified that Daredevils and Doubtful Minds have a relatively high degree of information search when taking into account the environmental conditions compared to Busy Bees, Lone Rangers and Informers' Friends. We formulate the second hypothesis:

> *Hypothesis 2: Daredevils and Doubtful Minds make less use of the overconfidence bias than Busy Bees, Lone Rangers and Informers' Friends.*

7.3 RESEARCH METHOD

The first step consisted of grouping the entrepreneurs into the five main categories described in Gibcus et al. (2008). We used the clusters defined in the previous study in order to arrive at the five groups of entrepreneurs. The distribution of entrepreneurs in the five categories is presented in Table 7.1.

Dependent Variables

To assess entrepreneurs' use of the representativeness heuristic and overconfidence bias in making strategic decisions, we developed a set of measures using the scripts of the interviews. Entrepreneurs were asked questions concerning their most important strategic decision of the last three years. The questions that are mainly taken into account were: 'How did you come to the idea for the decision?', 'Did you also have alternative ideas?', 'Did you look for information?' and 'Did you have any doubts

Table 7.1   Frequencies for the types of entrepreneurial decision-makers

	Frequency	Percentage
Daredevils	26	26.3
Lone Rangers	17	17.2
Doubtful Minds	12	12.1
Informers' Friends	21	21.2
Busy Bees	7	7.1

about the process; if yes, what were they?'. The degree of use of both variables is scored on a five-point scale, where 1 indicates a very low degree and 5 a very high degree.

We developed another set of coding rules on the basis of 10 transcripts that were coded by two separate coders, who discussed very thoroughly how they scored the transcripts and what information they used. This evaluation led to the formulation of several questions which were used to measure the variables. Four questions were devised to assess the degree of use of the representativeness heuristic. To measure the law of small numbers, two questions were asked: 'Does the decision-maker search and make use of additional information?' and 'Does the decision-maker mention more alternatives?'. A high amount of information use indicates that the possibility of generalizing from a small sample is reduced. Also, when more alternatives are considered, this implies a better thought-out decision-making process by the entrepreneur. This decreases the possibility that the entrepreneur has a tendency to generalize from a small sample. Insensitivity to predictability is measured with two questions: 'Is the decision-maker aware of the consequences of the alternatives?' and 'Does the respondent base the decision on a reliable estimation of the chances for success?'. When an entrepreneur scores high on both questions, he or she is highly sensitive to predictability.

We also developed four questions to derive a score for the level of overconfidence of the entrepreneur. Overestimation of one's own knowledge is measured with two questions: 'Does the decision-maker have doubts about his/her own knowledge and does he/she use additional external information?' and 'Is the text free from signs of overestimation of one's knowledge about the decision?'. When the individual is overconfident with respect to the appropriateness of his of her knowledge, he or she will not look for other information. This is measured with the first question. Furthermore, interviews were screened for phrases like 'I have so much experience, I don't need to involve other people', which can be seen as an indicator of overestimation of one's knowledge. Optimistic overconfidence is assessed by means of two questions: 'Does the respondent mention doubts about the decision?' and 'Is the text free from signs of overconfidence in the result of a decision?'. When an entrepreneur has a high level of this type of overconfidence, he or she is free from doubts concerning the results of the decision. This is assessed by means of the first question. The second question concerns an interpretation of the language used by the respondent. For example, one entrepreneur went bankrupt, but decided to start again in the same way and is sure that the results will now be great. This, points to an overestimation of the chances for success. Table 7.2 provides two illustrations of this procedure. The first respondent (no. 2528) has scores that are

Table 7.2   Illustration of measurement of dependent variables

Resp. no.	Scores	Indicators	Answers to the questions
2528	Representativeness 5	Law of small numbers	No information gathered, decision based on own experience, no influence from other people on decision
		Insensitivity to predictability	No alternatives mentioned Consequences are not mentioned No estimation of chances for success
	Overconfidence 5	Overconfidence of knowledge	No information search Trust own instinct and experience
		Optimistic overconfidence	No doubts concerning the success of the idea
610	Representativeness 2	Law of small numbers	Use of internal information, but no external information used Alternatives are considered
		Insensitivity to predictability	Consequences are mentioned Estimation of chances for success
	Overconfidence 4	Overconfidence of knowledge	No use of external information Indication of confidence in own knowledge
		Optimistic overconfidence	No doubts mentioned It has taken much time to reach a decision (implies doubts)

extreme on overconfidence and representativeness. The second respondent (no. 610) has more or less moderate scores on both variables.

The procedure was followed by two independent raters, who assessed overconfidence and the representativeness heuristic. To ensure the quality of the coding procedure and the reliability of the measurement, the inter-rater agreement (Cohen's kappa) is computed for both variables. The kappa for representativeness was 0.767 and for overconfidence, 0.6165. According to Bernard (2002), many researchers are satisfied with a kappa that exceeds 0.70, which is the case for representativeness. For overconfidence, the kappa is not completely satisfying. In drawing conclusions, the possibility of unreliable measurement must be taken into account. With respect to the measurement of representativeness, the raters disagreed in 18 cases. Rating the overconfidence resulted in 29 disagreements. The raters discussed the differences and subsequently agreed on the scores for the deviant cases; thereafter the agreement between the two raters improved considerably.

Control Variables

Age is added as a control variable. Age is supposed to have an influence on the way people process information, which consists of cognitive mechanisms and subjective opinions that people use to assist in making decisions (the use of biases and heuristics). Age is negatively correlated to the ability to integrate information (Taylor, 1975). This can be related to the fact that younger entrepreneurs are more open to new information and combine information more easily (Parker, 2006). Hence, it could be that younger entrepreneurial decision-makers make less use of heuristics and biases. Education of the entrepreneur is another control variable. This was included because the level of education can have an effect on the knowledge structures and the way in which entrepreneurs process information (Mitchell et al., 2002). Because the representativeness heuristic and overconfidence bias can be seen as a way of processing information, education could also have an influence on the relation between types of entrepreneurial decision-makers and the representativeness heuristic and the overconfidence bias.

Data Analysis

Analyzing the data consisted of testing the hypotheses by using independent *t*-tests. Independent sample *t*-tests were appropriate because a comparison was made on the mean scores of the continuous variables' overconfidence bias or representativeness heuristics, for two different groups (two clusters of types of entrepreneurs are stated in the hypotheses).

After each *t*-test, a covariance analysis was carried out in order to incorporate the control variables. This analysis allowed differences between the groups to be explored, while statistically controlling for age and education.

7.4   RESULTS

Of the total set of semi-structured interviews ($n = 109$), we had to reject several interviews since these did not contain enough information to measure the independent or dependent variables. Hence, we used 99 interviews. The mean age of the respondents is 46.28 years; 84 of the 99 respondents are male; 21 per cent held a university degree; 37 per cent finished a higher professional qualification. The mean entrepreneurial experience is 13.47 years, ranging from 0–40 years of experience, and the size class is measured by number of employees. The distribution of firm sizes is represented in Table 7.3, and the distribution with respect to industries is reflected in Table 7.4.

Table 7.3   Distribution of firm sizes

No. of employees	Frequency	Percentage
1–10	31	31.3
11–20	23	23.2
21–50	19	19.2
51–100	15	15.2
101–250	10	10.1
Missing	1	1.0
Total	99	100.0

Table 7.4   Distribution of industries

Industry	Frequency	Percentage
Manufacturing	9	9.1
Construction	11	11.1
Trade	7	7.1
Hotel and catering	7	7.1
Transport	8	8.1
Financial services	15	15.2
Business services	25	25.2
Personal services	16	16.1
Missing	1	1.0
Total	99	100.0

Table 7.5   Descriptives of dependent variables

	N	Mean	SD
Representativeness heuristic	99	3.48	1.358
Overconfidence bias	99	3.63	1.130

The results for our dependent variables show a mean value of 3.48 (SD 1.358) for the representativeness heuristic, and a mean value of 3.63 (SD 1.13) for the overconfidence bias (see Table 7.5). Table 7.6 presents the mean values and standard deviations of our dependent variables, representativeness heuristic and overconfidence bias, for each type of entrepreneurial decision-maker.

Hypotheses

Our first hypothesis was concerned with the influence of other people in making a strategic decision. We expected Informers' Friends and Busy Bees to make less use of the representativeness heuristic than Daredevils and Lone Rangers because of their inclination to rely more on the advice of other people in the decision-making process. An independent-samples t-test was conducted. There was no significant difference in scores for Informers' Friends and Busy Bees (M = 3.52, SD = 1.47) and Daredevils and Lone Rangers (M = 3.60, SD = 1.34). Although in the expected direction, the results were not significant.

Furthermore, we conducted a one-way analysis of variance between the two groups in order to compare the use of representativeness heuristic by

Table 7.6   Descriptives of dependent variables for each type of entrepreneur

Type of entrepreneurial decision-maker	Representativeness heuristic		Overconfidence bias	
	Mean	SD	Mean	SD
Daredevil	3.54	1.363	3.58	1.027
Lone Ranger	3.71	1.359	3.76	0.970
Doubtful Mind	3.00	1.348	3.08	1.165
Informers' Friend	3.57	1.502	3.95	1.244
Busy Bee	3.57	1.512	4.14	1.464

the two groups, while statistically controlling for age and education. We ensured that there were no violations of normality, linearity, homogeneity of variance, homogeneity of regression slopes and reliable measures of the covariates. The results of this analysis show that the difference between the two groups was not significant. Hence, Hypothesis 1 is not confirmed.

We also hypothesized that Daredevils and Doubtful Minds make less use of the overconfidence bias than do Busy Bees, Lone Rangers and Informers' Friends. We expected that those entrepreneurs who do not search for information might suffer from an overconfidence bias. Furthermore, a mismatch between the level of information search and the environmental conditions regarding a decision leads to the use of overconfidence biases. The independent-samples t-test was conducted to compare the use of the overconfidence bias for the two clustered groups. The difference between the two groups is significant ($t = 3.89$, $p < 0.05$), showing a significantly lower tendency to use overconfidence by Daredevils and Doubtful Minds (M = 3.42, SD = 1.08) as compared to Busy Bees, Lone Rangers and Informers' Friends (M = 3.91, SD = 1.16). The covariance analysis further demonstrated that the difference is still significant. Therefore, we can conclude that Hypothesis 2 is supported.

7.5   DISCUSSION AND CONCLUSIONS

The results of our study trigger several points for discussion. In our first hypothesis, we expected Daredevils and Lone Rangers to make less use of the representativeness heuristic than Doubtful Minds, Busy Bees and Informers' Friends, because they ask advice less often while making a strategic choice. Although the results are not significant, we cannot conclude that asking advice leads to a reduced sensitivity to the representativeness heuristic. A possible explanation for this finding might be related to the differences in the way entrepreneurs process information. According to the arguments presented in Chapter 3, an essential element of information processing is the development and use of cognitive representations under the influence of two information processing systems: heuristic and controlled. It may also be the case that asking for advice is actually another heuristic used by entrepreneurs while making a strategic choice. This means that they are not really engaged in extensive information processing, but rather use another cognitive short cut (what others think) to deal with the available information.

The second hypothesis was confirmed. Entrepreneurial decision-makers who are characterized by a misfit of economic condition and information search are more prone to fall into the overconfidence trap. This can be explained by the fact that a real misfit between the economic situation and information search can be generalized to a type of entrepreneurial decision-maker. Daredevils and Doubtful Minds are less susceptible to using the overconfidence bias than Lone Rangers, Busy Bees and Informers' Friends in making strategic decisions. Our results are in line with Forbes (2005), who argues that susceptibility to cognitive biases associated with entrepreneurial cognition may also be based on what entrepreneurs think about themselves. Thus, a difference in entrepreneurial self-efficacy between different types of entrepreneurs explains the differences in the use of the overconfidence bias.

Our study also has an important implication for policy makers. Although the use of cognitive biases and heuristics may be beneficial in some circumstances, it can lead to major problems in others (Tversky and Kahneman, 1974). However, it is still unclear to what extent the use of biases and heuristics in strategic decision-making remains stable over time. Some scholars argue that biases and heuristics are often applied in an unconscious manner (Tversky and Kahneman, 1981) and thus are relatively immune to change or modification. Alternatively, others have reasoned that decision biases can be corrected through training (for example, Agnoli, 1991; Russo and Schoemaker, 1992). Assuming that decision biases can be corrected through training, a focus on different types of entrepreneurial decision-makers can help to improve training programmes. Policy makers could customize some of the tools and instruments they use to facilitate start-up entrepreneurs to educate entrepreneurs and improve their decision-making skills.

Despite its merits, our study is not without limitations. First, the interviews did not contain much information about economic situation and innovativeness, indicating that those aspects are more susceptible to a subjective interpretation. Second, the level of inter-coder reliability could have been more convincing for overconfidence (although this problem was addressed when the two coders subsequently discussed their disagreements).

To overcome some of these problems, direct measures for the dependent variables could be developed. These can be derived from measures used in previous research. Busenitz and Barney (1997), for example, provided respondents with several scenarios to determine whether the representativeness heuristic was used. The overconfidence bias could be measured following the well-established format used by Simon et al. (2000) based on Fischhoff et al. (1977) and Russo and Schoemaker (1992). Furthermore, independent measures of the two components of the representative heuristic 'insensitivity to predictability' and 'the law of small numbers' could be used. Also, the overconfidence bias can be divided into two components: 'optimistic overconfidence' and 'overestimation of one's own knowledge'.

Our analysis strengthens the idea of using different types of entrepreneurial decision-makers in future research projects to clarify the relationship between types of entrepreneurial decision-makers and the use of biases and heuristics. The types of entrepreneurial decision-makers can be linked in future research to other heuristics and bias such as framing, counterfactual thinking, reasoning by analogy, sample-size neglect, overconfidence, excessive optimism, illusion of control, escalation of commitment, aversion to regret, planning fallacy, self-serving bias, confirmation bias, sunk cost fallacy and endowment effect.

In conclusion, from our study the assumed relationships derived from theory were only partly confirmed. This implies that the relation between entrepreneurial decision-makers and the use of cognitive bias and heuristics remains unclear and deserves further attention. However, the confirmed hypotheses revealed interesting findings. The influence of others in making a strategic decision decreases the use of the representativeness heuristic in strategic decision-making. We also showed that entrepreneurs with high confidence both in their skills about what it takes to be an entrepreneur and in the positive outcome of their decision, use the overconfidence bias more. Hence, our findings indicate that it makes sense to use a more differentiated approach torwards entrepreneurial decision-makers.

8. Risk, uncertainty and stakeholder involvement in entrepreneurial decision-making

Jaap van den Elshout and Patrick A.M. Vermeulen

8.1 INTRODUCTION

Every organization, large or small, faces strategic problems (Vennix, 1996). In order to cope with strategic problems, managers need to make strategic decisions (Noorderhaven, 1995). The outcomes of these strategic decisions shape the future of the organization. In small and medium-sized enterprises (SMEs), strategic decisions are the responsibility of one actor, the entrepreneur, and not a management team's responsibility as is often the case in large companies (Brouthers et al., 1998). Because entrepreneurs are central actors in the strategic decision-making in SMEs it is very likely that their individual traits play a very important role in shaping the strategic decision process. It has been stated that, as opposed to managers, entrepreneurs do not develop routines and often make decisions based on their intuition (ibid.), they are highly individualistic, have a high tolerance for uncertainty and are confident about their skills, knowledge and expertise (McGrath et al., 1992). Very often entrepreneurs have to identify business opportunities in the environment and make decisions that involve a considerable amount of risk and uncertainty. Perceived uncertainty and perceived risk are related concepts and often are obstacles for accurate strategic decision-making (Lipshitz and Strauss, 1997). Therefore, the way entrepreneurs perceive risks and uncertainty is a core element influencing their strategic choices.

Scholars agree that it is perceived, rather than objective, risk that drives the decision-maker to a particular behavioural pattern in strategic decisions (Dowling and Staelin, 1994). Uncertainty reflects the inability of the decision-maker to know all possible outcomes for the present multiple alternatives (Duncan, 1972; Bakker et al., 2007). When a decision-maker perceives a high degree of uncertainty, the natural tendency is to try to reduce it, by trying to look for additional information, using cognitive short cuts (cognitive heuristics and biases) or involving other agents in the decision-making process. Stakeholders are central agents that can be involved in the strategic decisions of entrepreneurs.

This chapter has two aims. First, we want to test the impact of risk perception and uncertainty on entrepreneurial decision-making processes. Second, we want to explore the extent to which the perception of risk and uncertainty leads to the involvement of stakeholders in entrepreneurial strategic decision-making (ESDM).

8.2 THEORETICAL FRAMEWORK AND HYPOTHESES

The success of SMEs heavily depends on the way entrepreneurs make strategic choices (Knight, 2000). In fast-changing and competitive environments, entrepreneurs face strong pressures to actively interpret opportunities and threats (Dess et al., 1997). The information available to the entrepreneur is often incomplete, which makes it likely that the perception of uncertainty is associated with strategic decision situations. In previous studies in large organizations, scholars have argued that there is a positive relation between perceived uncertainty and perceived risk (Lipshitz and Strauss, 1997). Managers who consider a decision to be uncertain perceive higher levels of risk. In SMEs, ambitious goals and high performance standards increase uncertainty and automatically the perceived risk about decisions (Baum and Locke, 2004). It is also possible that the lack of information, the confusion about alternatives and the inadequate understanding of certain strategic situations lead to higher levels of perceived risk and uncertainty (Lipshitz and Strauss, 1997). Hence, we formulate our first hypothesis:

Hypothesis 1: The perception of uncertainty in a strategic decision situation increases the perception of risk associated with that situation.

Earlier research suggested that entrepreneurial perception of risk and uncertainty is not only rooted in individual differences but is also influenced by contextual factors (for example, environmental uncertainty) or the amount of experience in the field of entrepreneurship (Forbes, 2005). More experienced entrepreneurs are likely to develop efficient strategies to deal with the lack of information and to be confident in making decisions when relevant information is not available (for more details, see Chapter 4). Therefore, it is very likely that experience has a negative impact on the perception of risk and uncertainty. The second hypothesis tested in this study is:

Hypothesis 2: Entrepreneurial experience has a negative influence on perceived uncertainty and perceived risk.

Perceived risk and uncertainty are often associated with negative emotions, and the decision-maker is motivated to reduce these feelings. A broader involvement of stakeholders could have a positive role in the reduction of uncertainty and thus on the decision-making process (Mitchell and Cohen, 2006). Freeman (1984) defines stakeholders as individuals or groups who can affect or are affected by the achievement of organizational objectives. In line with this definition, Boddy and Paton (2004) define stakeholders as individuals, groups or institutions who affect the organizational outcomes. Stakeholders not only affect the outcomes of the strategic decision-making, but may also affect the process itself.

By asking stakeholders to get involved in the strategic decision process, entrepreneurs increase their legitimacy and expand their knowledge base when making strategic choices. The literature is ambiguous about the relation between perceived uncertainty, perceived risk and different involved stakeholders in the strategic decision-making process. Sawyerr et al. (2003) state that entrepreneurs perceiving high uncertainty and risk during decision-making rely more on information from different stakeholders. Brouthers et al. (1998) found no evidence for this relationship. However, there seems to be a tendency in the literature to point towards a positive association between perceived risk and uncertainty on the one hand and stakeholder involvement on the other. Entrepreneurs who perceive high uncertainty and high risk are more likely to involve different knowledge sources because of more valuable insights others do not have (Simon et al., 2000; Jorrisen et al., 2002; Janney and Dess, 2006). These sources can convince an entrepreneur about the need for a strategic decision. Entrepreneurs who assume that a small involvement of stakeholders represents enough information may not adequately perceive the possibility of losses or acquire a full view of possible outcomes (Simon et al., 2000).

In a study of household investment decisions, Cho and Lee (2006) indicate that when perceived risk increases, consumers are more likely to have a higher number of involved stakeholders in the decision-making process. It seems that the higher the perceived uncertainty, the greater the need for information from the stakeholders (Jorissen et al., 2002; Forbes, 2005). To conclude, previous research showed a positive relation between perceptions of risk, uncertainty and the number of different involved stakeholders. This leads to the following hypothesis:

Hypothesis 3: The perception of risk and uncertainty in an entrepreneurial decision situation has a positive impact on the number of stakeholders involved in that particular decision.

As argued before, entrepreneurial experience is expected to have a negative influence on perceived risk and perceived uncertainty (Busenitz, 1999; Forbes, 2005). Experienced entrepreneurs will be less prone to higher perceptions of uncertainty and risk, because they have developed a rich knowledge base related to strategic decision-making. It is also expected that experienced entrepreneurs will involve a smaller number of stakeholders in the decision than entrepreneurs with less experience (Cooper et al., 1995), which is due to the fact that experienced entrepreneurs have already gained more knowledge over time and feel more confident about themselves (Busenitz, 1999). We formulate our fourth hypothesis:

Hypothesis 4: Entrepreneurial experience has a negative impact on the number of stakeholders involved in the decision situation.

Organizations manage their relations with stakeholders to enhance their value creation and to maximize their financial performance (Stavrou et al., 2006). Integrating relationships with multiple stakeholders leads to long-term decision outcomes (Post et al., 2002). Since organizations have limited resources, the process of identifying and prioritizing of stakeholders is important (Preble, 2005). This process is influenced by the power, legitimacy and urgency of each stakeholder (Mitchell et al., 1997; Post et al., 2002). Therefore, entrepreneurs should not underestimate the potential of stakeholders, since this could put the organizational continuity at risk. A large amount of stakeholder inclusion in the strategic decision-making process can lead to value creation and more opportunities for the organization (Vandekerckhove and Dentchev, 2005; Mitchell and Cohen, 2006). Ashmos et al. (1998) show that managers whose earlier decision outcomes were poor, had a larger variety of stakeholders involved in their subsequent strategic decision-making processes, which resulted in better outcomes.

Robson and Bennett (2000) found a positive relation between the number of different involved external advisers and decision outcomes. Similarly, Winn (2001) argued that in order to be successful it is important to have different stakeholders involved in the decision-making process. According to her, this leads to more knowledge and legitimacy for the organization. In line with Winn's arguments, other researchers point out that a broad stakeholder's participation is strongly related to more and better decision outcomes (Sawyerr et al., 2003; Choi and Shepherd, 2004; Gibb, 2006; Mitchell and Cohen, 2006). Hence, we formulate Hypothesis 5:

Hypothesis 5: The number of different stakeholders involved in the strategic decision has a mediating role in the relationship between perceived risk and uncertainty on the one hand and the quality of decision outcomes on the other.

8.3   METHODS

Sample

The data used in this study were collected by EIM Business and Policy Research (see Appendix). The data have been gathered from 1203 entrepreneurs from small firms in the Netherlands who are responsible for the management of the SME and the strategic decisions of the organization. The questionnaire focused on entrepreneurs in SMEs who, in the past three years, made at least one important decision regarding innovation, a project or something that was perceived as being extremely important. About 60 per cent of the entrepreneurs who were interviewed made some such important decision in the last three years and were therefore used in this research. After controlling for the questions 'How many employees does your company have?', 'Is your company a subsidiary of another company?', 'Are you responsible for making important decisions?' and 'Have you made one or more important decisions in the past three years?', about 40 per cent of the 1203 respondents were discarded. Because of missing values and incomplete questionnaires, 646 respondents remained in our sample (see Table 8.1).

Of the total number of respondents, 88 per cent were men. The mean age of the respondents was 44 years with a variance between 21 and 76 years. The average entrepreneurial experience was 15 years. Some 44 per cent of our sample have a higher professional education. The distribution of size class within SMEs used in this sample is shown in Table 8.2.

Table 8.1   Distribution of respondents

	Men	Women	Total
N (%)	1021 (84.9)	182 (15.1)	1203 (100)
Used in research (%)	581 (87.9)	80 (12.1)	661 (100)
Mean age in years (SD)	48.12 (56.67)	43.96 (8.83)	47.80 (53.23)
Mean experience in years (SD)	15.75 (13.74)	14.62 (9.55)	15.36 (13.74)

Table 8.2   Distribution of size classes

Employees	N (%)
0–10	276 (41.8)
11–50	266 (40.2)
51–100	119 (18.0)
Total	661 (100)

Measures

The questions from the telephone survey were constructed based on two qualitative pilot studies, performed in 2002 and 2003, and consisted of 22 in-depth interviews with entrepreneurs (see Chapter 5 and Appendix). The two independent variables 'perceived uncertainty' and 'perceived risk' were evaluated with a single item measure. Each question had a response category 'don't know/don't want to say' which was treated as a missing value. The variable perceived uncertainty contained six (0.8 per cent) missing values and perceived risk only two (0.2 per cent). These independent variables were measured on a metric level. The question 'perceived risk' was reverse coded.

The entrepreneurs were asked several questions to measure the number of different involved stakeholders in the decision-making process. In the questionnaire, the questions 'Who was influencing your decision?' and 'Which other persons or things influenced your decisions?' were the indicators for the determination of the number of different involved stakeholders. Five different stakeholders (family, employees, advisers, business relations in own branch and business relations in other branches) were explicitly referred to in the questionnaire, using the following response categories: 1 = yes, 2 = no and 3 = don't know/don't want to say. In a follow-up question the respondent could mention other stakeholders. In order to measure the number of different involved stakeholders, it was necessary to recode the answers ('yes' being 1 and 'no' being 0). The follow-up question was recoded by reading the answers of the respondents, checking this with the mentioned stakeholders in the previous question and subsequently putting the exact number of the named stakeholders in the cell. Adding up the scores on both questions created a new variable (total number of different involved stakeholders) on a continuous metric level. Table 8.3 provides an overview of the number of involved stakeholders. As indicated, the respondents were also able to name other possible stakeholders who

Table 8.3   Distribution of involved stakeholders

Type of stakeholder	N (%)
Advisers	288 (43.6)
Employees	224 (36.6)
Family	208 (31.5)
Business connections (own industry)	183 (27.7)
Business connections (other industry)	97 (14.7)
Other stakeholders	118 (17.9)

influenced the strategic decision-making process. Of all respondents, 18 per cent named other stakeholders, such as government, customers, branch organizations and clients.

To measure the dependent variable 'the quality of decision outcomes', the questions 'Has the decision led to the result which was expected?', 'Has the decision led to a higher turnover?' and 'Has the decision led to more profit?, were asked. The three questions were measured with 5-scale response categories. However, two response categories ('don't know/don't want to say' and 'not known') did not explain anything about decision outcomes. The response category 'to some extent' was added to the response category 'yes'. Therefore, the original 5-scale response categories were reduced to 2-scale response categories. This transformed the variable into a dichotomous variable.

The scale of decision outcomes, measured by three indicators, had an alpha of 0.613. However, since Cronbach's alpha coefficient is very sensitive to the number of used indicators (with short scales <10 indicators it is common to find 0.5) this scale (three indicators) represents a good internal consistency (Pallant, 2005). Finally, a sum score of the three questions produced the variable decision outcomes on a continuous scale. After checking for the total number of missing values (30 per cent), it was necessary to create a mean score on decision outcomes (Baarda and De Goede, 1999). This made it possible to create a more consistent and complete view of the decision outcomes.

8.4   RESULTS

The model was tested using AMOS structural equation modelling software version 6. A maximum likelihood procedure was used and the results are presented in Figure 8.1. The descriptive statistics are presented in Table 8.4.

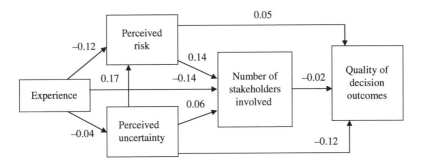

Figure 8.1   Results of the overall path model

Table 8.4   Means, standard deviations and inter-correlations

Variables	Mean	SD	1	2	3	4	5	6
1. Gender	1.12	0.33						
2. Education	3.28	1.66	0.12**					
3. Experience	15.61	13.30	−0.03	0.25**				
4. Perceived uncertainty	1.47	0.65	0.08*	0.04	−0.02			
5. Perceived risk	2.24	0.92	−0.01	−0.09*	−0.12**	0.17**		
6. Stakeholders	1.73	1.26	−0.10*	−0.19**	−0.16**	0.09*	0.17**	
7. Decision outcomes	0.69	0.35	−0.04	−0.08	−0.12**	−0.11**	0.02	−0.03

Note: $* p < 0.05$; $** p < 0.01$.

Two categories of fit indices were used in the analysis: absolute and incremental. The chi-square (9.06, $p < 0.003$) shows that the model is significantly different from the data. The variances implied in the theoretical model do not match the observed variances in the data. Further, the root mean square error of approximation (RMSEA) value is 0.11, which is higher than the value of 0.08, recommended for a fitting model (Browne and Cudeck, 1993). The incremental fit indices are NFI (Normal Fit Index) = 0.89, CFI (Comparative Fit Index) = 0.89 and TLI (Tucker–Lewis Index) = 0.78. The values of the incremental fit indices show that in relation to the null model, the theoretical one can be significantly improved.

The first hypothesis stating that the perception of uncertainty increases the perception of risk is fully supported by the data. When entrepreneurs experience uncertainty in a decision situation, it is very likely that they perceive that situation as also involving a considerable amount of risk. The second hypothesis states that entrepreneurial experience has a negative influence on the amount of uncertainty and risk perceived in a decision-making situation and it is partially supported by the data. The results support the idea that more-experienced entrepreneurs have a tendency to perceive more risk in their strategic choices. However, experience seems not to exert a significant influence on the amount of uncertainty associated with a strategic decision. The third hypothesis is partly supported. Whereas we hypothesized that risk and uncertainty perception have a positive influence on the number of stakeholders involved in the strategic choice, the data only support the fact that perceived risk has a positive and significant impact on the number of stakeholders involved in ESDM. In other words, when entrepreneurs perceive a high degree of risk in a strategic decision they tend to involve a higher number of stakeholders in the decision at hand. The fourth hypothesis was fully supported by the data, which means that entrepreneurial experience has a negative influence on the number of stakeholders involved in an ESDM. Finally, our last hypothesis was rejected. We did not find support for the proposition that the number of stakeholders involved in a strategic decision mediated the impact of risk and uncertainty perception on the quality of ESDM outcomes.

8.5 DISCUSSION AND CONCLUSION

In this study we explored the strategic decision-making processes in a sample of 661 entrepreneurs in the Netherlands using several key variables: perceived risk and uncertainty, number of stakeholders involved and entrepreneurial experience. Our results indicate a positive influence of perceived uncertainty on perceived risk. This is in line with earlier results (Lipshitz and Strauss, 1997; Baum and Locke 2004; Bakker et al., 2007), which showed that entrepreneurs who perceive a decision situation as uncertain will most likely perceive a considerable amount of risk involved. An explanation for this relation is that the lack of extensive knowledge and the limited search for alternatives in ESDM (Lipshitz and Strauss, 1997) associated with the fact that SMEs strive to achieve high goals in a complex environment (Baum and Locke, 2004) lead to the perception of uncertainty and ultimately to high risk involved in ESDM.

Entrepreneurial experience has a significant negative impact on the amount of perceived risk. The role of experience on perceived risk is probably explained by overconfidence (for more details, see Chapter 9). Through experience, entrepreneurs gain more confidence in their decisions and thus they are less likely to perceive a situation as risky. This explanation is also in line with the fact that experienced entrepreneurs do not involve a high number of stakeholders in the decision process. Experience, however, does not have a significant impact on perceived uncertainty, meaning that the relationship between experience and perceived risk can be explained by motivational rather than cognitive factors.

An important contribution of this study is the support for a positive relation between perceived risk and the number of different involved stakeholders. Based on earlier research it was expected that higher levels of perceived uncertainty and perceived risk would lead to a higher number of different stakeholders involved in the strategic decision-making process of entrepreneurs (Jorissen et al., 2002; Forbes, 2005; Cho and Lee, 2006). When perceiving risk and uncertainty, entrepreneurs feel less confident and tend to involve stakeholders in the decision process in order to gain legitimacy and a sense of certainty (Sawyerr et al., 2003; Forbes, 2005; Janney and Dess, 2006).

The results reported here do not support the expected positive relation between number of different involved stakeholders and decision outcomes (Dess et al., 1997; Robson and Bennett, 2000; Winn, 2001; Sawyerr et al., 2003; Choi and Shepard, 2004; Edelenbos and Klijn, 2005; Gibb, 2006; Mitchell and Cohen, 2006). The number of different stakeholders involved has no relation with decision outcomes. A possible explanation could be the size of the organizations. This research focused on SMEs with 100 employees, whereas other research focused on SMEs with up to 250 employees (Liagrovas, 1998; Knight, 2000; Winn, 2001; Sawyerr et al., 2003; Choi and Shepard, 2004; Sauner-Leroy, 2004; Edelenbos and Klijn, 2005; O'Regan et al., 2005). It is possible that in larger SMEs the decision-making process is more influenced by the power and legitimacy of stakeholders (Mitchell et al., 1997). One other reason is given by Sawyerr et al. (2003), who found that the age of an SME influences the relation between different involved stakeholders and the decision outcomes. The number of different stakeholders involved in the ESDM could have a greater impact during the early stages of existence because of the possible higher need for resources and legitimacy.

It was expected that decision outcomes would be positively influenced by the experience of the entrepreneur (Lee and Tsang, 2001; Collinson and Houlden, 2005; Janney and Dess, 2006). However, this research did not find support for this theoretical proposition. A plausible explanation is offered by Espedal (2006), who points out that entrepreneurs with successful experiences are extremely confident and more likely to use their routines from experiences. Another plausible explanation is the differences in the way that experience is utilized. Instead of looking at the number of years one has been an entrepreneur, looking at the quality of experiences (for example, practical, a narrow versus a wider focus of experiences) may lead to more interesting insights on the impact of experience on decision outcomes (Janney and Dess, 2006).

Our study is not without limitations. First, the respondents used in this questionnaire were sampled across eight different types of industries in the Netherlands. This raises the possibility of creating a complete view of reality within the Netherlands. Nevertheless, this research used a selected sample of Dutch SMEs with a maximum of 100 employees. A disadvantage of selective sampling is that it is less representative than an a-selective sample. Moreover, it seems that some industry branches were overrepresented, for example, small hotel and catering firms. Researchers found that industry characteristics affect decision outcomes (Baum and Locke, 2004), therefore a skewed representation across industries may bias the results of our study.

The second limitation is that the data were collected through telephone interviews. While these lower the non-response rate (that is, not completing or not returning the questionnaires), telephone interviews might lead to a superficial view that can soon change and it can lead to socially desirable answers. Moreover, the telephone questionnaire focused on one strategic decision taken by an entrepreneur in the last three years. This can lead to rather extreme scores. Individuals remember a decision with either extremely positive or extremely negative outcomes. Future research should use in-depth interviews that focus more on long-term implications of strategic decisions made by the entrepreneur.

A third limitation is the way in which the perceptions of risk and uncertainty were evaluated. A single-item evaluation has several limitations and further research should replicate the design with more extensive evaluations of these variables. Moreover, another limitation is related to the construct validity of the mediating variable (Baron and Kenny, 1986). Using a mediating variable that is measured by only one indicator can lower the construct validity of this study. Mediation variables should be measured by multiple independent measurements.

A fourth limitation is that the data reported here are a cross-sectional snapshot of the perceptions of entrepreneurs and the SMEs' conditions. This approach is not able to capture all the implications of a dynamic system over time and causality cannot be revealed. It is possible that entrepreneurs' perceptions of risk and uncertainty change over time because of the complexity in their environment. Future research should take a longitudinal approach, which considers complexity. This could more effectively capture specific cause and effect relationships in the model used in this research.

9. Entrepreneurial experience and innovation: the mediating role of cognitive complexity

Petru L. Curşeu and Dinie Louwers

9.1 INTRODUCTION

Innovation is a key process for small and medium-sized enterprise (SME) performance. In order to be effective and to remain on the market, entrepreneurs have to innovate. Previous research has explored several antecedents for organizational innovation, ranging from organizational factors (for example, size, structure) to group dynamics (for example, diversity, group processes) and individual characteristics (for example, creativity, education, experience). In SMEs, entrepreneurs are the central actors responsible for innovation, and often the decision to innovate is a strategic choice because it may have important consequences for organizational performance. Several authors have emphasized the important influence of entrepreneurial attributes on strategic decision-making and innovation processes in SMEs (Kimberley and Evanisko, 1981; Brouthers et al., 1998; Lee and Tsang, 2001; Westhead et al., 2005b).

Experience (expertise) is an important factor explored in a variety of studies that yielded mixed results. Entrepreneurial experience was found to have a positive relationship with responses to organizational changes in the environment (Westhead et al., 2005b), venture growth (Lee and Tsang, 2001) and information search (Cooper et al., 1995; Fredrickson and Iaquinto, 1989), which suggests that more-experienced entrepreneurs are more innovative than less-experienced ones. However, other researchers found a negative relationship between tenure and innovation in top management teams (for example, Bantel and Jackson, 1989) and between experience and information use of owners and managers of SMEs (Lybaert, 1998). Moreover, Kimberley and Evanisko (1981), Damanpour (1991) and Parker (2006) found no significant relationship between experience and innovation. Therefore, the relationship between entrepreneurial experience and innovation seems to be unclear. One explanation is that often experience is not directly measured, and several proxies such as age and education are used to quantify expertise. It is often argued that older decision-makers have more expertise than younger ones, and a high level of education is conducive for innovation; nevertheless it may be the case that their impact on innovation yields distinctive patterns. Also, the mechanisms through which experience is related to innovation may partially explain the mixed results. As argued in Chapters 3 and 4, experience and other demographic variables are rather distal factors that influence the decision effectiveness and innovation. More proximal, cognitive factors seem to mediate the impact of experience and demographics on decisional outcomes. The core aim of this chapter is to explore the role of cognitive complexity and sensitivity to the use of cognitive heuristics as mediators in the relationship between age, experience and education on the one hand and decision effectiveness and innovation on the other.

9.2 INNOVATION AND ESDM IN SMEs

In the contemporary competitive knowledge-based markets, innovation is increasingly seen as the most important way to create and maintain sustainable competitive advantages (Johannessen et al., 2001). SMEs are generally considered to be critical sources of innovation in an economy (Brouthers et al., 1998; Hoffman et al., 1998; Freel, 2000b; van Gils, 2005). Therefore, innovation in SMEs is a topic that has recently received a great amount of attention (Hoffman et al., 1998; Hadjimanolis, 2000).

Innovation is defined as the adoption of ideas, practices or objects that are perceived as being new to the adopting organization (Johannessen et al., 2001) and it is an essential way in which organizations react to environmental dynamics in a way that sustains organizational effectiveness and competitiveness (Damanpour and Evan, 1984; Damanpour, 1991; Damanpour and Goplakrishnan, 2001). Innovation can involve activities such as introducing new products, penetrating new markets, developing new supply sources, developing new organizational processes and practices, and creating new sales formats (for example, e-business) (Bhaskaran, 2006). Although in innovation research the distinction among different innovation types is often made, some scholars argue that studies which aggregate multiple types of innovations represent the total degree of organizational innovation better than studies which focus on one type of innovation (Damanpour, 1991). In the same vein, Siguaw et al. (2006) argue that it is more useful to look at total innovation than to adopt a narrow focus on the different types of innovation. Our research uses an inclusive perspective on innovation, and incorporates under the innovation umbrella both product and process innovations. Following Camisón-Zornoza et al. (2004), the focus of this research is on innovative output, which means that organizational innovation is conceptualized as the number of implemented process and product innovations, as perceived by the entrepreneur.

A key element in the study of innovation in SMEs is the study of the processes through which such enterprises actually decide to innovate (Hoffman et al., 1998). According to a Dutch report, in 80 per cent of Dutch SMEs, the entrepreneur plays a central role in the initiation, decision-making and implementation of innovations (CBS, 2006). The decision to innovate becomes a strategic choice for the SME and the attributes of the entrepreneur play a central role in this decision. Therefore, it is important to explore factors related to the entrepreneur in relation to SME innovation. Some authors have taken the characteristics of the entrepreneur, such as experience, into account as antecedents of innovation in SMEs (for example, Hoffman et al., 1998; Hadjimanolis, 2000; Romijn and Albaladejo, 2002; Westhead et al., 2005a, 2005b). However, research has led to mixed evidence about the importance of these entrepreneurial characteristics and the way in which they influence the decision to innovate (van Gils, 2005).

Age is a proxy often used to measure experience, and to a certain extent one may expect a positive association of age and experience (Taylor, 1975; Hitt and Tyler, 1991) based on the argument that expertise needs time to develop. As argued before, we expect a positive impact of experience on cognitive complexity and thus it is not unreasonable to argue that age also has a positive impact. Nevertheless, Taylor (1975) reports a negative association between age and the ability to integrate information in order to make an accurate choice in a simulated decision task. The author explains this negative association of age with cognitive complexity as a result of an increased sensitivity to cognitive heuristics and biases in older decision-makers. According to this study, older decision-makers are less confident, more susceptible to the negative effects of information overload and therefore develop less-complex representations about the decision situation.

Education is another variable often associated with experience, cognitive complexity and decision-making effectiveness. Entrepreneurs with a higher education have an extensive knowledge base and develop a more comprehensive understanding of the relevant factors in a decision situation (Hitt and Tyler, 1991). Therefore, highly educated entrepreneurs are expected to develop more-complex representations about a decision situation than entrepreneurs with a lower level of education.

As argued before (see Chapter 4 for more details) cognitive complexity is expected to mediate the impact of entrepreneurial characteristics on the quality of entrepreneurial strategic decision-making (ESDM) outcomes. The aim of Study 1 is to explore this claim.

9.3   STUDY 1

The purpose of this study is to test a mediation model in which the relationship between personal characteristics of the entrepreneur (level of education, age and experience as an entrepreneur) and ESDM outcomes (profit, turnover and satisfaction) is mediated by the cognitive complexity of the entrepreneur.

Sample and Procedure

For this study we used interview data that have been collected among a sample of 44 entrepreneurs in Romania. The interviews were conducted with entrepreneurs in SMEs who made at least one important strategic decision related to innovation in the past three years. The decision could be related to any innovation or project that was discontinuous (out of daily routine) and that was perceived to be important. Various questions were asked on the characteristics of the entrepreneur and the outcomes of the selected decision (see the interview details in the Appendix).

The interview data were used for the elicitation of the cognitive maps for all interviewed entrepreneurs independently (details of the procedure are described in Chapter 4). The complexity of the individual cognitive maps is evaluated using three indicators: map connectivity (the number of connections established between concepts), map diversity (the number of distinct types of relations established between the concepts based on the taxonomy proposed by Gómez et al. (2000) and the number of concepts used. The absolute map complexity index was computed based on the following formula: $ACMCo = NoC \times CMC \times CMD$ (for details, see Chapter 4). After the interview, entrepreneurs were asked to fill in a questionnaire consisting of a number of additional items concerning the perceived outcomes of the strategic choice described earlier as well as demographic information (age, level of education and years of experience as an entrepreneur). The scale concerning the quality of ESDM consisted of four items evaluating turnover, profit, general positive outcomes and satisfaction, with a Cronbach's alpha of 0.71.

Results

Means and standard deviations for both demographic data and the scores on cognitive complexity as well as on sensitivity to decision-making heuristics and biases are presented in Table 9.1.

The analyses in this study were conducted using AMOS structural equation modelling software version 6. The model was tested using the

Table 9.1   Means, standard deviations and correlations for Study 1

	Mean	SD	1	2	3	4
1. Age	39.61	9.32				
2. Level of education	3.60	1.07	0.04			
3. Experience as an entrepreneur	7.11	4.82	0.49***	0.01		
4. Cognitive complexity	5074.05	2509.32	−0.13	0.10	0.31	
5. Quality of ESDM	5.11	1.83	−0.26*	0.19	−0.11	0.25*

Note: *** $= p < 0.01$; * $= p < 0.10$.

maximum likelihood procedure. As the absolute fit indices show, the model fits the data well ($\chi^2 = 0.12$, $p = 0.72$, df $= 1$; RMSEA (Root Mean Square Error of Approximation $= 0.001$) and it is significantly different from a null model as indicated by the incremental fit indices (CFI Comparative Fit Index $= 1.00$, NFI Normed Fit Index $= 0.99$, TLI Tucker–Lewis Index $= 1.00$). The results of the path analysis are presented in Figure 9.1.

The model clearly provides evidence for cognitive complexity to be a mediator between the personal characteristics of the entrepreneur and the quality of ESDM outcomes. Proposition 1 formulated in Chapter 4, claiming a positive impact of cognitive complexity on ESDM effectiveness is fully supported. Concerning the antecedents in the model, the results are mixed. The effect of entrepreneurial experience on the quality of ESDM is partially mediated by cognitive complexity. The positive impact of experience on ESDM effectiveness is mediated by cognitive complexity, while the direct effect of experience on ESDM is negative. As argued in Chapter 4, experienced entrepreneurs are more likely to use a heuristic style of information processing and the impact of experience on cognitive complexity is positive, only to the extent to which it is associated with a high cognitive complexity. It is very likely that the negative impact of experience on the quality of ESDM is mediated by the use of general cognitive heuristics and biases.

Although in the expected direction, the impact of education on cognitive complexity is not significant. Nevertheless, the direct impact of education on the quality of ESDM outcomes is positive and significant, meaning that highly educated entrepreneurs perceive the quality of their decisions as being higher than entrepreneurs with a lower level of education. Another interesting result is that the impact of age on cognitive complexity is negative, which means that older entrepreneurs develop less-complex representations about the decision situation as compared to young entrepreneurs. This result is in line with previous studies (Taylor, 1975; Hitt and Tyler, 1991) and a possible explanation would be that older entrepreneurs use

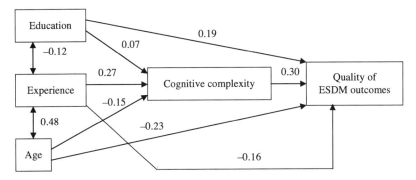

Figure 9.1   Results of the path analysis for Study 1

heuristics to simplify the knowledge domain to a greater extent than do younger entrepreneurs.

9.4   HEURISTICS, COGNITIVE COMPLEXITY AND INNOVATION IN SMEs

Cognitive models argue that experienced entrepreneurs are expected to be able to form more-complex representations than those of less-experienced entrepreneurs (for details, see Chapters 3 and 4). Cognitively complex entrepreneurs cover more aspects/events in the environment as well as a considerable number of possible connections among them. This increases the chances for the identification of business opportunities and increases the probability of innovation (Porac and Thomas, 1990). On the other hand, however, experienced entrepreneurs might be more sensitive to the use of general cognitive heuristics in decision-making. They may learn to trust their intuition and use indiscriminately general heuristics in specific decision situations. General heuristics are certain short cuts that actors use when processing information in uncertain and complex situations (for example, Busenitz, 1999). When general heuristics are used in specific decision situations, mental models are simplified, which can result in the overlooking of new opportunities in the environment, which decreases innovation (Schwenk, 1984; Barr et al., 1992). As argued in Chapter 4, two types of heuristic information processing can be distinguished. A first type emerges from experience and may have as a main consequence an increase in the complexity of cognitive structures formed in the working memory (WM). A second type, general heuristics (for example, overconfidence, representativeness), is identified in the decision-making literature and have as a main consequence an oversimplification of the decision situation. As argued in Chapter 4, the first type of heuristics may be beneficial for ESDM effectiveness if they emerge from an extensive experience and if they are used in very similar situations to the ones in relation to which they were formed. A first theoretical claim that will be tested is that the impact of general heuristics (second type) on ESDM effectiveness is negative and is mediated by cognitive complexity.

As argued above, the use of general heuristics plays a mediating role in the relationship between entrepreneurial attributes and cognitive complexity. An experienced entrepreneur tends to rely more on heuristics in decision-making (Taylor, 1975; Rerup, 2005), which results in the simplification of cognitive models. With respect to the use of overconfidence, Kaish and Gilad (1991) suggest that experience increases the confidence in own actions and decisions. With experience, entrepreneurs learn to trust their actions and decisions more, and because, in general, entrepreneurs are highly motivated to maintain a positive mood, they tend to give more weight to their successful experiences and try to forget unsuccessful ones, which makes them more confident about the knowledge they gained through time (Espedal, 2006). In addition, success stories are likely to accumulate, since they get more publicity compared to failures (Simon et al., 2000). Based on this overrepresentation of success stories in the past, experienced entrepreneurs are likely to overestimate their chances for success, which makes them more likely to become overconfident. Moreover, the overconfidence may lead to an increased use of representativeness bias. As argued in Chapter 3, entrepreneurs are likely to generalize from small samples, from their own experience, thereby violating general statistical rules. A possible outcome of overconfidence will be a heuristic processing of the statistical information available and a decrease in the use of proper analytical procedures to deal with this information.

Our argument here is that overconfidence mediates the relationship between entrepreneurial experience and the use of the representativeness heuristic. It is the trust in one's abilities, skills and expertise that makes a decision-maker rely more on intuition and thus be more sensitive to the general representativeness bias. When a decision-maker has little to no experience, it is very likely that the level of overconfidence is low, therefore he/she has to analyse the available data carefully and be less susceptible to the use of representativeness (Schwenk, 1988). This line of reasoning can be supported by several studies. Entrepreneurs with little experience were found to compensate the lower confidence by using more information and search more for opportunities in comparison with more-experienced entrepreneurs (Kaish and Gilad, 1991; Lybaert, 1998). This suggests that entrepreneurs with less experience are less sensitive to the representativeness heuristic than more-experienced entrepreneurs because of their low level of overconfidence.

Because representativeness involves the neglect of large samples of information (Busenitz, 1999) and the focus on one successful strategy narrows the vision of entrepreneurs (Espedal, 2006) it is very likely that the analysis of relevant information is restricted and information search gets concentrated within a specific domain (Westhead et al., 2005b). Therefore, crucial information and new opportunities will remain unnoticed, which inhibits actors from changing their cognitive models (Chattopadhyay et al., 2006). This will have a negative effect on cognitive complexity and ultimately on the propensity of the entrepreneur to innovate.

In addition to an indirect effect on innovation, overconfidence is also expected to foster innovation in a direct way. Individuals with greater overconfidence are less overwhelmed by the difficulties they face while making decisions and implementing them (Busenitz and Barney, 1997; Busenitz, 1999). Furthermore, when an entrepreneur shows confidence in the innovation that he or she has proposed, this will create commitment among others. This commitment enables implementation of the decision in the organization (Cooper et al., 1988; Busenitz and Barney, 1997), which makes innovation more likely. Research has indeed discovered that overconfidence positively influences innovation, such as the decision to enter a new market (Camerer and Lovallo, 1999) and to engage in risky product introductions (Simon and Houghton, 2003). In sum, a positive association between overconfidence and innovation can be expected.

Study 1, presented earlier, shows a negative impact of age on the quality of ESDM outcomes, and this result is in line with previous research (Taylor, 1975) showing that older decision-makers are less confident and less able to accurately integrate the available information. Moreover, other scholars have found evidence of a negative relationship between age and innovation (Bantel and Jackson, 1989; Parker, 2006). Based on this empirical evidence we hypothesize here a direct negative impact of age on cognitive complexity as well as an indirect negative effect, mediated by overconfidence. In other words we argue that older entrepreneurs score lower in cognitive complexity, and one factor responsible for this is the low confidence in decision-making situations. With respect to the impact of education level on innovation, Hambrick and Mason (1984) argue that innovation is positively associated with the level of education, and top managers with a higher education are more inclined to innovate as compared to top managers with a lower level. The level of education is also very likely to be positively associated with the level of overconfidence. To conclude, entrepreneurs with a higher education are expected to be more sensitive to overconfidence, but at the same time more innovative. Therefore, education has a direct positive impact on innovation and an indirect impact mediated by overconfidence and cognitive complexity.

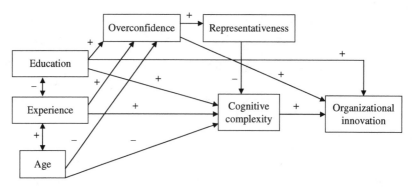

Figure 9.2   Overall theoretical model for Study 2

Finally, cognitive complexity is expected to have a positive impact on innovation. Complex cognitive schemas can contain much knowledge useful for gaining creative insights (Porac and Thomas, 1990). More elaborate cognitive models may also focus attention on opportunities in the environment (Westhead et al., 2005b). Chattopadhyay et al. (2006) propose that greater differentiation in the cognitive structures provides decision-makers with a greater number of distinct factors relevant to a problem. In addition, more integration of that relevant information will increase its usage in decision-making by increasing awareness of the important information and its interrelations. Shane and Venkataraman (2000) argue that people who are able to identify new means–ends relationships are more likely to discover entrepreneurial opportunities. These theoretical arguments support a positive relationship between cognitive complexity and innovation. Some studies indeed point towards a positive influence of cognitive complexity on innovation. For example, Barr et al. (1992) found that top managers who elaborated their cognitive models to incorporate environmental changes showed more signs of renewal in their strategies. Manimala (1992) found that the more innovative entrepreneurs were the ones with more contacts and more ideas. The model presented in Figure 9.2 summarizes the theoretical propositions advanced so far. The aim of Study 2 is to test this comprehensive model in a sample of Dutch entrepreneurs.

9.5   STUDY 2

Sample and Procedure

Semi-structured interviews were conducted with 109 entrepreneurs from the sample described in the Appendix. Some interviews did not provide valid information about decision-making, in particular about the use of cognitive heuristics and were excluded, which eventually led to a sample of 100 respondents.

The mean age of the respondents is 46.39 years. Eighty-five of the 100 respondents are male. A university degree is held by 20 per cent, and 38 per cent completed higher professional education. Mean entrepreneurial experience is 13.93 years, ranging from 0 to 40 years of experience.

Variables in the Model

Organizational innovation was evaluated through four questions in the telephone survey used to assess organizational innovation. They referred to both product and process innovations as perceived by the respondent. The questions were 'Has your company developed new products or services in the last three years?', 'Has your company introduced products or services that are new for your industry in the past three years?', 'Has your company developed new production or work processes in the past three years?' and 'Has your organization conquered new markets in the past three years?'. There were three response categories for these questions: yes, no and don't know. The last alternative was never chosen. There were no missing values on the items concerning innovation. An additive score was computed for the four items, to derive a general measure of innovation on a continuous scale.

Cognitive complexity is computed using the cognitive maps extracted from the interview transcripts. The transcripts of the semi-structured interviews are coded into cognitive maps, using a method described in Chapter 4. Absolute cognitive complexity was computed in a similar way to that in Study 1. Because the coding of the cognitive maps was performed in this study by two independent coders, we assessed the intercoder reliability by computing the intra-class correlation for the different components of cognitive complexity. For the number of concepts, the intra-class correlation coefficient is 0.998, for map connectivity it is 0.996, and for map diversity, 1.00. These values support a very good inter-rater reliability and thus the results can be used for further analyses.

Sensitivity to cognitive heuristics was evaluated using the procedure described in Chapter 7. The transcripts of the interviews are rated by two independent researchers to derive a qualitative measure of the sensitivity to the two heuristics: overconfidence and representativeness. Entrepreneurs were asked questions concerning their most important decision of the last three years. The questions that are mainly taken into account were: 'How did you come to the idea for the decision?', 'Did you also have alternative ideas?', 'Did you look for information?' and 'Did you have any doubts about the process; if yes, what were they?'. The degree of use of both heuristics is assessed on a five-point scale, where 1 indicates a very low degree and 5 a very high degree. To ensure the quality of the rating procedure and the reliability of the measurement, the inter-rater agreement (Cohen's kappa: Cohen, 1988) was computed for both variables. The kappa for representativeness was 0.767, and for overconfidence, 0.617. According to Bernard (2002), many researchers are satisfied with a kappa that exceeds 0.70, which is the case for representativeness. For overconfidence, the kappa is not completely satisfying. In drawing conclusions, the possibility of unreliable measurement must be taken into account.

Entrepreneurial experience was evaluated as the duration of experience in entrepreneurship. Following Reuber and Fischer (1999), the duration of entrepreneurial experience was measured by the number of years someone has been an entrepreneur. *Age* was also included in the research as an independent variable. *Education* of the entrepreneur is another independent variable used in the model. Level of education is measured on an ordinal scale with the question: 'What is your highest level of education?'. It has nine response categories, including 'don't know' and 'other, namely'. The data concerning level of education were treated as being measured on an interval level.

Results

The means, standard deviations and intercorrelations are presented in Table 9.2.

The analyses in this study were conducted using AMOS structural equation modelling software version 6. The model was tested using the

Table 9.2   Means, standard deviations and correlations for Study 2

	Mean	SD	1	2	3	4	5	6
1. Age	46.39	8.70						
2. Level of education	4.18	1.57	−0.02					
3. Experience as an entrepreneur	13.93	11.19	0.56**	−0.40**				
4. Representativeness	3.50	1.35	−0.09	−0.09	0.02			
5. Overconfidence	3.62	1.12	−0.03	0.17	0.01	0.38**		
6. Cognitive complexity	4565.03	1480.57	−0.03	0.02	−0.01	−0.28**	−0.09	
7. Innovation	1.90	1.43	0.04	0.25*	−0.06	−0.03	0.02	0.12

Note: ** = $p < 0.05$; * = $p < 0.10$.

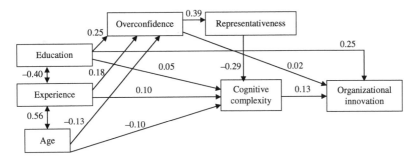

Figure 9.3   Path model results for Study 2

maximum likelihood procedure. The model is kept as simple as possible, due to the small sample ($n = 100$). As the absolute fit indices show, the model fits the data well ($\chi^2 = 4.66$, $p = 0.86$, df = 8; RMSEA = 0.001) and it is significantly different from a null model as indicated by the incremental fit indices (CFI = 0.98, NFI = 0.95, TLI = 0.99). The results of the path analysis are presented in Figure 9.3.

The data fully support the theoretical model and most of the hypothesized relations. The pattern of results is similar to the one reported in Study 1. Age has a negative impact on cognitive complexity, while the impact of experience and education is positive, yet not significant. The impact of cognitive complexity on innovation is positive and significant and the direct effect of education on innovation is also positive and significant. Therefore, the results support the contention that highly educated and cognitively complex entrepreneurs are more prone to innovate as compared to less-educated and cognitively simple entrepreneurs. A very important result is the mediating role of cognitive heuristics in the relationship between entrepreneurial demographic attributes and cognitive complexity. As hypothesized, entrepreneurial experience and level of education have a positive impact on the use of overconfidence, which in turn positively impacts on the use of the representativeness heuristic. Finally, the use of the representativeness heuristic has a strong negative effect on cognitive complexity. Although expected to be positive, the effect of overconfidence on innovations is not significant.

9.6   GENERAL DISCUSSION

The main goal of this research was to test whether cognitive complexity and sensitivity to overconfidence and representativeness mediate the relationship between entrepreneurial characteristics and organizational innovation.

The general model presented in Figure 9.2 was supported by the data. It has previously been argued that cognitive factors are better predictors of strategic changes than entrepreneurial characteristics (Barr et al., 1992). Our results are in line with this argument and show that the impact of experience and age on organizational innovation is fully mediated by the complexity of the cognitive representation developed in relation to the decision situation. Our data support what has previously been argued (ibid.; Hodgkinson et al., 1999): that cognitive representations are important antecedents for innovation in SMEs. Education, however, has a stronger direct effect on organizational innovation than the effect mediated by cognitive complexity. This direct effect, not mediated by cognitive complexity, may be explained in various ways. First, it may be related to a fashion of innovation established and communicated in higher education. In most of the educational programmes that specialize in business administration, innovation is described as a core driver of organizational performance. Innovation is good for company success! Second, the social network embeddedness of entrepreneurs may be a valid alternative explanation. It is very likely that highly educated entrepreneurs are engaged in social interactions with similar actors, and through these interactions they learn to value innovation more than entrepreneurs with a lower level of education.

A second aim of Study 2 was to provide more insights into the interplay between cognitive heuristics and cognitive complexity. Our results show that entrepreneurs who are sensitive to the representativeness heuristic develop in general less-complex cognitive models of their decision environment. Because the representativeness heuristic in particular results in the concentration of information search within a specific domain, which limits the amount of information that is collected and used, it also reduces the complexity of the cognitive representations formed in the WM. Entrepreneurs who are sensitive to the representativeness heuristic can be characterized by considering a low number of alternatives, using a limited amount of information, neglecting the consequences of their decisions and making no reliable estimation of their chances for success. In this way, they develop a rather simple cognitive model of the decision situation, which consists of a low number of concepts weakly interconnected.

Moreover, our results contribute to the cognitive heuristics debate. They clearly show that the general heuristics act as information processing mechanisms in an interdependent way. Overconfidence increases the chances that representativeness is used in a decision situation. This association implies that some entrepreneurs are in general more sensitive to the use of several general heuristics compared to others. Education and age are certainly factors that have an influence on the use of cognitive heuristics and cognitive complexity. Highly educated entrepreneurs are more likely to be overconfident than entrepreneurs with a lower level of education. Through this higher sensitivity to overconfidence, education has in fact a negative impact on cognitive complexity. We hypothesized that higher education provides entrepreneurs with a richer set of cognitive tools to make sense of their environment and enables them to see relationships between these various facts and events. Nevertheless, this direct effect of education on cognitive complexity was not supported by the data. A plausible explanation is that highly contextual factors (for example, specific factors associated with the decision to innovate) may play a more important role than the level of education in the formation and activation of cognitive representation in the WM space.

Age has a negative impact on both overconfidence and cognitive complexity. When entrepreneurs get older, their confidence in a decision grows weaker and the complexity of the cognitive representations decreases. A possible explanation is a decline in general cognitive abilities with age, meaning that in time entrepreneurs' ability to integrate information decreases (Bantel and Jackson, 1989). A main contribution of the empirical studies presented in this chapter refers to the implications of cognition on organizational innovation. Cognitive complexity mediates the effect of demographic characteristics on organizational innovation, which provides empirical support for the important role of entrepreneurial cognition in organizational innovation.

Limitations

Entrepreneurial experience is operationalized in this research simply as the duration of experience as an entrepreneur. However, the number of years that somebody has been an entrepreneur may not accurately reflect entrepreneurial experience. Reuber and Fischer (1999) acknowledge that a duration-based measure of experience has its limitations. It is argued that next to the amount or duration of experience it is also the type of experience that is important for the development of expertise (ibid.; Rerup, 2005; Westhead et al., 2005a, 2005b). Westhead et al. argue that experience in a variety of domains creates a broad knowledge corridor, which resembles high cognitive complexity. On the contrary, when an entrepreneur has accumulated experience in a narrow area, she/he will concentrate search within a specific domain (ibid.). These differential effects of broad versus narrow experience have been overlooked in our empirical studies. Similarly, it has been recognized that the amount of successful experience is of importance (Cahill, 1998; Rerup, 2005; Espedal, 2006). According to Espedal, successful experience will reinforce routines and lead to a narrowing of the focus. In contrast, entrepreneurs who have had unsuccessful experiences will feel the need to revise their routines (ibid.). These results are in line with the role of emotion in ESDM (see Chapter 3, for more details). They need to collect new information and search for alternatives. In this way, unsuccessful experiences may reduce the use of heuristics and increase cognitive complexity. Further research should further address the role of emotions in cognitive complexity.

Our model tested the linear relationship between variables. In some of the cases (see especially the rather small values of some path coefficients) the possibility of the existence of curvilinear relationships between the variables may not be ruled out. Shepherd et al. (2003) show that for inexperienced capitalists, performance increased by gaining experience; nevertheless, after several years of experience, performance reached an optimum and decreased thereafter. In the same way, the possibility of a curvilinear relationship between cognitive complexity and organizational innovation must be taken into account. It was proposed that cognitive complexity has a positive effect on organizational innovation. However, a very high level of cognitive complexity might instead inhibit innovation. The introduction of innovations usually involves multiple problems (Busenitz and Barney, 1997). Dealing with all these problems will postpone decisions and will be quite overwhelming (ibid.). To be innovative, it might be important to just act quickly instead of taking every single aspect of the situation into account. This implies that a certain level of simplification may be necessary in order to engage in innovation. Therefore, there seems to be an optimum of cognitive complexity.

10. Social capital, cognitive complexity and the innovative performance of SMEs

Daniëlle G.W.M. van Gestel

10.1 INTRODUCTION

Small and medium-sized enterprises (SMEs) can be seen as the engines of economic development (Brouthers et al., 1998; de Jong, 2004). The success of these firms is influenced by the strategic decisions made by entrepreneurs. Innovations are often the result of such strategic choices and are important sources for SMEs' competitiveness. As indicated by van Gils (2005), it is crucial for SMEs to innovate since enterprises that innovate have higher long-term returns and are more likely to survive over time.

Since the 1980s and in close association with the theoretical and methodological developments in social network analysis, the importance of social relationships of the entrepreneur for SME effectiveness has received considerable attention (Cope et al., 2007). This perspective focuses on the fact that economic activity is embedded in society and very often the most innovative entrepreneurs are part of a large social network (ibid.) from which they get valuable information, financial and often emotional support. In their recent work, Anderson et al. (2007) indicated that individuals with strong social relationships are able to achieve more compared to when they act alone. Cooke and Wills (1999) showed that the presence of social relationships can contribute to the availability of information, something that could reduce the uncertainties that entrepreneurs are facing. The presence of social capital, which can be seen as resources based on group membership, relationships or networks of influence (Inkpen and Tsang, 2005) seems to be valuable for entrepreneurs. Cope et al. (2007) argue that entrepreneurial growth can be realized by identifying individual opportunities, but it is also influenced by the social relationships of the entrepreneur. Despite the fact that it is repeatedly argued that the presence of social capital can make contributions to the entrepreneurial success, less attention has been paid to empirically testing the mechanisms through which social capital impacts on SME innovation and effectiveness (Cooke and Wills, 1999).

A key factor linking social capital to innovation in SMEs is the fact that entrepreneurs embedded in large social networks have access to more information than entrepreneurs deciding alone (ibid.; Moran, 2005). Therefore, entrepreneurs embedded in social networks seem to make more informed strategic choices involving innovation. Through their social ties, entrepreneurs are able to identify opportunities in their surroundings, by integrating the information available in the social network (Shane and Venkataraman, 2000). The capability of the entrepreneur to integrate information and use it in the process of strategic decision-making is referred to as 'cognitive complexity'. Cognitive complexity indicates the richness of the representation developed by an individual about a particular decision situation (Curşeu and Rus, 2005). It represents the way of thinking of the entrepreneur and his/her identification of the environment (Kiesler and Sproull, 1982) and it might explain the impact of social capital on SME innovation. The aim of this chapter is to test the mediating role of cognitive complexity on the relationship between the presence of social capital and innovation in SMEs.

10.2   THE INNOVATIVE PERFORMANCE OF SMEs

To date, little attention has been paid to innovation in the context of small firms (Freel, 2000a) and major innovations were traditionally associated with large firms (Hadjimanolis, 2000). While large firms enjoy benefits with capital-intensive industries associated with greater market power and resources, small firms are more successful when they are able to exploit behavioural advantages in industries with a large amount of skilled labour (Freel, 2000a; Hadjimanolis, 2000). Because of these differences, large firms and SMEs have to adopt different innovation strategies. The strength of the small company lies not in its resources, but rather in a more flexible way of organizing and in the decision-making behaviour of the entrepreneur. It is difficult for SMEs to secure financial resources, to spread their risks appropriately and to attract technically qualified labour (Freel, 2000b). Nevertheless, small firms have unique advantages associated with organizational flexibility and motivated management (Vossen, 1998). Further, SMEs often lack bureaucracy which relates to efficient, usually informal communication systems and adaptability because of nearness to markets (Freel, 2000a, 2000b; Hadjimanolis, 2000).

In the context of SMEs, an innovation can be seen as 'the generation of a new idea and its implementation into a new process, product or procedure in a group or organization, that is new for the relevant actors and it has to be advantageous for the individual, the group or the society as a whole' (Joma et al., 2001: 5). The idea that can be transformed into an innovation can be formed with totally new knowledge or can be a changing way of thinking with respect to an already existing decision.

In the innovation literature, a common distinction is made between radical and incremental innovations. Radical innovations are innovations that cause discontinuities on a micro and a macro level (Garcia and Calantone, 2002), meaning that they are fundamental changes which have a great impact on the market. Radical innovations present clear differences from existing practices. They create a high degree of uncertainty in organizations and industries, because of the fact that they 'sweep away significant parts of previous investments in technical skills and knowledge, designs, production techniques, plants and equipment' (Popadiuk and Choo, 2006: 305). Incremental innovations can be defined as 'products that provide new features, benefits, or improvements to the existing market' (Garcia and Calantone, 2002: 123). Incremental innovations are more about the refinement, adoption and enhancement of existing products and services. They are usually low in cost and breadth of impact but occur much more frequently than radical innovations.

In operational terms, this chapter focuses on the innovative performance of SMEs. Hinloopen (2003) described innovative performance as the innovative 'products' of firms which are determined by the interaction with actors in the environment. Rothwell (1991) indicated that high innovative performance of firms can be characterized by a proactive search for new ideas. As stated by Popadiuk and Choo (2006), the innovation is generated in the continuous process of information gathering, combined with an always challenging vision of the entrepreneur.

The innovative performance of an SME is influenced by a number of underlying organizational and entrepreneurial traits (Freel, 2000a; Hadjimanolis, 2000). Overall, the most common variables indicative of firm strategy towards innovative outputs are: R&D expenditure, use of external finance, managerial focus, use of external networks, employee involvement, training and education, documented innovation plans, organizational structure, graduate employment, customer knowledge and inter-firm collaboration (Freel, 2000b; Hadjimanolis, 2000; Bhattacharya and Bloch, 2004; De Jong and Vermeulen, 2006). Note that these variables are not exhaustive, but they provide an overview of determinants that are important for innovative performance in SMEs. In this study we focus on the relationship between the use of external networks, employee involvement (two determinants that measure social capital) and the innovative performance of SMEs. In the next section, two types of innovation that specify the relationship between social capital and innovative performance of SMEs are presented.

10.3   SOCIAL CAPITAL AND THE INNOVATIVE PERFORMANCE OF SMEs

Social capital as a term developed during the last decades of the 20th century and has rapidly become an important concept in organization studies (Burt, 1997). The unique features of this form of capital make it an important asset for the organization (Moran, 2005). Cooke and Wills (1999) indicated that the work of economist Glenn Loury (1977 in Cooke and Wills, 1999: 222) gives a general definition of social capital by stating it as 'naturally occurring social relationships to promote or aid the development of valued skills or characteristics'. Burt (1997) further elaborated on this vision by indicating that it is an asset that resides in an individual's social relationships. The work of Coleman (1988) focuses more on the fact that social capital is a structural feature of a society, facilitating individual actions. Social capital is therefore a valuable asset which comes from the access to resources because of the actors' social relationships (Moran, 2005). In this chapter, social capital is defined as a 'set of resources made available to an individual through social relationships within the social structure of the network and in the formal and informal structure of the organization' (Oh et al., 2006: 570).

Social capital impacts on the innovative performance of SMEs in three ways: through influence, solidarity and information made available to the entrepreneur through social relationships (Adler and Kwon, 2002). The aspect of influence becomes visible when individuals accumulate obligations from others in the network and have to 'pay back' these commitments at a later point in time. As Burt (1992) clearly stated, the individual who spans disconnected networks (structural holes) is the most influential actor in the field. The second aspect, solidarity, refers to trust and goodwill that is created in social relationships and enhances the condition of the relationship (Adler and Kwon, 2002). Less bureaucracy and closer relationships, which are common in small businesses, improve solidarity and contribute to cooperation (Hausman, 2005). The third aspect of social capital relates to the information available to the entrepreneur. Through the availability of actors in their surroundings, entrepreneurs gain access to valuable information which can be used to achieve competitive advantages (Zhao and Aram, 1995).

Cooke and Wills (1999) indicated that the connections with actors external to the SME create efficient information channels and entrepreneurial learning. Having more external contacts increases access to different ideas and alternative solutions (Moran, 2005). Besides relationships within the social structure of the network, internal relationships (within the SME) are also critical in entrepreneurial decision-making. Employees have unique knowledge and are closely connected to the market. From this perspective, they have valuable information for the entrepreneur which can contribute to innovation and the progress of the SME.

Innovation is an iterative process of information processing activities which requires input from members of various functions playing different roles (Frishammer and Hörte, 2005). Therefore, both external and internal social relationships contribute to a higher pool of knowledge in the entrepreneurial decision to innovate. To make it possible to gather information from various sources, the boundaries of an organization must be permeable. This calls for regular contacts with other parties, which includes both formal and informal contacts but without any obligations involved (De Jong and Vermeulen, 2006). Besides the importance of using the external environment, the involvement of employees plays a crucial role in the innovative performance of SMEs (Freel, 2000a; De Jong and Vermeulen, 2006). Oerlemans et al. (1998) also focused on this aspect by saying that the knowledge necessary for innovations can be optimally acquired via external and internal sources. Frontline employees are close to the market and have information about customers and competitors (Freel, 2000a). Better market understanding and awareness of the needs of customers can result in enhanced competitive advantages of SMEs (Hadjimanolis, 2000). By listening to employees, ideas and possibilities become visible to the entrepreneur (Hausman, 2005). Furthermore, this stimulates the creativity of employees, which results in higher innovative outputs (Freel, 2000a).

As stated by Lipparini and Sobrero (1994) and Oerlemans et al. (1998), incremental innovations are about the refinement and enhancement of products and services. Vermeulen (2005) also indicated that incremental innovations are an extension of existing products of a company. For these innovations, a firm's existing resources and capabilities are important, and require routine procedures. This might imply that for incremental innovations the involvement of employees is more valuable than for radical innovation. With respect to radical innovations, often highly skilled employees are required (Veryzer, 1998). In SMEs, there are fewer possibilities (in comparison with large firms) to educate employees via intensive training and education programmes (Freel, 2000b) or to attract new ones, due to limited internal resources (Freel, 2000a). Despite this, SMEs will probably have sufficient knowledge and resources at their disposal for managing incremental innovation projects (Vermeulen, 2005). Employees are able to provide the information needed to enhance the competences of the SME (Elfring and Hulsink, 2003). The involvement, knowledge and skills of employees can be seen as preconditions for incremental innovations in SMEs (De Jong and Vermeulen, 2006). This leads to the following hypothesis:

Hypothesis 1a: The involvement of employees is beneficial for incremental innovations.

As was mentioned earlier, incremental innovations are improvements of existing products or processes. It can be assumed that information is shared easily when it involves incremental innovations. Radical innovations can be characterized by exploration and require a significant change in the business context (Popadiuk and Choo, 2006). Most of the time, radical innovations are confronted with a great deal of uncertainty (Hadjimanolis, 2000). As Elfring and Hulsink (2003: 414) stated: 'It's a bumpy ride rather than a linear process'. They showed the need for external linkages that support the entrepreneur in the innovation process. Other firms in the vicinity of the SME can provide valuable information which is necessary to 'fuel innovation' (Hausman, 2005). Radical innovations often require outsiders, as insiders are likely to be blinded by existing practices (Elfring and Hulsink, 2003). The above indicates the importance of external actors in the social network of the entrepreneur with respect to both types of innovations. This results in the following hypothesis:

Hypothesis 1b: The presence of external relations is beneficial for both incremental and radical innovations.

10.4 THE MEDIATING ROLE OF ENTREPRENEURIAL COGNITIVE COMPLEXITY

Cognitive complexity is an attribute which describes information processing in a cognitive system (Curşeu and Rus, 2005). It refers to the complexity of the cognitive representation activated in the working memory of the decision-maker and it can be described via two closely related processes: cognitive differentiation and integration. An individual with a high cognitive complexity is, for example, able to differentiate a system into many different components and then make connections among them to integrate these components into actions. In addition, when an individual is able to differentiate a system into different elements he/she is able to make more precise and refined decisions (ibid.). Thus, persons with a high cognitive complexity are able to analyse a situation into many separate elements and then explore connections and possible relationships among these elements. This multidimensional way of thinking results in an individual who is more aware of the environment, more flexible to adapt to changes, a more efficient decision-maker and ultimately a more frequent innovator (Calori et al., 1994).

In SMEs, it is the entrepreneur who must have the ability to decompose and integrate social capital to make sense of the complex situations imposed by the dynamic organizational environment in which most of the SMEs exist. When more social capital is present, the entrepreneur can identify more elements and integrate these when making a decision. When perceiving more stimuli from actors within a particular domain, multiple perspectives can be applied (Curşeu and Rus, 2005) which results in higher cognitive complexity of the entrepreneur. Hodgkinson and Johnson (1987, in Porac and Thomas, 1990) also noticed that managers who had more contact with the environment developed a more complex representation of the environment. Socializing events can shape the goals, resources and behaviour of the entrepreneur (Westhead et al., 2005a, 2005b). The second hypothesis is:

Hypothesis 2: The presence of social capital (both internal and external) has a positive impact on the cognitive complexity of the entrepreneur.

As stated by Westhead et al. (2005a, 2005b), highly cognitive complex individuals are more creative, which is positively associated with higher innovative outputs. Furthermore, individuals with high cognitive complexity tend to have perceptions of the environment that are less black and white and are more able to integrate information into a decision. Individuals with high cognitive complexity tend to be more flexible in creating new distinctions and, overall, see more possibilities. As explained by Westhead et al. (2005a), more-elaborate cognitive models might focus more attention on possibilities in the environment than less-detailed cognitive models. Calori et al. (1994) indicated with their research that the CEO's cognitive complexity should match the complexity of the environment in order to have a positive effect on performance.

With her research on project leaders, Green (2004) explored the possibility that the higher their ability to integrate information, the more likely it is that specific project problems are identified. Furthermore, Barr et al. (1992) found that top managers with more-elaborate cognitive models were more aware of environmental changes and could therefore show more renewal in their strategies. Barr et al.'s. and Green's studies were exploratory with respect to the ability to integrate information and process this for decision-making. More research needs to be done to specify the relationship between the cognitive complexity of the entrepreneur and strategic decision-making. Despite this, it seems reasonable to assume that when the entrepreneur has a higher ability to differentiate the differing perspectives and integrate these into a decision, a higher innovative performance of SMEs would occur. Therefore, the following hypothesis is derived:

Hypothesis 3: Cognitive complexity has a positive impact on the innovative performance (both radical and incremental) of SMEs.

As indicated earlier, innovative performance in SMEs is an outcome of an iterative process of information processing activities that is supported by the presence of social capital. It requires input from members of various functions (internal and external) playing different roles (Frishammar and Hörte, 2005). The growth of knowledge in an organization depends on the capacity of the management to absorb the information needed and combine this with individual knowledge (Nonaka and Takeuchi, 2003). Entrepreneurs have an enormous impact on the strategic directions adopted by their firms and their resulting performance. In contrast to large firms, in SMEs there is no distinction between the board of directors responsible for the strategic directions and operational managers who handle the daily business of the organization (Hausman, 2005). In SMEs, this role is fulfilled by the entrepreneur or a small group of people. The presence of social capital available via the social relationships of the entrepreneur and the possibility of integrating the information, are important with respect to the decisions that are made. The uniqueness of the cognitive representations of the entrepreneur can help to explain the differences in innovative performance of SMEs. Therefore, the following hypothesis is formulated:

Hypothesis 4: The cognitive complexity of the entrepreneur mediates the relationship between the presence of social capital and the innovative performance of SMEs.

10.5 METHOD

Sample

In this research, EIM data were used (see Appendix). The sample was limited to entrepreneurs who have no more than 250 employees. In line with the definition of CBS (2006), SMEs were defined as follows: micro, 0–10 employees; small, 11–100; and medium sized, 101–250. The distribution of the sample across the different size classes was as follows: micro, 34.8 per cent; small, 54.8 per cent; and medium, 10.4 per cent. The median age of the respondents was 45 years, varying from 26 to 66 years. The mean number of years that the respondent was an entrepreneur could be determined at 13 years (range 0–40 years). A large number of the entrepreneurs were men (86 per cent) and more than half of them had a high educational level (university degree, 20.4 per cent, higher professional education, 37.0 per cent).

Measures

Diverse questions were posed to the entrepreneur via the telephone questionnaire. In order to measure the dependent variables of this research, entrepreneurs were asked to indicate whether their firm had achieved an organizational innovation during the last three years. Thus a total view of the innovative outputs developed by the SME could be obtained. A differentiation was made between products that are new to the firm, those that are new to the market and those that are new to the industry. Besides new products, new working processes that were developed for the company were also measured. If new markets and industries were addressed, innovations were referred to as 'radical innovations' due to their important micro and macro implications (Garcia and Calantone, 2002). Incremental innovations were defined as products that are new to the firm and new working processes.

The presence of social capital is rather difficult to operationalize because of its high level of abstraction (Flora et al., 1997). However, it was possible to make a distinction between the external orientation of the entrepreneur and the involvement of employees (Frishammar and Hörte, 2005; Oh et al., 2006). Decisions are influenced through the availability of actors in their internal and external environments. These actors provide the entrepreneur with access to valuable information which can be used to achieve competitive advantages via strategic decision-making (Zhao and Aram, 1995; De Carolis and Saparito, 2006). With respect to the external orientation, a number of different contacts that were influencing the decision could be indicated. For measuring the involvement of employees, the entrepreneur had to indicate whether employees were influencing strategic choices and the processes of renewal.

The presence of social capital was viewed from an egocentric network perspective. This means that only the linkages of one person (ego) were taken into account. In practice, it means that the ego's self-report about his or her network was researched (Friedman and Aral, 2001). The individual level of social capital has received a lot of attention with respect to the outcome for the individual actor (for example, Krackhardt, 1990), although less research has been conducted with respect to the outcome of the organizational unit as a whole (Leana and van Buren, 1999; Moran, 2005). For that reason, it is interesting to look at the relationships of the entrepreneur and the outcomes for the SME in the form of innovative performance.

For measuring cognitive complexity, the qualitative data were used (see Appendix). The data were coded in cognitive maps (see Chapter 4 for more details). A double check on these maps was made in order to make sure that all the elements from the transcript were included. The absolute cognitive complexity was computed using the formula: $ACMCo = NoC \times CMC \times CMD$ (see Chapter 4 for more details). Before calculating this score, it was controlled for extreme values but no outliers were identified. Since two coders were used to evaluate the structure of the cognitive maps, intercoder reliability was estimated using the intra-class correlation coefficient and the lowest value is 0.982, showing a high degree of agreement in the two evaluations.

10.6   RESULTS

The relationships between the variables were tested via AMOS structural equation modelling software version 6. A maximum likelihood procedure was used and the results are presented in Figure 10.1.

The descriptive statistics are presented in Table 10.1. Two categories of fit indices were used in the analysis: absolute fit indices and incremental fit indices. The chi-square (2.14, $p < 0.34$) shows that the whole model is not significantly different from the data. The variances implied in the theoretical model match the observed variances in the data. Further, the root mean square error of approximation (RMSEA) is 0.02, which is lower than the value of 0.08, recommended for a fitting model (Browne and Cudeck, 1993). The incremental fit index, which is reflected by the normed fit index (NFI),

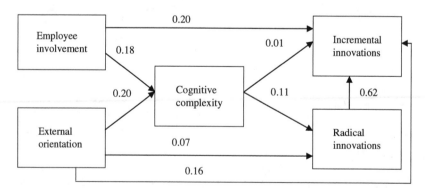

Figure 10.1   Results of the path model

Table 10.1 Descriptive statistics and correlations

	Mean	SD	1	2	3	4	5	6
1. Age	45.97	8.68						
2. Experience	13.29	11.13	0.58**					
3. Employee involvement	1.37	0.63	−0.12	−0.24*				
4. External orientation	1.26	1.06	0.01	0.01	0.13			
5. Cognitive complexity	4602.54	1494.59	0.01	−0.01	0.17	0.21*		
6. Radical innovations	0.81	0.76	0.02	−0.02	−0.01	0.08	0.14	
7. Incremental innovations	1.09	0.79	0.02	−0.07	0.18	0.15	0.15	0.63**

Note: * Correlation is significant at the 0.05 level (2-tailed). ** Correlation is significant at the 0.01 level (2-tailed). $N = 107$.

is 0.97. The ideal value of this index is set at a value > 0.90. This means that, in relation to the null model, the model cannot be significantly improved.

The data show that employee involvement has a positive impact on incremental innovation, therefore Hypothesis 1a is supported by the data. Concerning the impact of external orientation, it is significant only on the incremental innovation, therefore Hypothesis 1b is only partially supported in that the impact of external orientation on radical innovation is not significant (yet it is in the hypothesized direction). Hypothesis 2 is fully supported by the data. Both employee involvement and external orientation are beneficial for cognitive complexity. Cognitive complexity, however, seems to foster only radical innovation, therefore Hypothesis 3 is only partially supported in that it also states a positive impact of cognitive complexity on incremental innovation. Although the data offer support for the hypothesized model, the fourth hypothesis is not supported by the data. The cognitive complexity of the entrepreneur does not function as a mediator in the relationship between the presence of social capital and the innovative performance of the entrepreneur.

10.7 DISCUSSION

This study explored the relationship between the personal network of the entrepreneur, identified here as social capital, the information processing capabilities of the entrepreneur, that is, the cognitive complexity, and the innovative performance of SMEs. As argued earlier in this chapter, SMEs often operate in an uncertain environment. Because very often entrepreneurs do not have access to extensive information sources (Gibcus et al., 2008), they are backed up by actors in their environment who influence their decision-making process. As shown here, social capital contributes to the availability of information, and it has a positive impact on the innovative performance of SMEs. This is valid especially with respect to incremental innovations. The involvement of employees in the strategic decision to innovate is beneficial for incremental innovations. Employees are able to provide information which is needed to improve the products and services of the SMEs (Hausman, 2005). They are familiar with the processes in the organization and are able to make contributions to it.

Further, the results showed that incremental innovations were also positively influenced via the external relations of the entrepreneur. Incremental innovations are very valuable for the SME but do not directly influence the market and other SMEs. With respect to external actors (that is, advisers or other SMEs), it can be assumed that information for product development or efficiency of working processes is therefore easily shared. The fact that both external and internal relationships are positively connected to incremental innovations, confirmed the importance of these groups for entrepreneurs in SMEs. Moreover, if SMEs introduce radical innovations, they are also involved in incremental ones. Once a radical innovation is introduced it is very likely that the SME will implement ways to improve it and thus implement incremental innovations.

The data show a positive impact (yet not significant) of external social capital on radical innovation. Radical innovations often require outsiders to support this type of innovation. External parties are able to provide the entrepreneur with information and prevent him/her from being blinded by his/her own practices (Elfring and Hulsink, 2003). The lack of significance may be explained by what Lipparini and Sobrero (1994) call the 'lonely innovator perspective'. For radical innovations, which contain fundamental changes, entrepreneurs often innovate alone and rely less on their social capital because they want to introduce 'the breaking news' themselves. Taylor and Thorpe (2004) show that entrepreneurs feel highly responsible for the success of their firm. They suggested an isolated decision-making process where success was dependent on the entrepreneurs' cognitive skills and abilities rather than on the range or quality of his/her social relationships. They used the following quote to indicate the above: 'This is my job, to make decisions; others depend on me to make the right decisions' (ibid.: 207).

Another explanation may be that small firms often suffer from having a small-sized network (Hausman, 2005). It is possible that a relative shortage of innovative information is available in this network, which is necessary for radical innovations (ibid.). The contacts of the entrepreneur are a valuable attribute with respect to innovations, but they have no exhaustive sources of new information. Burt (1992) explained this by saying that a small-sized network often shows signs of conformity between the network members. This might explain the absence of a positive relationship between external relations of the entrepreneur and radical innovations. It shows that, as indicated by Hadjimanolis (2000), innovativeness of SMEs is strongly conditioned by the context in which they are embedded.

Coming back to the whole model that was tested here, emphasizing the mediating role of cognitive complexity in the relationship between social capital and innovative performance, it is not possible to draw definite conclusions. Cognitive complexity seems beneficial for radical innovations, yet not for incremental ones. This result emphasizes the role of entrepreneurial cognition in the innovative performance of the SMEs, yet it does not fit exactly the predictions formulated earlier. Another important result reported here is that the presence of social capital leads to more complex representations about the strategic choice to innovate. Entrepreneurs who have a better contact with their surroundings (for example, social networks) develop a more complex representation of the environment. They have more possibilities of identifying different elements and integrating these when making a decision.

Although this research did not solve completely the theoretical puzzle concerning the role of cognitive complexity in entrepreneurial strategic decision-making, the importance of cognitive processes in entrepreneurial research must not be undervalued. More research is necessary to further explore this relationship. The main implication of the results reported here is that the presence of social relationships is likely to enhance the incremental innovative performance of SMEs. The personal network of the entrepreneur seems to be of great value for the performance of the SME. With respect to employees, it is important that responsibilities are delegated and that they are involved in the decision-making process (Hausman, 2005). When these tasks are shared, important insights of the employees may be used to come to a better decision. As Hausman (ibid.: 778) explained, 'delegating authority to other firm members encourages creativity and poises the firm to capitalize on diverse solutions'.

The external orientation of the entrepreneur also needs to be emphasized. SMEs can supplement their innovation process via external information that becomes available. Therefore, the SME must be permeable, at least to absorb ideas from outside and to broaden the vision of the entrepreneur. Decision-making can be supported when a better understanding of the environment of the SME is taken into account.

10.8   LIMITATIONS AND FUTURE RESEARCH DIRECTIONS

Several limitations have to be addressed at this stage. A first question concerns the measurement of social capital. In order to do this, data that were used in this research were aggregated answers from several dichotomous items. This is not always disadvantageous because dichotomous questions usually result in better response rates (Churchill, 1999 in Gibcus et al., 2008) and less-biased answers (De Jong and Vermeulen, 2006). Unfortunately, they also provided the researcher with less-sophisticated information regarding the topic at hand. Especially with respect to social capital, it did not capture much of the depth that lies in this variable.

A second limitation is the cross-sectional nature of the study. It is important that the data are collected more frequently and to ensure that the evaluations of the social capital precede the evaluation of cognitive complexity and the strategic decision to innovate. The semi-structured interviews focused on the most important decision concerning innovations that had been made by the entrepreneur in the past three years. However, Popadiuk and Choo (2006) indicated that innovations come from a sequence of decisions. Therefore, the whole sequence regarding innovative performance of SMEs should be revealed and explored, social capital can be measured more extensively and cognitive complexity can be assessed with respect to the total strategic decision-making process regarding innovations.

The third limitation is related to the environment of the entrepreneur. Calori et al. (1994) found that a higher cognitive complexity of the entrepreneur is not always beneficial for organizational performance. The cognitive complexity of the entrepreneur must match the level of environmental complexity to have a positive effect on organizational performance. It was assumed that the environment of the entrepreneur can be typified as very dynamic and uncertain (Gibcus et al., 2008). However, when the opposite is the case, high cognitive complexity could even inhibit innovation. Therefore, it would be interesting to identify whether, under conditions of high environmental dynamism, high cognitive complexity would positively affect innovative performance. It seems clear that the environment of the entrepreneur must be taken into account in order to explain more fully the interesting phenomenon of cognitive complexity.

11. Cognitive complexity, industry dynamism and risk taking in entrepreneurial decision-making

Sjoerd Bosgra

11.1 INTRODUCTION

In recent years, a consensus seems to have emerged among scientists in various fields that the theories and models of strategic decision-making are not universally applicable to both large firms and small and medium-sized enterprises (SMEs) (Papadakis et al., 1998). SMEs typically do not possess the manpower or the mechanisms to constantly screen the environment for information. Decision-making is usually the task of a single individual (that is, the entrepreneur). Consequently the risks that are involved in entrepreneurial strategic decision-making are carried by the entrepreneur. In this respect, the chances of entrepreneurial failure are generally higher than the chances of success. Liles (1974) suggested that besides the financial risks of business failure, the risks involved in entrepreneurial decision-making are much broader and span areas such as psychic well-being and family relations.

Yet, entrepreneurs accept those risks and for decades scientists have been intrigued by the functioning of the entrepreneurial mind (Busenitz, 1999). Initially, research in this field was based on the assumption that entrepreneurs show higher natural tendencies to take risks (that is, risk propensity) (McClelland, 1961; Collins and Moore, 1964), but despite a handful of studies that do indeed find some support for such assumptions (for example, Sexton and Bowman, 1984; Begley and Boyd, 1987b), the growing unanimity among scientists is that managers and entrepreneurs do not show structural differences in their natural tendencies to take risks (Brockhaus, 1980; Low and MacMillan, 1988; Ray, 1994; Busenitz, 1999). As researchers sought for alternative points of view on entrepreneurial strategic decision-making (ESDM), on many occasions, cognitive interpretations turned out to be the most proximal explanatory factors for ESDM effectiveness (Palich and Bagby, 1995). Although the cognitive approach to ESDM is a young and developing perspective, an increasing number of scholars use cognitive concepts and methods in the study of ESDM (Busenitz and Barney, 1997; Busenitz, 1999; Keh et al., 2002).

Cognitive complexity is a new concept that may contribute to a better understanding of ESDM. It refers to an individual's information processing capabilities (Schröder et al., 1967). Rather than focusing on the content of decision-making, the concept of cognitive complexity addresses the structural configuration of a decision-maker's mental representation of a decision situation. Cognitive complexity has been linked to a number of variables (for an overview, see Chapter 4), which suggests that cognitive complexity acts as a mediator between an entrepreneur's tendency to take risks and the outcome of his/her decision-making. But despite the keen attention being given to cognitive complexity and cognitive interpretations of ESDM, to the best of our knowledge cognitive complexity has to date not been scientifically linked to entrepreneurial risk-taking behaviour in a direct sense. This chapter reports on a study that empirically investigates to what extent the level of cognitive complexity of individual entrepreneurs is related to their risk-taking behaviour.

However, the investigated relationship between entrepreneurs' cognitive complexity and their risk-taking behaviour may not be as modest as suggested. The predominant interpretation of individual cognitive complexity is that it is content specific (Schröder et al., 1967) and consequently, when investigating the conceivable effect of cognitive complexity on decision-making, the setting in which it takes place deserves further specification. In addition, decision context plays a much more important role in entrepreneurial decision-making than in large firm settings (Simon and Houghton, 2002). This decision context is to a large extent determined by the dynamics of the industry in which an organization operates (Glazer and Weiss, 1993) and the relationship between cognitive complexity and risk-taking behaviour is therefore investigated within the context of industry dynamism.

11.2 THE EFFECT OF COGNITIVE COMPLEXITY ON RISK-TAKING BEHAVIOUR

Definitions of cognitive complexity differ among scholars in the field (Crockett, 1965; Curşeu and Rus, 2005). With respect to the cognitive representational system, cognitive complexity refers to the structural complexity of an individual's cognitive system (ibid.). Individuals who exhibit high levels of cognitive complexity have the ability to understand differences, they apply different points of view, they perceive contradictions, they are better able to deal with duality and they have a more complete view of their environment in the sense that they are able to distinguish the important factors that play a role and the relationships between those factors. A person who exhibits a relatively low level of cognitive complexity (that is, cognitive simplicity) will instead have a relatively limited number of constructs at his/her disposal and a rather black and white perception of the environment.

Streufert and Swezey (1986) related cognitive complexity directly to decision-making by defining it as the ability to differentiate perspectives and to integrate them into a decision. In this definition, the ability to differentiate perspectives refers to the aforementioned number of constructs, and the ability to integrate these perspectives into a decision refers to the different links between these concepts (Curşeu and Rus, 2005). In this chapter, cognitive complexity is therefore conceptualized by the two dimensions of differentiation and integration in a set of cognitive representations.

Strategic decision-making in SMEs is characterized by high levels of uncertainty and the strategic decisions therefore involve higher levels of risk than in large firms (Covin and Slevin, 1989). Especially in entrepreneurial decision-making, all the possible outcomes of a strategic decision can rarely be known, let alone their probabilities. Baird and Thomas (1985) argue that if information about the consequences of a strategic decision and the probabilities of these consequences is incomplete, uncertainty necessarily involves risk. Since this information is seldom complete, it is asserted that entrepreneurial risk-taking behaviour can be seen as the act of making a decision that involves a level of risk and uncertainty. The conceptualization of risk is thus to be directed at the entrepreneur's risk assessment of the decision situation rather than the descriptive label for the curvature of the utility function. In accordance with this argument, risk will be conceptualized as the individual entrepreneur's assessment of risk and uncertainty involved in a strategic decision.

One reason why entrepreneurs engage in risky actions is that they lack necessary information in a decision situation (Gibcus et al., 2008). In accordance with this view, Kahneman and Lovallo (1993) assert that decision-makers tend to develop an inside view on the decisions they face. In their argument, decision-makers isolate the focal situation from future situations and they ignore statistics from past situations, resulting in incoherent and unjustified patterns of risk behaviour. At the same time they conclude: 'The adoption of an outside view, in which the problem at hand is treated as an instance of a broader category . . . may facilitate the application of a consistent risk policy' (ibid.: 29–30). Taking into consideration that lack of necessary information or the refusal to incorporate the available information into a decision increases risk taking, it is arguable that having a more complete view on a decision situation or being able to absorb the information at hand into a decision, will decrease risk taking. Liles (1974), for example, concludes that whether or not an entrepreneur will make a decision that involves a relatively high degree of risk, to a large extent depends on how well the possible consequences of that decision have been evaluated. Those consequences can only properly be evaluated if the variables that play a role in the decision situation and the relations between those variables, are known. Being able to apply multiple perspectives on a decision situation will reduce the chance of overseeing or neglecting those variables. Therefore, the extent to which entrepreneurs are able to differentiate between perspectives on that decision situation and to integrate these perspectives into a decision (Streufert and Swezey, 1986), will influence their risk behaviour. Hence, we suggest that entrepreneurs who have a high level of cognitive complexity will generally have a better understanding of their organizational environment, and their decisions will therefore involve lower levels of perceived uncertainty and risk. Likewise, the decisions of entrepreneurs with a lower level of cognitive complexity will be based on a limited comprehension of the situation at hand and will therefore involve higher levels of risk. The first hypothesis is thus formulated as follows:

Hypothesis 1: Cognitive complexity has a negative effect on risk-taking behaviour in ESDM.

11.3   INDUSTRY DYNAMISM AND ITS MODERATING EFFECT

However, the expected relationship between cognitive complexity and risk-taking behaviour partly depends on the setting in which it takes place. First, because the context in which a decision takes place plays a much more important role in small firms than it does in larger firms (Simon and Houghton, 2002). Large firms have structures that enable rational decision-making (Brouthers et al., 1998) and the effects that the decision context might have can thus be reduced. Entrepreneurial decision-making is distinctively restricted to one decision-maker and SMEs have less-rational structures. ESDM is much more sensitive to contextual influences as compared to other types of strategic decisions. Second, the concept of cognitive complexity is contingent on its conceptual domain (Schröder et al., 1967); entrepreneurs may employ a higher level of cognitive complexity in a situation that is closely related to their expertise, whereas they may display a lower complexity in situations where they possess little expertise.

Whether the environment in which an organization operates is characterized by relative dynamism or stability determines to a large extent the strategic considerations of the decision-maker. Dynamic environments are generally characterized by a relatively high in- and outflow of organizations, whereas in static environments, the number of newcomers and exits as a proportion of the total population is relatively low (Verhoeven et al., 2005). The dynamism of the organizational environment is largely determined by the industry in which an organization operates (Lei et al., 1996). Industry dynamism thus determines to a large extent the strategic decision-making context, and when investigating the impact of cognitive complexity on decision-making, this influence ought to be considered. In a large empirical study, Miller and Friesen (1983) investigate the relation between industry dynamism and strategic decision-making. Their data support the hypotheses that decision-makers who find themselves in dynamic environments need to put more effort into processing information about the environment. The process of strategic decision-making in such organizations, as opposed to organizations in more static environments, requires continuous evaluation of the environment and decisions that are based on this evaluation. Moreover, compared to static environments, in these dynamic environments, there is a greater need to continuously make fundamental decisions about strategy in order to survive (ibid.). These findings imply that, contrary to static environments, taking strategic risks is an absolute necessity to survive in dynamic environments. However, in order to come to an effective strategic decision, decision-makers in such environments need to process large amounts of information and incorporate that information into their decision.

Entrepreneurial cognitive complexity is defined as the ability of an entrepreneur to distinguish perspectives and to integrate those perspectives into a decision (Streufert and Swezey, 1986). Thus it is arguable that cognitively complex entrepreneurs in dynamic industries are better able to evaluate their environment and to incorporate that evaluation into a strategic decision, whereas their cognitively simple counterparts in such industries will base their fundamental strategic decisions on an incomplete view of the organizational environment. Given their poor evaluation of the environment, it is presumed that cognitively simple entrepreneurs will not judge a necessary risk as such in a dynamic environment.

Likewise, in static environments they will likely take risks that are unaccounted for. At the same time, because of their better understanding of the environment resulting from their thorough evaluation, cognitively complex entrepreneurs operating in such a dynamic industry will see the necessity of taking a risk when they need to, and they will more easily recognize when there is no need to take large strategic risks. The conceivable negative impact of cognitive complexity on risk-taking behaviour is therefore expected to be negatively moderated by industry dynamism. The second hypothesis is thus formulated as follows:

Hypothesis 2: The relation between cognitive complexity and risk-taking behaviour is negatively moderated by the dynamism of the industry in which the organization operates.

11.4   METHOD

Sample

For this study, an extensive dataset was available from EIM Business and Policy Research (see Appendix). The qualitative data were gathered by means of semi-structured interviews with 109 entrepreneurs of SMEs with 1–250 employees. These interviews were coded into cognitive maps on the basis of which cognitive complexity was measured for each entrepreneur (for details on cognitive mapping, see Chapter 4). The data regarding risk taking were gathered through the use of a computer-assisted telephone survey. The data that were used to compute industry dynamism for each of the eight industries were gathered from the Central Bureau of Statistics (CBS) in Voorburg, the Netherlands.

Procedure

The cognitive complexity of the 109 entrepreneurs was calculated using the formula for relative cognitive complexity (as described in Chapter 4) on the cognitive maps (cognitive complexity equals the product of the number of links in a cognitive map and the number of different types of links, divided by the total number of concepts in the map). It calculates the complexity of a cognitive map in relation to the number of concepts in the map.

The concept of risk-taking behaviour was calculated by means of both a quantitative and a qualitative measure. From the telephone survey we used data related to the size of the risk that entrepreneurs took in making their focal decision. A Likert scale with five options provides the respondent with options ranging from 'very large risk' to 'hardly any or no risk'. The last option is 'do not know/do not want to say'. Furthermore, we used a question related to the level of perceived uncertainty that was involved in the decision. Again, a Likert scale provides five options to the question 'How convinced were you of your decision?', ranging from 'very convinced' to 'severe doubts'. Besides these quantitative measures, there are questions in the semi-structured interview that measure the level of risk and uncertainty that were involved in the decision. The level of risk is indicated by the question 'What were the risks you took by making this decision?', and the level of uncertainty by the question 'Did you have doubts about the idea?'. Through the process of coding, the qualitative answers were fit into the same options that the respondent was given in the survey for both concepts. The average of the quantitative and qualitative scores determines the score on risk-taking behaviour.

The analysis of the dynamism variable and its subsequent hypothesized moderating effect is based on seven industries: manufacturing, construction, trade, hotel and catering, transport, financial services and commercial services. The data for this variable were gathered from the CBS in Voorburg. A formula was introduced for the evaluation of industry dynamism. Such formulae are not new in this line of research, but they each have their shortcomings with regard to this setting. For example, Kim and Lim (1988) approach dynamism from the organizational perspective. Such a measure would not be adequate for the broader industry dynamism (Snow and Hambrick, 1980). To be more specific, whereas number of competitors is an indicator for dynamism in the organizational context (that is, the more direct competitors, the more turbulent the environment), in the broader sectoral setting, dynamism is relative to the total number of companies operating in that particular industry (that is, the more organizations operate in a certain industry, the less dynamism is constituted by the number of entrants and exits). Nieuwenhuijsen and Nijkamp (2001) acknowledge that dynamism is constituted by the number of entrants and exits and relative to the total population of organizations in an environment, but they conceptualize dynamism as the sum of the number of entrants and the number of exits. Verhoeven et al. (2005) calculate industry dynamism relative to the total population, by taking the percentages of entrants and exits in the population, but their calculations of what they refer to as 'industry turbulence' are based on the sum of absolute numbers.

However, if we not only acknowledge the relativity of dynamism to the total population, but also take this population into account in our calculations, industry dynamism should be constituted by the product of the number of entrants and number of exits, divided by the total number of companies operating in that industry. This results in the following formula:

$$\delta I = \frac{N_n \times N_x}{N_t},$$

where δI (delta I) is industry dynamism, N_n is the total number of entrants, N_x is the total number of exits and N_t is the total number of companies operating in that particular industry. In this way, relatively smaller industries that witness many newcomers and many bankruptcies will have a high dynamism score, whereas a relatively large industry with few new foundings and few exits will have a low score on dynamism. In industries that are

Table 11.1 Industry dynamism scores per industry

Industry	Nn	Nx	Nt	δI
Manufacturing	1,700	3,470	46,605	126.57
Construction	5,100	5,610	81,690	350.24
Trade	8,200	14,920	164,590	743.33
Hotel and catering	1,100	3,190	36,650	95.74
Transport	1,400	2,805	27,925	140.63
Financial services	1,990*	3,445	14,665	467.48
Commercial services	13,300	19,720	158,650	1653.17

Note: * Estimated score.

characterized by a relatively high dynamism, in order for their organization to survive, decision-makers have to continuously interpret their environments and adjust the strategy of the company accordingly (Shepherd, 1999). Table 11.1 is a representation of the dynamism scores of the seven remaining industries.

Finally, the research model was controlled for the variables firm size and years of experience of the entrepreneur.

11.5 RESULTS

To test the hypotheses, a three-step regression analysis was carried out. In the first step, risk-taking behaviour was regressed on the two control variables size of the organization ($\beta1$) and experience of the entrepreneur ($\beta2$). In the second step, risk-taking behaviour was regressed on cognitive complexity ($\beta3$) and industry dynamism ($\beta4$) separately. In the third and final step, risk-taking behaviour was regressed on the cross-product term of cognitive complexity and industry dynamism ($\beta5$).

Table 11.2 shows the means, standard deviations and the correlations between all variables included in the study. The correlations between the majority of the variables were generally low (ranging from 0.001 to 0.021).

First, the control variable size of the organization (measured in number of employees) shows a significant and negative correlation with industry dynamism. This finding suggests that on average, dynamic industries consist of smaller firms than do static industries. Given that industry dynamism = [(number of entrants) (number of exits)]/total population, this finding can be explained by the rapid coming and going of organizations – 50–80 per cent of all SMEs cease to exist within the first five years of their

Table 11.2   Correlations and descriptive statistics for all variables

Variable	Mean	SD	1	2	3	4
1. Size	40.90	57.63				
2. Experience	13.57	11.07	−0.01			
3. Cognitive complexity	4.81	0.50	0.07	−0.04		
4. Industry dynamism	841.17	662.24	−0.21**	0.17*	0.08	
5. Risk-taking behaviour	2.68	0.58	−0.01	−0.02	−0.19**	−0.05

Note: $** = p < 0.05$; $* = p < 0.1$.

founding (Busenitz, 1999). It is arguable that, because of the higher competition, these failure rates are higher in dynamic environments as compared to static ones. Dynamic environments will thus be characterized by a relatively less mature, not fully grown population of organizations, having negative implications for the average size of the organization.

Second, the entrepreneurial experience shows a positive correlation with industry dynamism, yet it is not statistically significant. This finding can be interpreted in two ways. On the one hand, experienced entrepreneurs may be attracted by dynamic industries, because their accumulated business sense enables them to recognize opportunities in rapidly changing markets and stimulates them to enter these markets. On the other hand, hostile takeovers are more likely to take place in dynamic industries (Hill and Hansen, 1991) and because of their knowledge of the industry, it could be argued that these takeovers will more often be executed by experienced entrepreneurs at the cost of their inexperienced counterparts than the other way around. This would result in a generally more experienced population of entrepreneurs in dynamic environments. However, this interpretation contradicts the negative correlation between industry dynamism and organizational size.

Finally, cognitive complexity is significantly and negatively correlated with risk-taking behaviour. In the regression analysis, neither size of the organization ($\beta 1 = -0.011$, $p = 0.838$), nor experience of the entrepreneur ($\beta 2 = -0.020$, $p = 0.912$) were found to have a significant effect on risk-taking behaviour in the first model.

The second step in the regression analysis reveals a significant and negative impact of cognitive complexity on risk-taking behaviour. Hypothesis 1 is therefore supported ($\beta 3 = -0.204$, $p = 0.042$). Furthermore, the analysis reveals that 5 per cent of the variance (R-square) in risk-taking behaviour is explained by this model. Hypothesis 2 was tested in the third step of the regression analysis ($\beta 5$). The final step in the regression analysis revealed no significant effect of industry dynamism on the relation between cognitive complexity and risk-taking behaviour ($\beta 5 = -0.091$; $p = 0.375$).

Table 11.3   Results of the regression analysis for risk-taking behaviour

Variables	Step 1	Step 2	Step 3
Control			
Size (β1)	−0.011	−0.006	−0.002
Experience (β2)	−0.020	−0.002	0.003
Independent			
Cognitive complexity (β3)		−0.204*	−0.390*
Industry dynamism (β4)		−0.049	−0.071
Interaction			
CC×Industry dynamism (β5)			−0.091

Note: * = $p < 0.05$. Entries represent standardized coefficients (β).

When plotted, the outcomes of the interaction effect yielded effects contrary to what was expected. To illustrate, the interaction for risk-taking behaviour is presented in Figure 11.1. This pattern shows that in dynamic industries, cognitively complex entrepreneurs tend to make decisions that involve lower levels of risk, whereas cognitively simple entrepreneurs tend to take higher risks. In more stable environments, entrepreneurs with high cognitive complexity take more risks than their cognitively simple counterparts. Hypothesis 2 is thus not supported.

11.6   DISCUSSION

There are fundamental differences in the strategic decision-making process between managers of large firms and entrepreneurs in SMEs (Gibcus et al., 2008) and there is a growing consensus among scientists in the fields of organization and strategic management that the validity of the dominant theories of strategic decision-making is limited in entrepreneurial settings (Brouthers et al., 1998; Busenitz, 1999). Research into the cognitive predictors of entrepreneurial decision-making has flourished in recent years and has yielded encouraging results. This vein of research has mainly focused on the biases and heuristics that entrepreneurs employ in their decision-making. Without disparaging to these valuable contributions towards building a cognitive perspective on entrepreneurial decision-making, these biases and heuristics are all proxies for information processing and refer to the content of a decision. Surprisingly few efforts have been made to explore the effects of the structural composition of entrepreneurs' cognitive representation of a decision situation on their decision-making.

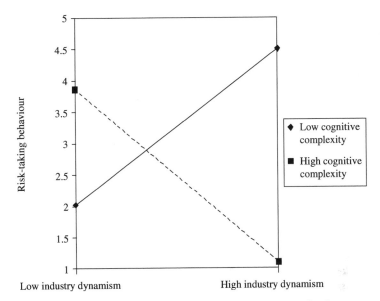

*Figure 11.1   Interactive effects of cognitive complexity and industry
dynamism on risk-taking behaviour*

This study bridges this apparent gap by revealing a significant and negative impact of entrepreneurial cognitive complexity on risk-taking behaviour. Entrepreneurs who are able to apply multiple perspectives to a decision
situation and to integrate these perspectives into their decision, generally
take lower risks than their cognitively simple counterparts. The more elaborate the cognitive framework of entrepreneurs regarding a decision situation at hand, the lower the risks involved in the decision they will make.

Furthermore, this research adds to the 'timid choices and bold forecasts'
argument put forward by Kahneman and Lovallo (1993), in which they
state that decision-makers are cognitively biased to isolate their decisions
from future situations and tend to ignore statistics from the past. Because
of the integration of multiple perspectives into their decision-making, the
findings of this study suggest that the Kahneman and Lovallo argument
applies to cognitively complex entrepreneurs less than to the cognitively
simple ones. Their conclusion that a broader view of the decision at hand
may result in a more consistent risk policy is therefore supported. However,
we now have a clearer understanding of the cognitive functioning behind
this assertion, namely that differentiating and integrating multiple perspectives into a decision leads to lower risk taking. Furthermore, our results
reveal a theoretical mechanism that is in line with Liles's (1974) conclusion
that a careful evaluation of the possible consequences of a risky decision

determines to a large extent whether or not an entrepreneur will make that decision.

Another contribution of this research lies in the linking of content-specific cognitive complexity to entrepreneurship. Allinson et al. (2000) state that the cognitive approach to entrepreneurship deals with entrepreneurs' preference for a mechanism by means of which they gather, process and evaluate information. Indeed, when focusing on biases and heuristics, entrepreneurial preferences are analysed. However, these preferences are developed over time and are relatively stable over different situations. Given the previously discussed conception of cognitive complexity as being specific to its conceptual domain (Curşeu and Rus, 2005), the revealed effect of cognitive complexity on risk-taking behaviour opposes the cognitive perspective on entrepreneurship. Entrepreneurs who have a high cognitive complexity in an area that is closely related to their expertise, may well have a notably lower cognitive complexity in areas that are not or are only remotely related to their expertise. This suggests that the cognitive approach to entrepreneurship is much broader than a collection of cognitive preferences or routines, namely that it also deals with more 'fluid' cognitive aspects that are largely determined by their context. On a broader basis, this chapter underlines the growing conception of the cognitive perspective as a better predictor of entrepreneurial strategic behaviour than the currently predominant puristic view on strategy (Dutton and Jackson, 1987). It adds to the growing notion that rational and political lines of reasoning are not as applicable to entrepreneurial decision-making as they are to larger firms (Brouthers et al., 1998). The results can also be interpreted as a further undermining of classical risk theories. Furthermore, this chapter helps to answer the apparent paradox of entrepreneurs taking higher risks, but not having higher risk propensities (Busenitz, 1999), by providing a statistically supported argument from the cognitive framework.

Although the main hypothesis of this chapter was confirmed, the expected interaction effect of industry dynamism on the relation between cognitive complexity and risk-taking behaviour was found not to be statistically supported. When plotted, the interaction effect even turned out to produce effects contrary to the hypothesized effect. Several reasons may account for this. In the first place, there might simply be no interaction of industry dynamism on the main effect and the slopes may just be a random outcome of the entered coefficients. In that case, the effect of cognitive complexity on risk-taking behaviour would not be as contingent on its decision-making context as was previously put forward. If cognitive complexity has a negative impact on entrepreneurial risk-taking behaviour, no matter the context, this interpretation would yield a more universal applicability of the main effect. However, plotting the interaction effects, the slopes suggest that in dynamic industries, cognitively complex entrepreneurs tend to make decisions that involve lower levels of risk, whereas cognitively simple entrepreneurs tend to take higher risks. In more-stable environments, entrepreneurs with high cognitive complexity take higher risks than their cognitively simple counterparts. A possible explanation for this is the difference in the perception of risk between the cognitively complex and simple entrepreneurs. Due to their limited understanding of the decision situation, in turbulent environments, cognitively simple entrepreneurs may perceive the risk involved in any decision as high, whereas their poor understanding does not affect their perception of risk to a large extent in more static environments.

Other than the theoretical interpretations, there are some methodological considerations that might have accounted for the lack of statistical support for the expected interaction. First, although based on a careful examination of the available literature and including all the dimensions of which industry dynamism is constituted (that is, number of new entrants, number of exits and total population (Verhoeven et al., 2005) the formula that was introduced to compute industry dynamism has not been tested before. Another possible explanation for the rejection of the expected moderation of industry dynamism is the fact that dynamism has been conceptualized in a way that shows low similarity with the conceptualization of the independent and the dependent variable. Cognitive complexity was measured on the personal level and risk-taking behaviour was evaluated as the individual perception of risk involved in a decision by the entrepreneur.

A final explanation for the lack of support of the moderating variable lies in the conceptualization of the dependent variable. In the qualitative and the quantitative dataset, entrepreneurs were asked to focus on one strategic decision that they took. However, when talking about risk-taking behaviour, it is possible to focus on not only the level of risk involved in a decision, but also the frequency of the decision-making. To illustrate: if an entrepreneur has made one single strategic decision that involves a certain level of risk and his/her cognitive complexity is evaluated by means of the cognitive representation of that decision situation, a comparison can be made and a causal relationship can be found. But the evaluation of an effect of a nationwide industry characteristic such as industry dynamism on two 'snapshot' variables is a lot more problematic. The inclusion of a dimension of frequency in the concept of entrepreneurial risk-taking behaviour could have increased the comparability of the moderator variable on the one hand and the independent and dependent variable on the other.

11.7   RECOMMENDATIONS AND FUTURE RESEARCH DIRECTIONS

The first recommendation for future research is to use this effect as a starting-point for a design that will warrant a higher level of generalizability, by the application of a longitudinal design, a random sample, an adequate sample size and the collection of a unique dataset for that setting. In this chapter, the effect of cognitive complexity on risk-taking behaviour was tested only within the entrepreneurial framework, but in addition to replicating this research in a broader empirical setting, it would be interesting to investigate the same effect within a sample of strategic decision-makers in larger organizations and analyse the differences between the groups. The confirmed hypothesis was controlled for size of the organization, but only within the sample of SMEs. In addition to a reconfirmation of this main effect in a broader setting, this research calls for the exploration of more cognitive antecedents of entrepreneurial risk-taking behaviour and the exploration of more consequences of cognitive complexity.

A second recommendation for further research is the use of the introduced formula for computing industry dynamism. The available formulae measure industry dynamism on the organizational level (Kim and Lim, 1988) but they do not include the multiplication of entrants and exits (Verhoeven et al., 2005). Moreover, the absolute score on dynamism is often not related to the total population of organizations operating in a particular industry (Nieuwenhuijsen and Nijkamp, 2001). If industry dynamism is to be evaluated on a level that exceeds the scope of direct competition, the introduced formula is therefore highly recommended.

Because of the indicative purpose of this chapter, these recommendations need to be approached with caution. However, the confirmation of the impact of cognitive complexity on entrepreneurial strategic decision-making could well have a practical relevance. This suggestion could contribute to the awareness of entrepreneurs about their risk-taking behaviour and increase their consciousness of their strategic decision-making. An important consideration for entrepreneurs to take into account is that cognitive complexity is content specific.

The adoption of a consistent risk policy (Kahneman and Lovallo, 1993) may foster successes in a content area that is closely related to an entrepreneur's field of expertise. However, this should not lead entrepreneurs to believe that the same effect will necessarily take place in a conceptual domain where they possess less expert knowledge. Likewise, practitioners who operate in the entrepreneurial sector, such as private equity investors and strategy consultants, may benefit from knowing that entrepreneurs' risk taking is related to their expertise. In addition, this research has an obvious relevance for the entrepreneurs themselves in helping them to realize that their risk-taking behaviour is partly determined by their cognitive representation of the decision situation. This chapter may thus help establish an awareness among entrepreneurs that a better understanding of the problem at hand may lower the risks involved in their strategic decision-making.

12. Conclusions: an outline of ESDM research

Petru L. Curşeu and Patrick A.M. Vermeulen

To understand why and how entrepreneurs act in order to be successful we first have to understand how they think. This claim has been stated repeatedly in the entrepreneurial literature, however to date, most of the empirical research focuses on cognitive heuristics and biases used by entrepreneurs. The aim of this book was to further explore some of the cognitive underpinnings of entrepreneurial strategic decision-making (ESDM). Several problems were addressed and some theoretical propositions were put forward in the theoretical chapters presented in Part I, some of which were tested in the empirical studies presented in Part II. The chapters of the book answer a few interesting problems that have arisen in entrepreneurial cognition literature (for example, how is the decision situation represented in the cognitive system of the decision-maker?) and at the same time raises new ones that await their answers (or being addressed at all!). The most relevant insights of the book are summarized in a set of nine main problems associated with ESDM:

1. To what extent is ESDM a rational process and to what extent is this process similar to strategic decisions in large companies?
The rationality debate dominates decision-making research. The basic assumptions (for example, omniscience, logic-based thought processes) of classical rationality perspectives on decision-making give more room to an instrumental (for example, existence of a specific aim and a belief system that drives decision-making behaviour) or procedural (for example, information-gathering strategies) view on rationality (Dean and Sharfman, 1993; Shafir and LeBoeuf, 2002). ESDM deviates from what is defined as 'a rational process' in at least two ways. First, because of the high degree of complexity involved in most strategic issues, complete information concerning the alternative available is often missing. SMEs often operate in very dynamic environments in which business opportunities occur in an often unpredictable way, therefore entrepreneurs have to decide quickly and implement decisions at a much faster pace as compared to managers in

large corporations. Second, entrepreneurs often lack decision rules, norms and routines used in larger corporations as fundamental decision-making tools that will ensure a rational analysis of the alternatives and their consequences.

Therefore, when making strategic choices, entrepreneurs: (i) do not have all the information related to the alternatives to be considered in the decision process at their disposal, (ii) often have to decide under high time pressure and (iii) often lack structured procedures and protocols to support the decision process. All these factors as well as other contextual constraints force the entrepreneur to make a quick decision, knowing that relevant information is missing. In this line of reasoning, the only aspect of rationality left in ESDM is the fact that it is an intentional and goal-directed cognitive process. As a consequence, general decision-making models are likely to be inaccurate in explaining how entrepreneurs decide in strategic matters. This calls for more descriptive models, accounting for entrepreneurial-specific factors, to explain how strategic choices are made and implemented in small and medium-sized enterprises (SMEs). These models have to account for entrepreneurial attributes (common characteristics shared by small-business owners), situational characteristics (for example, highly dynamic and unpredictable environments), organizational (for example, employee participation, the use of decision support systems) as well as larger societal factors (for example, entrepreneurs' embeddedness in a social network) involved in the decision-making process. Because entrepreneurs are often solitary decision-makers, it is very likely that entrepreneurial attributes play a much more important role in ESDM as compared to SDM in large companies.

2. What types of entrepreneurial decision-makers are there and how do they differ in the way they approach an ESD?

A substantial amount of entrepreneurial literature explored the shared characteristics of entrepreneurs, trying to identify a unique set of traits that distinguish entrepreneurs from other decision-makers. Although successful to a certain extent (see, for example, entrepreneurial self-efficacy) this approach does not overrule the possibility that a certain amount of variability still exists in the ways in which entrepreneurs decide. Gibcus et al. (2008) introduce a taxonomy that distinguishes five types of entrepreneurs based on the distribution of several factors related to the decision situation. Two chapters in this book propose studies designed to validate this taxonomy. Using an algorithmic-level analysis, the study presented in Chapter 6 shows that the five types use different strategies when making high-stake decisions. Substantial differences are observed in the way the decision is initiated, the way in which the information is gathered and the way in which the alternatives are evaluated. The empirical study reported in Chapter 7 shows that these entrepreneurial types differ in their sensitivity to over-confidence bias. These empirical results show that differences in the decision-making styles of entrepreneurs boil down to a set of underlying cognitive factors.

The implications of these empirical results are far-fetched. The main implication for research is that the patterns of attributes associated with different decision-making styles need to be considered when exploring ESDM. The homogeneity assumption for entrepreneurial traits could be misleading. Probably the most important practical implication concerns the design of cognitive training programmes for decision-makers in SMEs. A significant proportion of SMEs disappear from the market in their first years of existence (Camerer and Lovallo, 2000). The failures are generally due to defective decision-making. Improving the quality of decision-making processes in entrepreneurship is an important aspect closely related to economic growth. In order to improve the quality of ESDM, policy makers need to customize the training programmes for the specific needs of different entrepreneurial groups.

3.   What makes a good entrepreneurial decision?

A very simple and straightforward answer to this question would be: a decision is good to the extent to which it is rational. Due to the multitude of approaches used to define rationality and the lack of agreement in the field, it is easier to find and study situations in which a decision is irrational. However, using rationality as a criterion to evaluate the quality of a decision does not allow us to completely unfold the complexity of issues involved in the quality of strategic decisions. A strategic decision is always situated in a specific context, therefore it is not only the decision-maker (and his/her rationality) that matters. Based on the theoretical analyses and empirical results presented in this book, the quality of a strategic choice should be analysed by looking at the whole array of contextual factors associated with the decision, including the typical characteristics of the entrepreneur, the organization and the environment in which the SME operates. It is therefore the analysis of the decision-maker in context that leads to a comprehensive understanding of decision quality. A particular aspect that needs (re)consideration in the study of ESDM is the influence of cognitive heuristics on decisional outcomes. In the entrepreneurial literature, the use of cognitive heuristics is traditionally associated with a deviation from rational decision-making. However, it is the use of heuristics in context that makes them detrimental to or beneficial for the quality of ESDM.

The empirical studies that addressed the issue of ESDM effectiveness used as indicators: increase in turnover and profit as a result of the strategic choice and the entrepreneurs' satisfaction in relation to the decision. Nevertheless, a more complete approach on decision quality should also include more objective evaluations of decision processes and outcomes.

4. What is the role of heuristic (automatic) and analytic (controlled) information processing modes in ESDM?

When entrepreneurs make strategic choices they can use different strategies to analyse the information available. One strategy is for entrepreneurs to take a quick glance at the arguments and then decide based on their intuition, or they can explore the information thoroughly and think carefully about all the aspects involved in the decision. In line with the fact that ESDM often involves very complex problem domains, one may argue that systematic information processing should be the preferred strategy in such situations. Nevertheless, in some instances a strategic choice needs to be made quickly and the decision-maker has no time for extensive consideration of the available information. Therefore, are rapid strategic decisions based on intuition less accurate than decisions in which no time constraint is imposed on the decision-maker who is able and motivated to process thoroughly all the information available? This is a core question that was addressed in this book by using insights from dual-process models of information processing. Our core argument is that ESDM is the result of the interplay between intuitive/heuristic (System 1) and analytical (System 2) reasoning. This interplay results in the formation of cognitive representations in the working memory (WM) space and it is the accuracy and appropriateness of these representations that explain the outcomes of the decision processes.

The high stake involved in strategic decisions makes the process very sensitive to affect infusion, and since entrepreneurs in general have a tendency to avoid negative emotions and maintain a positive mood, it is very likely that intuitive or heuristic information processing is the dominant mechanism in ESDM. Moreover, the context in which entrepreneurs have to make strategic choices is often dynamic, unpredictable and demands quick actions. Hence, heuristics are often used in order to cope with these situational characteristics. Finally, specific entrepreneurial cognitive attributes favour the use of intuition and heuristic processing in ESDM. Heuristic information processing refers to: (i) the activation of holistic schemas from the long-term memory, schemas that were developed previously while the decision-maker was dealing with similar decisions or (ii) the use of general cognitive biases that affect a wide area of cognitive processes. The activation of schemas in the WM space is quick and allows the entrepreneur to quickly make analogies with previous decision situations and to make an intuitive choice based on these analogies. The quality of intuitive decisions is high, to the extent to which: (i) the entrepreneur uses heuristics developed through experience and not general biases that lead to the over-simplification of the decision situation and (ii) the use of heuristics is highly context specific and heuristics are not generalized to a large array of decision situations. The use of analytical reasoning (controlled information processing) can overrule the negative influences of general heuristics on ESDM. Further research should explore the way in which these two information processing modes interact in ESDM. It is very likely that highly successful ESDM is the result of an accurate use of expertise-related heuristics and an efficient management of controlled cognitive processes on the use of general cognitive heuristics and biases. This successful interplay of these two information processing modes leads to the development of complex cognitive representations in relation to a specific decision situation. A core argument presented in the literature so far (Dane and Pratt, 2007) and tested in several empirical studies presented in this book is that a highly complex cognitive representation formed in the WM is beneficial for the quality of ESDM outcomes.

5. How are strategic decisions represented in the cognitive system of the decision-maker, and which characteristics of these representations lead to a high-quality decision?

A core problem in the decision-making literature in general is the scarce evidence for the influence of cognitive representations on the quality of decision-making outcomes (Hastie, 2001). In a similar vein, strategy scholars showed little interest in exploring the way in which strategic issues are cognitively represented and which are the main antecedents for these representations. In entrepreneurship research, Baron and Ward (2004) raised the theoretical challenge of exploring whether entrepreneurs form cognitive representations that are different from other decision-makers. To date, little empirical work has been done to explore these highly relevant issues. This book explores a particular way in which knowledge can be represented in the cognitive system of the decision-maker, namely conceptual networks. The main argument of this representational approach is that knowledge can be represented as interconnected concepts in a network. Concepts are thus the nodes of the network, and the relationships among them are represented by lines. Such a representational structure has the benefit of being able to incorporate a wide range of concepts and relations. Moreover, conceptual networks can represent explicit as well as implicit knowledge structures.

Cognitive complexity is the main characteristic of these representations and it refers to the richness of the conceptual network formed in relation to a specific decision situation. Cognitive complexity is illustrative for both the degree of differentiation and integration of a cognitive representation. Because, in general, strategic decisions involve a high degree of complexity, we argued that cognitive complexity is beneficial for the quality of decision outcomes. Three empirical studies presented in this book tested this theoretical claim and showed that the complexity of the cognitive representations developed in relation to a particular decision is indeed beneficial (i) for the quality of the outcomes, both financial and with regard to the satisfaction of the decision-maker and (ii) for the innovative performance of the SME. We can therefore conclude that cognitive complexity is a main antecedent of ESDM quality. Cognitive complexity, however, is just one of the characteristics of cognition that has an impact on decision-making. Further research should explore other characteristics of the cognitive representations formed in the WM space and their influence on the quality of decision-making outcomes as well as the complex relationship between cognitive complexity and decision outcomes.

6. What methods will allow us to elicit, represent and evaluate the structural characteristics of entrepreneurial cognition?

A core issue addressed in this book was the way in which the cognitive representations formed in the WM space can be elicited and represented. It has been a challenge for the cognitive scientists to gain access into the unseen information processing of the human cognitive system. If cognitive structures are such important elements in information processing, a central question is how can we accurately evaluate these structures? Cognitive mapping is one way in which cognitive representations have been explored so far in the cognitive sciences. Drawing its inspiration from graph theory, cognitive mapping is a process that represents cognitive structures as sets of interconnected concepts, or cognitive maps.

Several chapters in this book use an ideographic variant of cognitive mapping to transform the interview transcripts into cognitive maps. A four-step procedure described in Hodgkinson and Clarkson (2005) is used here as an elicitation and representation technique. The procedure starts with the knowledge elicitation procedure, which consists of extensive interviews or the collection of other written documents describing the decision situation. Cognitive maps are then derived from these written documents by first extracting the core concepts and the relationships among them (first-order concepts and connections) and the secondary concepts and relationships are used to give specificity to the structure of the map. The structural characteristics of these maps are then coded and analysed, and focused on three indicators: number of concepts used, number of connections and types of connections established among the concepts. Finally, the complexity of the cognitive maps is computed using different formulae, which are illustrative of the richness of the cognitive representations developed by entrepreneurs in relation to a particular strategic decision.

Further research should address alternative ways in which other types of cognitive representations (in addition to conceptual networks) used in ESDM can be assessed. The development of valid and reliable methods for the elicitation and representation of cognitive structures is essential both for theory, in that it allows insights into the cognitive space of the decision-maker, and practice, because it can be used as an accurate diagnostic tool, based on which decision training can be designed.

7. How do demographic variables and cognitive heuristics influence cognitive complexity and ESDM effectiveness?

Some of the empirical studies presented in this book explore antecedents of cognitive complexity in ESDM. One of the arguments presented in the theoretical discussion is that demographic variables (for example, age, education) are antecedents of cognitive complexity. The empirical results show that, for example, older entrepreneurs develop less-complex cognitive representations about the decision situation than younger entrepreneurs. Also, more-experienced entrepreneurs develop more-complex representations compared to less-experienced ones. Moreover, an important empirical result presented here concerns the mediating role of cognitive heuristics (both general and expertise related) in the relationship between demographic variables and cognitive complexity. When the use of overconfidence and representativeness is taken into account, the influence of age on cognitive complexity can be decomposed into a direct negative influence (probably explained by a decline of cognitive abilities with age) and an indirect small positive influence mediated by overconfidence and representativeness. Older entrepreneurs are less overconfident and this leads to a lower sensitivity to representativeness bias, which in turn is beneficial for cognitive complexity. Also, the experience as an entrepreneur has both a direct positive influence on cognitive complexity (probably explained by the use of highly contextual expertise-related cognitive heuristics) as well as an indirect negative influence, mediated by overconfidence and representativeness. The two general heuristics considered here are strongly interconnected, and overconfidence seems to strengthen the use of representativeness.

These results open promising research directions into the complex role of cognitive complexity as a mediating factor between entrepreneurial demographics and the quality of decision outcomes. Moreover, a theoretical argument presented in the book is that the influence of entrepreneurial-specific motivational factors (for example, self-efficacy, cognitive motivation and tolerance for ambiguity) on the quality of decision outcomes is explained by cognitive complexity. It is also important that further research explores the interplay between general and expertise-related heuristics as antecedents of cognitive complexity.

8. How does the social capital of the entrepreneur impact on cognitive complexity and ESDM effectiveness?

Although in SMEs strategic choices are usually made by the entrepreneur alone (the entrepreneur as a rugged individualist, McGrath et al., 1992), she/he is not the only actor involved in the decision process. The perspective of the entrepreneur embedded in larger social structures (for example, relations with SME employees or with external actors) is one of the facets of ESDM explored in this book. The empirical results presented here show that both the involvement of employees as well as the presence of external network ties are beneficial for cognitive complexity. This means that the social capital of the entrepreneur is a central antecedent of cognitive complexity. Further research should explore the influence of the entrepreneur's position in a social network (for example, degree of centrality, filling structural holes) as well as the influence of the characteristics of the entrepreneur's social network (for example, presence of weak ties, density) on cognitive complexity and the quality of decision outcomes.

We argue that a relational approach has much potential for future research efforts to contribute to the literature on ESDM. In particular, the structural position of the entrepreneur in an advice network may exert a strong influence on the quality of decision-making. A central position in a social network or a position in which the entrepreneur fills structural holes are likely to enrich the cognitive structures developed by the entrepreneur. In these structural positions, the entrepreneur acts as a connecting actor between different sources of information, and thus has better access to a large pool of knowledge that will most probably be reflected in her/his cognitive complexity and ultimately on the quality of her/his strategic choices. At a different level of analysis (for example, network level), the structural characteristics of the advice network in which the entrepreneur is embedded may exert influences on the quality of the decision-making process. Better-connected (more-dense) networks and networks with several weak ties may facilitate knowledge exchange and integration and thus offer their members a strategic advantage as compared to decision-makers embedded in less-dense networks, or networks with less-weak ties.

9. How would a unified theory of ESDM integrate the factors related to information processing, motivational attributes and the role of emotions in ESDM?

A final contribution of this book is the integration into a unitary theoretical framework of several factors related to ESDM. The model presented in

Chapter 3 integrates motivational attributes, emotions and information processing modes that influence ESDM. Situational cues are perceived from the environment and through the activation of two information processing modes (automatic and controlled), implicit and explicit knowledge representations are activated from the long-term memory into the working memory. Emotions influence the activation of knowledge representation, in several ways. First, information congruent with the emotional state experienced at a certain point is processed more extensively than information not associated with an emotional state, therefore information with emotional value plays an important role in ESDM. Second, experiencing negative emotions leads to more-extensive and -analytical processing of the information available, while positive emotions lead to the use of intuitive reasoning in ESDM. Third, implicit knowledge representations stored in the long-term memory are often associated with an emotional content and these combined cognitive/emotional structures are activated in a holistic fashion in ESDM. The decision-maker forms a representation about the decision situation in the WM space and this representation explains the influence of motivational attributes and information processing modes on the outcomes of ESDM.

This integrative model opens some fruitful research directions in entrepreneurial cognition. First, the model acknowledges the role of emotions in ESDM. The mechanisms through which emotions impact on ESDM as well as the interplay between emotions and cognition in ESDM are still heavily under-researched in entrepreneurial literature. A key proposition to be tested in empirical studies refers to the moderating role of positive and negative emotions on the use of intuition and rational analysis in ESDM. Another relevant aspect is the context-dependent role of emotional states on information processing effectiveness. It is very likely that in strategic decisions with no time constraints, the positive role of negative emotions on ESDM effectiveness is strengthened (because they trigger extensive information processing and maximize the use of available information), while in conditions in which decisions have to be made under time pressure, the negative role of positive emotions on ESDM effectiveness is reduced because the use of intuition in these conditions may lead to satisfactory results.

Second, the model advances the proposition that cognitive complexity acts as a mediator in the relationship between motivational attributes and the quality of ESDM outcomes. High self-efficacy increases the chances of information search and it is beneficial for the quality of ESDM because it increases the complexity of the cognitive representations developed in the WM space. Tolerance for ambiguity is very likely to have the opposite effects. If a decision-maker has a high tolerance for ambiguity (she/he is comfortable making decisions when knowing that relevant information is missing), it is very likely that the complexity of the cognitive representations developed about a particular decision situation is lower due to the 'jump to conclusions' kind of strategy used. Cognitive motivation is likely to be beneficial for the quality of ESDM outcomes because of the increased appetite of individuals high in cognitive motivation for cognitive activities (problem solving, decision-making).

Finally, the role of controlled and automatic information processing modes in ESDM needs further attention. Ultimately it is the interplay between these two information processing modes that leads to the knowledge activation process in the WM. The exploration of the interplay has both a theoretical and a practical relevance. The theoretical relevance lies in the fact that the distinction between the controlled and automatic information processing modes may explain the mixed results of entrepreneurial literature on the use of heuristics and biases. The practical relevance lies in the possibility of adjusting the functioning of the heuristic/intuitive information processing mode by guided and controlled information processing. Based on these insights, policy makers can design training strategies to increase the control of System 2 over System 1 and increase the effectiveness of ESDM.

Appendix

As we have already mentioned in the preface of this book, the data on which the empirical chapters in this volume are based have been collected by or in collaboration with EIM Business and Policy Research. The data were collected in three steps. First, two pilot studies covering a total of 22 in-depth interviews were conducted by researchers from EIM. Second, on the basis of these pilot studies and a literature review, a survey was constructed and administered in Dutch small and medium-sized enterprises (SMEs). Third, 109 entrepreneurs who also participated in the survey were interviewed by eight student teams that each consisted of three students. In order to ensure comparative data, the students were provided with a semi-structured interview guide that included eight leading questions and 24 follow-up questions. The student teams were closely supervised by a researcher from EIM and one of the editors of the book. In the remainder of this appendix we describe each of these data collection stages in more detail.

PILOT STUDIES

EIM carried out two pilot studies on the decision-making process by SMEs, in 2002 and 2003, consisting of 22 in-depth interviews with entrepreneurs. The first pilot study had a very exploratory character, whereas the second was of a more confirmatory nature. For the first pilot study, entrepreneurs were selected from the EIM SME Panel. This panel was set up and is controlled by EIM. Its major objective is to collect information about knowledge, attitudes and opinions of entrepreneurs with respect to various (government) policy-related issues. In each round, about 2000 companies were interviewed by means of computer-assisted telephone interviewing (CATI). The entrepreneur or the general manager of the company provided the answers. The EIM SME Panel consists of Dutch companies with fewer than 100 employees, distributed equally across three size classes (0–9, 10–49 and 50–99 employees) and eight sectors. The eight sectors distinguished are manufacturing, construction, trade, hotel and catering, transport, financial services, business services and personal services.

During the second measurement in 2002, the panel included four questions about decision-making: (i) 'Did you make one or more strategic decisions in the last three years?'; (ii) 'If yes: could you give a short description of your last strategic decision?'; (iii) 'Did this decision work out positively or negatively?'; and (iv) 'Are you satisfied with the result of your decision?'. Ten entrepreneurs were selected from the EIM SME Panel who were willing to elaborate on their strategic decision-making during an in-depth interview. EIM selected 10 decision-making entrepreneurs who took a strategic decision that resulted in a clear discontinuity in the course of the organization. For practical reasons the selected SMEs were not distributed across the whole country; they belonged to several sectors and the decisions concerned various matters. Focusing on recent decisions of strategic importance, the first pilot tried to recover what the decision-making process in small firms looked like. The interview script was inspired by Mintzberg et al. (1976); it contained open-ended questions only (How did the idea come along? How did you experience complexity? How many alternatives did you consider?).

The set-up of the second pilot study was somewhat different from that of the first. It was decided not to interview the same members of the EIM SME Panel about their decision-making process, but instead a new panel was created to select the case studies by using a telephone survey. The sample consisted of 200 completed telephone interviews. All 200 SMEs have a minimum of one and a maximum of 99 employees. The persons spoken to were always the directors/owners, that is, those who were making the important decisions. The survey was distributed equally across the following sectors: manufacturing, construction, trade, hotel and catering, transport, financial services, business services and personal services. Forty-nine entrepreneurs agreed to have a discussion (face-to-face interview) with one of the researchers about their decision-making process. Of these 49, 12 were selected for an in-depth interview. The selection consisted of six entrepreneurs with a 'go' decision, two with a 'no-go' decision and four with ideas or plans that possibly will result in a strategic decision. During the interviews the entrepreneurs were asked about relevant facts and motives that finally resulted or will result in the decision.

QUANTITATIVE DATA

In the second stage, survey data were collected. Commissioned by the Dutch Ministry of Economic Affairs, this survey aimed to collect descriptive statistics and explore how decisions in SMEs are made. It focused on those entrepreneurs in small enterprises who had taken at least one important decision in the past three years. The decision could be related to any innovation or project that was discontinuous (out of daily routine) and that was perceived to be important. Various questions were asked concerning the characteristics of the entrepreneur and the selected decision.

The data were collected by CATI among 1200 SMEs within the Netherlands. The sample was limited to entrepreneurs in SMEs, that is, firms with no more than 100 employees. Respondents were sampled across eight industries: manufacturing, construction, trade, hotel and catering, transport, financial services, business services and personal services (such as beauty parlours, fitness centres and hairdressing salons). The firms were equally distributed across the eight industries. The size class of a firm was measured by full-time equivalents of employees. The distribution of the sample across size classes was as follows: 0–4 employees, 25.6 per cent; 5–9 employees, 15.0 per cent; 10–19 employees, 28.9 per cent; 20–49 employees, 12.8 per cent; and 50–99 employees, 17.8 per cent. About 60 per cent of the interviewed respondents had made an important decision in the past three years. The median of the investments related to the decision was 100,000 euros. Because outlying and incomplete cases were discarded from the analysis, eventually 646 respondents were included in the sample used in this book. All respondents were responsible for the management of the day-to-day business and the strategic decisions of the firm. The median age of respondents was 44 years (range: 21–76). Almost 88 per cent of respondents were men and 13 per cent had a university degree.

Note that our data are not completely representative of the small-business population in the Netherlands. For example, 5.2 per cent of the small firms in the Netherlands belong to the hotel and catering industry, whereas 12.5 per cent of the small firms in the sample used for this book represent this industry. This means that small firms in the hotel and catering industry are overrepresented. Also note that the descriptive statistics in this book provide no reliable estimation of population figures. However, for the goal of this study this is not considered problematic.

QUALITATIVE DATA

In the third stage, data were collected using face-to-face interviews that were conducted with a subsample (109 respondents) of the SME entrepreneurs from the survey. In contrast to the survey data, the data from these interviews are more extensive and detailed and hence very suitable for capturing cognitions. The interviews were conducted by student teams from Erasmus University, Rotterdam, from March to May 2003 as part of a project coordinated by one of the editors. Like the research reported upon in Gibcus et al. (2008), these interviews were part of a larger research project on SMEs of EIM Business and Policy Research. Each interview was conducted by two researchers and took about 60–90 minutes. The interviews, conducted in Dutch, consisted of two parts. The first part, the part used in this book, dealt with decision-making. The second part dealt with innovation. Each part was semi-structured, in the sense that a set of questions to be posed was constructed prior to the interviews (some main questions and a number of follow-up ones). The first part on decision-making dealt with one specific strategic decision and extensively explored the different facets and events that were involved. The researchers sent written reports of the interviews they conducted to the interviewed entrepreneurs for corrections. Nearly all interviewees approved the report without corrections.

References

Adler, P.S. and S.W. Kwon (2002), 'Social capital; prospects for a new concept', *Academy of Management Review*, **27** (1), 17–40.

Agnoli, F. (1991), 'Development of judgmental heuristics and logical reasoning: training counteracts the representativeness heuristic', *Cognitive Development*, **6** (1), 195–217.

Allais, M. and O. Hagen (1979), *Expected Utility Hypotheses and the Allais Paradox*, Dordrecht: Reidel.

Allinson, C.W., E. Chell and J. Hayes (2000), 'Intuition and entrepreneurial behavior', *European Journal of Work and Organizational Psychology*, **9** (1), 31–43.

Alloy, L.B. and L.T. Abramson (1982), 'Learned helplessness, depression, and the illusion of control', *Journal of Personality and Social Psychology*, **42** (6), 1114–26.

Anderson, A., J. Park and S. Jack (2007), 'Entrepreneurial social capital: conceptualizing social capital in new high-tech firms', *International Small Business Journal*, **25** (3), 245–72.

Ardichvili, A., R. Cardozo and S. Ray (2003), 'A theory of entrepreneurial opportunity identification and development', *Journal of Business Venturing*, **18** (1), 105–23.

Ashby, W.R. (1965), *An Introduction to Cybernetics*, New York: Wiley.

Ashfort, B.E. and F. Mael (1989), 'Social identity theory and the organization', *Academy of Management Review*, **14** (1), 20–39.

Ashmos, D.P., D. Duchon and R.R. McDaniel Jr (1998), 'Participation in strategic decision making: the role of organizational predisposition and issue interpretation', *Decision Sciences*, **29**, 25–51.

Atkinson, J.W., J.R. Bastian, R.W. Earl and G.H. Litwin (1960), 'The achievement motive, goal-setting, and probability preferences', *Journal of Abnormal and Social Psychology*, **60** (1), 27–36.

Axelrod, R. (1976), *The Nature of Decision*, Princeton, NJ: Princeton University Press.

Baarda, D.B. and M.P.M. De Goede (1999), *Statistiek met SPSS voor Windows, inleiding elementaire statistiek en handleiding voor het verwerken en analyseren van onderzoeksgegevens met SPSS voor Windows*, (Statistics with SPSS for Windows, introduction to basic statistics and guide to processing and analyzing data with SPSS for Windows), Groningen: Stenfert Kroese.

Baird, I.S. and H. Thomas (1985), 'Toward a contingency model of strategic risk taking', *Academy of Management Review*, **10** (2), 230–43.

Bakker, R.M., P.L. Curşeu and P. Vermeulen (2007), 'Cognitive factors in entrepreneurial strategic decision making', *Cognition, Brain, Behavior*, **11** (9), 195–219.

Bandura, A. (1977), 'Self-efficacy: toward a unifying theory of behavioral change', *Psychological Review*, **84** (2), 191–215.

Bandura, A. (1986), *Social Foundations of Thought and Action: A Social Cognitive Theory*, Englewood Cliffs, NJ: Prentice-Hall.

Bandura, A. and R. Wood (1989), 'Effect of perceived controllability and performance standards on self-regulation of complex decision making', *Journal of Personality and Social Psychology*, **56** (5), 805–14.

Bankova, A. (1991), *Introduction to Management*, Sofia: Sofia University Press.

Bantel, K.A. and S.E. Jackson (1989), 'Top management and innovations in banking: does the composition of the top team make a difference?', *Strategic Management Journal*, **10** (1), 107–24.

Barbosa, S.D., M.W. Gerhardt and J.R. Kickul (2007), 'The role of cognitive style and risk preference on entrepreneurial self-efficacy and entrepreneurial intentions', *Journal of Leadership and Organizational Studies*, **13** (4), 86–104.

Barnes, J.H. (1984), 'Cognitive biases and their impact on strategic planning', *Strategic Management Journal*, **5** (2), 129–37.

Baron, R.A. (1998), 'Cognitive mechanisms in entrepreneurship: why and when entrepreneurs think differently than other people', *Journal of Business Venturing*, **13** (4), 275–94.

Baron, R.A. (1999), 'Counterfactual thinking and venture formation: the potential effects of thinking about what might have been', *Journal of Business Venturing*, **15**, 78–91.

Baron, R.A. (2004), 'The cognitive perspective: a valuable tool for answering entrepreneurship's basic "why" questions', *Journal of Business Venturing*, **19** (3), 221–39.

Baron, R.M. and D.A. Kenny (1986), 'The moderator-mediator variable distinction in social psychological research: conceptual, strategic, and statistical considerations', *Journal of Personality and Social Psychology*, **51**, 1173–82.

Baron, R.A. and T.B. Ward (2004), 'Expanding entrepreneurial cognition's toolbox: potential contributions from the field of cognitive science', *Entrepreneurship, Theory, Research and Practice*, **28**, 553–74.

Barr, P.S., J.L. Stimpert and A.S. Huff (1992), 'Cognitive change, strategic action, and organizational renewal', *Strategic Management Journal*, **13** (special issue), 15–36.

Baum, J.R. and E.A. Locke (2004), 'The relationship of entrepreneurial threats, skills, and motivation to subsequent venture growth', *Journal of Applied Psychology*, **89**, 587–98.

Bazerman, M.H. (1986), *Managerial Decision Making*, New York: John Wiley.

Bazerman, M. (1999), *Smart Money Decisions*, New York: Wiley.

Beattie, R. (1999), 'The creative entrepreneur: a study of the entrepreneur's creative processes', in P.D. Reynolds, W.D. Bygrave, S. Manigart, C.M. Mason, G.D. Meyer, H.J. Sapienza and K.G. Shaver (eds), *Frontiers of Entrepreneurship Research*, Babson Park, MA: Babson College, pp. 138–51.

Begley, T.M and D.P. Boyd (1987a), 'A comparison of entrepreneurs and managers of small business firms', *Journal of Management*, **13** (1), 99–108.

Begley, T.M. and D.P. Boyd (1987b), 'Psychological characteristics associated with performance in entrepreneurial firms and smaller businesses', *Journal of Business Venturing*, **2** (1), 79–93.

Bell, D. (1982), 'Regret in decision-making under uncertainty', *Operations Research*, **30** (5), 961–81.

Bell, D.E., H. Raiffa, A. Tversky and R. Gillett (1988), *Decision Making: Descriptive, Normative, and Prescriptive Interaction*, Cambridge: Cambridge University Press.

Benos, A.V. (1998), 'Aggressiveness and survival of overconfident traders', *Journal of Fiancial Markets*, **1** (3/4), 353–83.

Bernard, H.R. (2002), 'Content analysis', in H.R. Bernard (ed.), *Research in Anthropology: Qualitative and Quantitative Methods*, Walnut Creek, CA: AltaMira Press, pp. 476–83.

Bhaskaran, S. (2006), 'Incremental innovation and business performance: small and medium-size food enterprises in a concentrated industry environment', *Journal of Small Business Management*, **44** (1), 64–80.

Bhattacharya, M. and H. Bloch (2004), 'Determinants of innovation', *Small Business Economics*, **22**, 155–62.

Bhide, A.V. (2000), *The Origin and Evolution of New Business*, Oxford and New York: Oxford University Press.

Bieri, J. (1955), 'Cognitive complexity–simplicity and predictive behavior', *Journal of Abnormal and Social Psychology*, **51** (2), 263–8.

Birley, S. and P. Westhead (1993), 'A comparison of new businesses established by "novice" and "habitual" founders in Great Britain', *International Small Business Journal*, **12** (1), 38–60.

Boddy, D. and R. Paton (2004), 'Responding to competing narratives: lessons for project managers', *International Journal of Project Management*, **22**, 225–33.

Boland, R.J., J. Singh, P. Salipante, J.D. Aram, S.Y. Fay and P. Kanawattanachai (2001), 'Knowledge representations and knowledge transfer', *Academy of Management Journal*, **44** (2), 393–417.

Bougon, M.G. (1992), 'Congregative cognitive maps: a unified dynamic theory of organization and strategy', *Journal of Management and Studies*, **29** (3), 369–89.

Bourgeois, L. and K. Eisenhardt (1988), 'The politics of strategic decision-making in high velocity environments: towards a mid-range theory', *Academy of Management Journal*, **31** (4), 737–70.

Brief, A.P. and H.K. Downey (1983), 'Cognitive and organizational structures: a conceptual analysis of implicit organizing theories', *Human Relations*, **36**, 1065–90.

Brockhaus, R.H. (1980), 'Risk taking propensity of entrepreneurs', *Academy of Management Journal*, **23** (3), 509–20.

Brouthers, K., F. Andriessen and I. Nicolaes (1998), 'Driving blind: strategic decision-making in small companies', *Long Range Planning*, **31** (1), 130–38.

Browne, M.W. and R. Cudek (1993), 'Alternative ways of assessing model fit', in K. Bollen and S. Long (eds), *Testing Structural Equation Models*, Newbury Park, NJ: Sage, pp. 136–62.

Budner, S. (1962), 'Intolerance of ambiguity as a personality variable', *Journal of Personality*, **30**, 29–50.

Burt, R.S. (1992), *Structural Holes: The Social Structure of Competition*, Cambridge, MA: Harvard University Press.

Burt, R.S. (1997), 'The contingent value of social capital', *Administrative Science Quarterly*, **42**, 339–65.

Busenitz, L.W. (1999), 'Entrepreneurial risk and strategic decision making: it's a matter of perspective', *Journal of Applied Behavioral Science*, **35** (3), 325–40.

Busenitz, L.W. and J. Barney (1997), 'Differences between entrepreneurs and managers in large organizations: biases and heuristics in strategic decision-making', *Journal of Business Venturing*, **12** (1), 9–30.

Butler, R. (2002), 'Decision making', in A. Sorge (ed.), *Organization*, London: Thomson Learning, pp. 224–51.

Cacioppo, J.T. and R.E. Petty (1982), 'The need for cognition', *Journal of Personality and Social Psychology*, **42** (1), 116–31.

Cacioppo, J.T., R.E. Petty, J.A. Feinstein and W.B.G. Jarvis (1996), 'Dispositional differences in cognitive motivation: the life times of individuals varying in need for cognition', *Psychological Bulletin*, **119** (2), 197–253.

Cahill, D.J. (1998), 'Organizational decline and innovation: are entrepreneurs a special case?', *Academy of Management Review*, **23** (3), 387–8.

Calori, R., G. Johnson and P. Sarnin (1994), 'CEOs' cognitive maps and the scope of the organization', *Strategic Management Journal*, **15** (6), 437–57.

Camerer, C. and D. Lovallo (1999), 'Overconfidence and excess entry: an experimental approach', *American Economic Review*, **89** (1), 306–18.

Camerer, C.F. and D. Lovallo (2000), 'Overconfidence and excess entry: an experimental approach', in D. Kahneman and A. Tversky (eds), *Choices, Values and Frames*, Cambridge and New York: Cambridge University Press, pp. 414–23.

Camisón-Zornoza, C., R. Lapiedra-Alcamí, M. Segarra-Ciprés and M. Boronat-Navarro (2004), 'A meta-analysis of innovation and organizational size', *Organization Studies*, **25** (3), 331–61.

Campbell, C. (1992), 'A decision theory model for entrepreneurial acts', *Entrepreneurship Theory and Practice*, **17** (1), 21–7.

Cannon-Bowers, J., E. Salas and S. Convers (1993), 'Shared mental models in expert team decision making', in N.J. Castellan Jr. (ed.), *Individual and Group Decision Making: Current Issues*, Hillsdale, NJ: Lawrence Erlbaum, pp. 221–46.

Cantillon, R. (1755 [1964]), *Essai Sur la Nature du Commerce en General* (Essay on the Nature of Commerce), New York: Augustus M. Kelley.

Carland, J.W., F. How, W.R. Boulton and J.A.C. Carland (1984), 'Differentiating entrepreneurs from small business owners: a conceptualization', *Academy of Management Review*, **9** (2), 354–9.

Carley, K.M. (1986), 'An approach for relating social structure to cognitive structure', *Journal of Mathematical Sociology*, **12** (2), 137–89.

Carley, K. (1993), 'Coding choices for textual analysis: a comparison of content analysis and map analysis', *Sociological Methodology*, **23** (1), 75–126.

Carley, K.M. (1997), 'Extracting team mental models through textual analysis', *Journal of Organizational Behavior*, **18** (special issue), 533–58.

Carley, K.M. and M. Palmquist (1992), 'Extracting, representing, and analyzing mental models', *Social Forces*, **70** (3), 601–36.

Carver, C. (1997), 'The internal–external scale confounds internal locus of control with expectancies of positive outcomes', *Personality and Social Psychology Bulletin*, **23** (6), 580–85.

Casson, M. (1982), *The Entrepreneur: An Economic Theory*, London: Gregg Revivals.

CBS (2006), *Kennis en economie 2006: onderzoek en innovatie in Nederland* (Knowledge and economy 2006: research and innovation in the Netherlands), Voorburg/Heerlen: Centraal Bureau voor de Statistiek.

References

Chandler, A. (1962), *Strategy and Structure: Chapters in the History of the Industrial Enterprise*, Cambridge, MA: MIT Press.

Chandler, G.N., J. Dahlqvist and P. Davidsson (2002), 'Opportunity recognition processes: a taxonomy and outcome implications', *Frontiers of Entrepreneurship Research* (conference proceedings), Babson College, Wellesley, MA.

Charness, G., E. Karni and D. Levin (2007), 'Individual and group decision making under risk: an experimental study of Bayesian updating and violations of first-order stochastic dominance', *Journal of Risk and Uncertainty*, **35** (2), 129–48.

Chattopadhyay, P., G.P. Hodgkinson and M.P. Healey (2006), 'Of maps and managers: toward a cognitive theory of strategic intervention', *Academy of Management Best Conference Paper 2006*, Managerial and Organization Cognition division (MOC) of the Academy of Management, pp. B1–B6.

Chen, C.C., P.G. Greene and A. Crick (1998), 'Does entrepreneurial self-efficacy distinguish entrepreneurs from managers?', *Journal of Business Venturing*, **13** (4), 295–316.

Cho, J. and J. Lee (2006), 'An integrated model of risk and risk-reducing strategies', *Journal of Business Research*, **59**, 112–20.

Choi, Y.R. and D.A. Shepherd (2004), 'Entrepreneurs' decisions to exploit opportunities', *Journal of Management*, **30** (3), 377–95.

Christensen, P.S., O.O. Madsen and R. Peterson (1994), *Opportunity Identification: The Contribution of Entrepreneurship to Strategic Management*, Aarhus: Aarhus University Institute of Management.

Christensen-Szalanski, J.J.J., D.E. Beck, C.M. Christensen-Szalanski and T.D. Koepsell (1983), 'Effects of expertise and experience on risk judgments', *Journal of Applied Psychology*, **68** (2), 278–84.

Cohen, J.W. (1988), *Statistical Power Analysis for the Behavioural Sciences*, Hillsdale, NJ: Lawrence Erlbaum.

Coleman, J. (1988), 'Social capital in the creation of human capital', *American Journal of Sociology*, **94**, 95–120.

Collins, O.F. and D.G. Moore (1964), *The Enterprising Man*, East Lansing, MI: Bureau of Business and Economic Research.

Collinson, S. and J. Houlden (2005), 'Decision-making and market orientation in the internationalisation process of small and medium sized enterprises', *Management International Review*, **45** (4), 413–36.

Cooke, P. and D. Wills (1999), 'Small firms, social capital and the enhancement of business performance through innovation programs', *Small Business Economics*, **13**, 219–34.

Cooper, A.C., T. Folta and C.Y. Woo (1995), 'Entrepreneurial information search', *Journal of Business Venturing*, **10** (2), 107–20.

Cooper, A.C., C.Y. Woo and W.C. Dunkelberg (1988), 'Entrepreneurs' perceived chances for success', *Journal of Business Venturing*, **3** (2), 97–108.

Cope, J., S. Jack and M.B. Rose (2007), 'Social capital and entrepreneurship', *International Small Business Journal*, **25** (3), 213–19.

Coronges, K.A., A.W. Stacy and T.W. Valente (2007), 'Structural comparison of cognitive associative networks in two populations', *Journal of Applied Social Psychology*, **37** (9), 2097–129.

Cossette, P. and M. Audet (1992), 'Mapping of an idiosyncratic schema', *Journal of Management Studies*, **29** (3), 325–47.

Covin, J.G. and D.P. Slevin (1989), 'Strategic management of small firms in hostile and benign environments', *Strategic Management Journal*, **10** (1), 75–87.

Covin, J.G. and D.P. Slevin (1991), 'A conceptual model of entrepreneurship as firm behavior', *Entrepreneurship Theory and Practice*, **16** (1), 7–25.

Crockett, W.H. (1965), 'Cognitive complexity and impression formation', in B.A. Maher (ed.), *Progress in Experimental Personality Research*, New York: Academic Press, pp. 47–90.

Cummins, D., D. Carson and A. Gilmore (2001), 'Marketing decision-making competencies for SMEs', paper presented at Academy of Marketing Conference, 28 June–1 July, Cardiff.

Curşeu, P.L. (2006), 'Need for cognition and rationality in decision-making', *Studia Psychologica*, **48** (2), 141–56.

Curşeu, P.L. and S. Boroş (2004), *Femeia manager: între reprezentare şi realitate socială* (The women manager: between social representation and social reality), Cluj-Napoca: ASCR Press.

Curşeu, P.L. and D. Rus (2005), 'The cognitive complexity of groups: a critical look at team cognition research', *Cognitie, Creier, Comportament* (Cognition, Brain, Behavior), **9** (4), 681–710.

Curşeu, P. L., S.G.L. Schruijer and S. Boroş (2007), 'The effects of groups' variety and disparity on groups' cognitive complexity', *Group Dynamics: Theory, Research and Practice*, **11** (3), 187–206.

Cyert, R. and J. March (1963), *A Behavioural Theory of the Firm*, Englewood Cliffs, NJ: Prentice-Hall.

Daft, R.L. and K.E. Weick (1984), 'Toward a model of organizations as interpretation systems', *Academy of Management Review*, **9** (2), 284–95.

Damanpour, F. (1991), 'Organizational innovation: a meta-analysis of effects of determinants and moderators', *Academy of Management Journal*, **34** (3), 555–90.

Damanpour, F. and W.M. Evan (1984), 'Organizational innovation and performance: the problem of "organizational lag"', *Administrative Science Quarterly*, **29** (3), 392–409.

Damanpour, F. and S. Gopalakrishnan (2001), 'The dynamics of the adoption of product and process innovations in organizations', *Journal of Management Studies*, **38** (1), 45–65.

Dane, E. and M.G. Pratt (2007), 'Exploring intuition and its role in managerial decision making', *Academy of Management Review*, **32** (1), 33–54.

Davis, T.R.V. and F. Luthans (1980), 'A social learning approach to organizational behavior', *Academy of Management Review*, **5** (2), 281–90.

De Carolis, D.M. and P. Saparito (2006), 'Social capital, cognition, and entrepreneurial opportunities: a theoretical framework', *Entrepreneurship Theory and Practice*, **1**, 41–56.

De Jong, J.P.J. and P.A.M. Vermeulen (2006), 'Determinants of product innovation in small firms', *International Small Business Journal*, **24** (6), 587–609.

Dean, J.W. and M.P. Sharfman (1993), 'Procedural rationality in the strategic decision-making process', *Journal of Management Studies*, **30** (4), 587–610.

Dean, J.W. and M.P. Sharfman (1996), 'Does decision process matter? A study of strategic decision-making effectiveness', *Academy of Management Journal*, **39** (2), 368–96.

Dellabarca, R. (2000), 'Understanding the "opportunity recognition processes" in entrepreneurship, and consideration of whether serial entrepreneurs undertake opportunity recognition better than novice entrepreneurs', University of Cambridge: MBA Dissertation.

Dess, G., G. Lumpkin and J. Covin (1997), 'Entrepreneurial strategy making and firm performance: tests of contingency and configurational models', *Strategic Management Journal*, **18** (9), 677–95.

Dickson, P. (1992), 'Toward a general theory of competitive rationality', *Journal of Marketing*, **56** (1), 69–83.

Dougherty, D. (1992), 'A practice-centered model of organizational renewal through product innovation', *Strategic Management Journal*, **13** (special issue), 77–92.

Douglas, E.J. and D.A. Shepherd (1999), 'Entrepreneurship as a utility maximizing response', *Journal of Business Venturing*, **15** (1), 231–51.

Dowling, G.R. and R. Staelin (1994), 'A model of perceived risk and intended risk handling activity', *Journal of Consumer Research*, **21**, 119–54.

Downs, R.M. and D. Stea (1977), *Maps in Minds: Reflections on Cognitive Mapping*, New York: Harper & Row.

Drucker, P. (1985), 'The discipline of innovation', *Harvard Business Review*, **63** (3), 67–72.

Duncan, R.B. (1972), 'Characteristics of organizational environments and perceived uncertainty', *Administrative Science Quarterly*, **17** (3), 313–27.

Duncan, W. (1989), *Great Ideas in Management*, San Francisco, CA: Jossey-Bass.

Dunn, J.C., S. Lewandowski and K. Kirsner (2002), 'Dynamics of communications in emergency management', *Applied Cognitive Psychology*, **16** (6), 719–37.

Dutton, J.E. and S.E. Jackson (1987), 'Categorizing strategic issues: links to organizational action', *Academy of Management Review*, **12** (1), 76–90.

Edelenbos, J. and E.H. Klijn (2005), 'Managing stakeholder involvement in decision making: a comparative analysis of six interactive processes in the Netherlands', *Journal of Public Administration Research and Theory*, **16**, 417–46.

Eden, C., F. Ackerman and S. Cropper (1992), 'The analysis of cause maps', *Journal of Management Studies*, **29** (3), 309–24.

EIM (2004), *Kleinschalig ondernemen 2004* (Small-scale entrepreneurship 2004), Zoetermeer: EIM Business and Policy Research.

Eisenhardt, K. (1989), 'Making fast strategic decisions in high velocity environments', *Academy of Management Journal*, **32** (3), 543–76.

Eisenhardt, K. (2000), 'Paradox, spirals, ambivalence: the new language of change and pluralism', *Academy of Management Review*, **25** (4), 703–5.

Eisenhardt, K. and M.J. Zbaracki (1992), 'Strategic decision making', *Strategic Management Journal*, **13** (1), 17–37.

Elbanna, S. (2006), 'Strategic decision-making: process perspectives', *International Journal of Management Review*, **8** (1), 1–20.

Elbanna, S. and J. Child (2007), 'The influence of decision, environmental and firm characteristics on the rationality of strategic decision-making', *Journal of Management Studies*, **44** (4), 561–91.

Elfring, T. and W. Hulsink (2003), 'Networks in entrepreneurship: the case of high-technology firms', *Small Business Economics*, **21**, 409–22.

Ellsberg, D. (1961), 'Risk, ambiguity and the savage axioms', *Quarterly Journal of Economics*, **75** (1), 643–99.

Espedal, B. (2006), 'Do organizational routines change as experience changes?', *Journal of Applied Behavioral Science*, **42** (4), 468–90.

Festinger, L. (1957), *A Theory of Cognitive Dissonance*, Stanford, CA: Stanford University Press.

Fischhoff, B., P. Slovic and S. Lichtenstein (1977), 'Knowing with certainty: the appropriateness of extreme confidence', *Journal of Experimental Psychology: Human Perception and Performance*, **3** (4), 552–64.

Fiske, S. and S. Taylor (1991), *Social Cognition*, New York: McGraw-Hill.

Flora, J.F., J. Sharp and C. Flora (1997), 'Entrepreneurial social infrastructure and locally initiated economic development in the nonmetropolitan United States', *Sociological Quarterly*, **38** (4), 623–45.

Forbes, D.P. (1999), 'Cognitive approaches to new venture creation', *International Journal of Management Reviews*, **1** (4), 415–39.

Forbes, D.P. (2005), 'The effects of strategic decision-making on entrepreneurial self-efficacy', *Entrepreneurship Theory and Practice*, **29** (5), 599–626.

Forgas, J.P. (1995), 'Mood and judgment: the affect infusion model (AIM)', *Psychological Bulletin*, **117** (1), 39–66.

Forgas, J. P. and J.M. George (2001), 'Affective influences on judgments and behavior in organizations: an information processing perspective', *Organizational Behavior and Human Decision Processes*, **86** (1), 3–34.

Forlani, D. and J. Mullins (2000), 'Perceived risks and choices in entrepreneurs' new venture decisions', *Journal of Business Venturing*, **15** (4), 305–22.

Fredrickson, J.W. (1984), 'The comprehensiveness of strategic decision processes: extension, observations, future directions', *Academy of Management Journal*, **27** (3), 445–66.

Fredrickson, J.W. and A.I. Iaquinto (1989), 'Inertia and creeping rationality in strategic decision processes', *Academy of Management Journal*, **32** (3), 516–42.

Fredrickson, J.W. and T.R. Mitchell (1984), 'Strategic decision processes: comprehensiveness and performance in an industry with an unstable environment', *Academy of Management Journal*, **27** (2), 399–423.

Freel, M.S. (2000a), 'Strategy and structure in innovative manufacturing SMEs: the case of an English region', *Small Business Economics*, **15**, 27–45.

Freel, M.S. (2000b), 'Barriers to product innovation in small manufacturing firms', *International Small Business Journal*, **18** (2), 60–80.

Freeman, R.E. (1984), *Strategic Management: A Stakeholder Approach*, Boston, MA: Pitman.

Frese, M., M. van Gelderen and M. Ombach (2000), 'How to plan as a small scale business owner: psychological process characteristics of action strategies and success', *Journal of Small Business Management*, **38** (4), 1–18.

Friedman, S.R and S. Aral (2001), 'Social networks, risk-potential networks, health, and disease', *Journal of Urban Health: Bulletin of the New York Academy of Medicine*, **78** (3), 411–18.

Frishammar, J. and S.A. Hörte (2005), 'Managing external information in manufacturing firms: the impact on innovation performance', *Journal of Product Innovation Management*, **22**, 251–66.

Gaglio, C.M. (1997), 'Opportunity identification: review, critique, and suggested research directions', in J. Katz (ed.), *Advances in Entrepreneurship, Firm, Emergence, and Growth*, Greenwich, CT: JAI Press, pp. 139–202.

Garcia, R. and R. Calantone (2002), 'A critical look at technological innovation typology and innovativeness terminology: a literature review', *Journal of Product Innovation Management*, **19**, 110–32.

Gartner, W.B., B.J. Bird and J.A. Starr (1992), 'Acting as if: differentiating entrepreneurial from organizational behavior', *Entrepreneurship Theory and Practice*, **16** (3), 13–31.

Gibb, A. (2006), 'Making markets in business development services for SMEs: taking up the Chinese challenge of entrepreneurial networking and stakeholder relationship management', *Journal of Small Businesses and Enterprise Development*, **13**, 263–83.

Gibcus, P., P.A.M. Vermeulen and J.P.J. de Jong (2008), 'Strategic decision-making in small firms: a taxonomy of small business owners', forthcoming in *International Journal of Entrepreneurship and Small Business*.

Gilad, B. (1982), 'On encouraging entrepreneurship: an interdisciplinary approach', *Journal of Behavioral Economics*, **11** (1), 132–63.

Gilmore, A. and D. Carson (2000), 'The demonstration of a methodology for assessing SME decision making', *Journal of Research in Marketing*, **2** (2), 108–24.

Gingerenzer, G., P.M. Todd and ABC Group (1999), *Simple Heuristics that Make Us Smart*, Oxford and New York: Oxford University Press.

Ginsberg, A. (1990), 'Connecting diversification to performance: a sociocognitive approach', *Academy of Management Review*, **15** (3), 514–35.

Ginsberg, A. and A. Bucholtz (1989), 'Are entrepreneurs a breed apart? A look at the evidence', *Journal of General Management*, **15** (2), 32–40.

Gioia, D.A. and C.C. Manz (1985), 'Linking cognition and behavior: a script processing interpretation of vicarious learning', *Academy of Management Review*, **10** (3), 527–39.

Glazer, R. and A.M. Weiss (1993), 'Marketing in turbulent environments: decision processes and the time-sensitivity of information', *Journal of Marketing Research*, **30** (4), 509–21.

Gómez, A., A. Moreno, J. Pazos and A. Sierra-Alonso (2000), 'Knowledge maps: an essential technique for conceptualisation', *Data and Knowledge Engineering*, **33** (2), 169–90.

Goss, D. (2007), 'Reconsidering Schumpeterian opportunities, *International Journal of Entrepreneurial Behaviour and Research*, **13** (1), 3–18.

Green, G.C. (2004), 'The impact of cognitive complexity on project leadership performance', *Information and Software Technology*, **46** (3), 165–72.

Griffin, D.W. and C.A. Varey (1996), 'Towards a consensus on overconfidence', *Organizational Behavior and Human Decision Processes*, **65** (3), 227–31.

Gustafsson, V. (2006), *Entrepreneurial Decision-making: Individuals, Tasks, and Cognitions*, Cheltenham, UK and Northampton, MA, USA: Edward Elgar.

Hadjimanolis, A. (2000), 'An investigation of innovation antecedents in small firms in the context of a small developing country', *R&D Management*, **30** (3), 235–45.

Hall, J. and C. Hofer (1993), 'Venture capitalists' decision criteria in new venture evaluation', *Journal of Business Venturing*, **8** (1), 25–42.

Hambrick, D.C. and L.M. Crozier (1985), 'Stumblers and stars in the management of rapid growth', *Journal of Business Venturing*, **1** (1), 31–45.

Hambrick, D.C. and P.A. Mason (1984), 'Upper echelons: the organization as a reflection of its top managers', *Academy of Management Review*, **9** (2), 193–206.

Hamel, G. (2000), *Leading the Revolution*, Boston, MA: Harvard Business School Press.

Harris, R. (1998), 'Introduction to decision making', VirtualSalt, July 2, http://www.virtualsalt.com/crebook5.htm, April 2007.

Harrison, E.F. (1987), *The Managerial Decision-making Process*, Boston, MA: Houghton Mifflin.

Hastie, R. (2001), 'Problems for judgment and decision making', *Annual Review of Psychology*, **52**, 653–83.

Hausman, A. (2005), 'Innovativeness among small businesses: theory and propositions for future research', *Industrial Marketing Management*, **34**, 773–82.

Hébert, R.F. and A.N. Link (1982), *The Entrepreneur*, New York: Praeger.

Hewstone, J., W. Stroebe and G.M. Stephenson (1996), *Introduction to Social Psychology*, Oxford: Blackwell.

Hill, C.W.L and G.S. Hansen (1991), 'A longitudinal study of the cause and consequences of changes in diversification in the U.S. pharmaceutical industry 1977–1986', *Strategic Management Journal*, **12** (1), 187–99.

Hinloopen, J. (2003), 'Innovation performance across Europe', *Economics of Innovation and New Technology*, **12** (2), 145–61.

Hitt, M.A. and B.B. Tyler (1991), 'Strategic decision models: integrating different perspectives', *Strategic Management Journal*, **12**, 327–51.

Hodgkinson, G.P., N.J. Bown, A.J. Maule, K.W. Glaister and A.D. Perman (1999), 'Breaking the frame: an analysis of strategic cognition and decision making under uncertainty', *Strategic Management Journal*, **20** (10), 977–85.

Hodgkinson, G.P. and G.P. Clarkson (2005), 'What have we learned from almost thirty years of research on causal mapping? Methodological lessons and choices for the information systems and information technology communities', in V.K. Narayanan and D.J. Armstrong (eds),

Causal Mapping for Research in Information Technology, Hershey, PA: Idea Group, pp. 46–79.

Hodgkinson, G. P., J.A. Maule and N.J. Bown (2004), 'Causal cognitive mapping in the organizational strategy field: a comparison of alternative elicitation procedures', *Organizational Research Methods*, **7** (1), 3–26.

Hoffman, K., M. Parejo, J. Bessant and L. Perren (1998), 'Small firms, R&D, technology and innovation in the UK: a literature review', *Technovation*, **18** (1), 39–55.

Hofstede, G. (1980), *Culture's Consequences: International Differences in Work Related Values*, Beverly Hills, CA: Sage.

Hogarth, R.M. (1987), *Judgement and Choice: The Psychology of Decisions*, New York: John Wiley.

Hornaday, J. and J. Aboud (1971), 'Characteristics of successful entrepreneurs', *Personnel Psychology*, **24** (3), 141–53.

Hough, J.R. and M.A.White (2003), 'Environmental dynamism and strategic decision-making rationality: an examination at the decision level', *Strategic Management Journal*, **24** (5), 481–9.

Huczynski, A. and D.A. Buchanan (2007), *Organizational Behaviour: An Introductory Text*, 6th edn, New York: Prentice-Hall.

Huff, A.S. (1990), *Mapping Strategic Thought*, Chichester: Wiley.

Huff, A.S. and R.K. Reger (1987), 'A review of strategic process research', *Journal of Management*, **13** (2), 211–36.

Iederan, O., P.L. Curşeu and P.A. Vermeulen (2007), 'Effective decision-making: the role of cognitive complexity in entrepreneurial strategic decisions', Internal Research Report, Department of Organization Studies, Tilburg University.

Inkpen, A.C. and E.W.K. Tsang (2005), 'Social capital, networks and knowledge transfer', *Academy of Management Review*, **30** (1), 146–65.

Jackson, D., L. Hournay and N. Vidmar (1972), 'A four-dimensional interpretation of risk taking', *Journal of Personality*, **40** (3), 483–501.

Janis, I.L. (1989), *Crucial Decisions: Leadership in Policymaking and Crisis Management*, New York: Free Press.

Janney, J.J. and G.G. Dess (2006), 'The risk concept for entrepreneurs reconsidered: new challenges for the conventional wisdom', *Journal of Business Venturing*, **21**, 385–400.

Jenkins, M. and G. Johnson (1997), 'Entrepreneurial intentions and outcomes: a comparative causal mapping study', *Journal of Management Studies*, **34** (6), 895–920.

Johannessen, J., B. Olsen and G.T. Lumpkin (2001), 'Innovation as newness: what is new, how new, and new to whom?', *European Journal of Innovation Management*, **4** (1), 20–31.

Joma, R.J., J. van Engelen and R. ten Cate (2001), *Kenniscreatie in beweg-ing: Kennisontwikkeling voor duurzame innovatie* (Knowledge creation in motion: developing knowledge for sustainable innovation), Groningen: NIDO.

Jorrisen, A., E. Laveren, R. Martens and A. Reheul (2002), 'The relation-ship between management accounting systems, firm strategy, perceived environmental uncertainty, networking, CEO characteristics and perfor-mance in SMEs', *Entrepreneurship and Small Businesses*, **16**, 688–709.

Juslin, P., A. Winman and H. Olsson (2000), 'Naive empiricism and dog-matism in confidence research: a critical examination of the hard–easy effect', *Psychological Review*, **107** (2), 384–96.

Kahneman, D. and D. Lovallo (1993), 'Timid choices and bold forecasts: a cognitive perspective on risk taking', *Management Science*, **39** (1), 17–31.

Kahneman, D., P. Slovic and A. Tversky (1982), *Judgement Under Uncertainty: Heuristics and Biases*, Cambridge and New York: Cambridge University Press.

Kaish, S. and B. Gilad (1991), 'Characteristics of opportunities search of entrepreneurs versus executives: sources, interests, general alertness', *Journal of Business Venturing*, **6** (1), 45–61.

Katz, J.A. (1992), 'A psychosocial cognitive model of employment status choice', *Entrepreneurship Theory and Practice*, **17** (1), 29–37.

Keh, H.T., M.D. Foo and B.C. Lim (2002), 'Opportunity evaluation under risky conditions: the cognitive processes of entrepreneurs', *Entrepreneurship Theory and Practice*, **27** (2), 125–48.

Kelley, H.H. (1973), 'The processes of causal attribution', *American Psychologist*, **28** (2), 107–28.

Kelly, G.A. (1955), *The Psychology of Personal Constructs*, New York: Norton.

Khatri, N. and H. Ng (2000), 'The role of intuition in strategic decision-making', *Human Relations*, **53** (1), 57–86.

Kiesler, S. and L. Sproull (1982), 'Managerial response to changing envi-ronments: perspectives on problem sensing from social cognition', *Administrative Science Quarterly*, **27** (4), 548–70.

Kim, L. and Y. Lim (1988), 'Environment, generic strategies and perfor-mance in a rapidly changing country: a taxonomic approach', *Academy of Management Journal*, **31** (4), 802–27.

Kimberley, J.R. and M.J. Evanisko (1981), 'Organizational innovation: the influence of individual, organizational and contextual factors on hospi-tal adoption of technological and administrative innovations', *Academy of Management Journal*, **24** (4), 689–713.

Kirzner, I. (1973), *Competition and Entrepreneurship*, Chicago, IL: University of Chicago Press.

Kirzner, I. (1979), *Perception, Opportunity and Profit*, Chicago, IL: University of Chicago Press.

Klein, J.H. and D.F. Cooper (1982), 'Cognitive maps of decision-makers in a complex game', *Journal of the Operational Research Society*, **33** (1), 63–71.

Knight, F. (1921), *Risk, Uncertainty and Profit*, Boston, MA: Houghton Mifflin.

Knight, G. (2000), 'Entrepreneurship and marketing strategy: the SME under globalization', *Journal of International Marketing*, **8**, 12–32.

Krackhardt, D. (1990), 'Assessing the political landscape: structure, cognition, and power in organizations', *Administrative Science Quarterly*, **35** (2), 342–69.

Krueger, N.F. (2000), 'The cognitive infrastructure of opportunity emergence', *Entrepreneurship Theory and Practice*, **24** (3), 5–23.

Kunreuther, H., R. Meyer, R. Zeckhauser, P. Slovic, B. Schwartz, C. Schade, M.F. Luce, S. Lippman, D. Krantz, B. Kahn, and R. Hogarth (2002), 'High stakes decision making: normative, descriptive and prescriptive considerations', *Marketing Letters*, **13** (3), 259–68.

Laibson, D. and R. Zeckhauser (1998), 'Amos Tversky and the ascent of behavioral economics', *Journal of Risk and Uncertainty*, **16** (1), 7–47.

Lang, J.R., J.E. Dittrich and S.E. White (1978), 'Managerial problem solving models: a review and a proposal', *Academy of Management Review*, **3** (October), 854–66.

Langfield-Smith, K. (1992), 'Exploring the need for a shared cognitive map', *Journal of Management Studies*, **29** (3), 349–68.

Lawler, E.J. (2001), 'An affect theory of social exchange', *American Journal of Sociology*, **107** (2), 321–52.

Leana, C.R. and H.J. van Buren (1999), 'Organizational social capital and employment practices', *Academy of Management Review*, **24** (3), 538–55.

Leaptrott, J. (2006), 'The dual process model of reasoning and entrepreneurial decision-making: a field study of new childcare ventures', *Journal of Applied Management and Entrepreneurship*, **11** (2), 17–31.

Lee, D.Y. and E.W.K. Tsang (2001), 'The effects of entrepreneurial personality, background and network activities on venture growth', *Journal of Management Studies*, **38** (4), 583–602.

Lei, D., M.A. Hitt and R. Bettis (1996), 'Dynamic core-competences through meta-learning and strategic context', *Journal of Management*, **22** (4), 549–69.

Leland, J.W. (1998), 'Similarity judgments in choice under uncertainty: a reinterpretation of the predictions of regret theory', *Management Science*, **44** (5), 659–72.

Levander, A. and I. Raccuia (2001), *Entrepreneurial Profiling – A Cognitive Approach to Entrepreneurship*, Stockholm: Stockholm Business School.

Liagrovas, P. (1998), 'The White Paper on growth, competitiveness and employment and Greek small and medium sized enterprises', *Small Business Economics*, **11**, 201–14.

Lichtenstein, S., B. Fischhoff and L. Phillips (1982), 'Calibration of probabilities: the state of art to 1980', in Kahneman et al. (eds), pp. 306–44.

Liles, P.R. (1974), *New Business Ventures and the Entrepreneur*, Homewood, IL: Richard D. Irwin.

Lipparini, A. and M. Sobrero (1994), 'The glue and the pieces: entrepreneurship and innovation in small-firm networks', *Journal of Business Venturing*, **9**, 125–40.

Lipshitz, R. and O. Strauss (1997), 'Coping with uncertainty: a naturalistic decision-making analysis', *Organizational Behavior and Human Decision Processes*, **69**, 149–63.

Loasby, B. (1976), *Choice, Complexity and Ignorance: An Enquiry into Economic Theory and the Practice of Decision-making*, Cambridge: Cambridge University Press.

Loasby, B. (1998), 'Decision premises and economic development', paper presented at Druid Summer Conference, Bornholm, 9–11 June.

Loomes, G. and R. Sugden (1982), 'Regret theory: an alternative theory of rational choice under uncertainty', *Economic Journal*, **92** (368), 805–24.

Lord, R.G. and K.J. Maher (1990), 'Alternative information-processing models and their implications for theory, research and practice', *Academy of Management Review*, **15** (1), 9–28.

Low, M. and I. MacMillan (1988), 'Entrepreneurship: past research and future challenges', *Journal of Management*, **14** (2), 139–61.

Lybaert, N. (1998), 'The information use in an SME: its importance and some elements of influence', *Small Business Economics*, **10** (2), 171–91.

Lyon, D., G. Lumpkin and G. Dess (2000), 'Enhancing entrepreneurial orientation research: operationalizing and measuring a key strategic decision-making process', *Journal of Management*, **26** (5), 1055–85.

Mador, M. (2000), 'Strategic decision-making process research: are entrepreneur and owner managed firms different?', *Journal of Research in Marketing and Entrepreneurship*, **2** (3), 215–34.

Manimala, M.J. (1992), 'Entrepreneurial heuristics: a comparison between high PI (pioneering–innovative) and low PI ventures', *Journal of Business Venturing*, **7** (6), 447–504.

March, J.G. and H.A. Simon (1958), *Organizations*, New York: McGraw-Hill.

March, J.G. and H.A. Simon (1993), 'Organizations revisited', *Industrial and Corporate Change*, **2** (3), 299–316.

Masters, R. and R. Meier (1988), 'Sex differences and risk-taking propensity of entrepreneurs', *Journal of Small Business Management*, **26** (1), 31–5.

Mathieu, J.E., T.S. Heffner, G.F. Goodwin, E. Salas and A. Cannon-Bowers (2000), 'The influence of shared mental models on team process and performance', *Journal of Applied Psychology*, **85** (2), 273–83.

McCarthy, A., F. Schoorman and A. Cooper (1993), 'Reinvestment decisions by entrepreneurs: rational decision-making or escalation of commitment?', *Journal of Business Venturing*, **8** (1), 9–24.

McClelland, D. (1961), *The Achieving Society*, New York: Van Nostrand.

McGrath, R.G. (1999), 'Falling forward: real options reasoning and entrepreneurial failure', *Academy of Management Review*, **24** (1), 13–30.

McGrath, R., I. MacMillan and S. Scheineberg (1992), 'Elitists, risk-takers, and rugged individualists? An exploratory analysis of cultural differences between entrepreneurs and non-entrepreneurs', *Journal of Business Venturing*, **7** (2), 115–35.

Messick, D. and M. Bazerman (1996), 'Ethical leadership and the psychology of decision-making', *Sloan Management Review*, **37** (winter), 9–22.

Miller, D. and P.H. Friesen (1983), 'Strategy-making and environment: the third link', *Strategic Management Journal*, **4** (3), 221–35.

Miner, J.B. and N.S. Raju (2004), 'Risk propensity differences between managers and entrepreneurs and between low- and high-growth entrepreneurs: a reply in a more conservative vein', *Journal of Applied Psychology*, **89** (1), 3–12.

Mintzberg, H., D. Raisinghani and A. Théorêt (1976), 'The structure of unstructured decision processes', *Administrative Science Quarterly*, **21** (2), 246–75.

Mintzberg, H. and F. Westley (2001), 'Decision-making: it's not what you think', *MIT Sloan Management Review*, **42** (3), 89–93.

Mitchell, R.K., B.R. Agle and D.J. Wood (1997), 'Toward a theory of stakeholder identification and salience: defining the principle of who and what really counts', *Academy of Management Review*, **4**, 853–86.

Mitchell, R.K., L.W. Busenitz, B. Bird, C.M. Gaglio, J.S. McCullen, E.A. Morse and J.B. Smith (2007), 'The central question in entrepreneurial cognition research 2007', *Entrepreneurship Theory and Practice*, **31** (1), 1–27.

Mitchell, R.K., L.W. Busenitz, T. Lant, P.P. McDougall, E.A. Morse and J.B. Smith (2002), 'Toward a theory of entrepreneurial cognition: rethinking the people side of entrepreneurship research', *Entrepreneurship Theory and Practice*, **27** (2), 93–104.

Mitchell, R.K. and B. Cohen (2006), 'Stakeholder theory and the entrepreneurial firm', *Journal of Small Business Strategy*, **17**, 1–15.

Moran, P. (2005), 'Structural vs. relational embeddedness. Social capital and managerial performance', *Strategic Management Journal*, **26**, 1129–51.

Mullins, J. (1996), 'Early growth decisions of entrepreneurs: the influence of competency and prior performance under changing market conditions', *Journal of Business Venturing*, **11** (2), 89–105.

Nieuwenhuijsen, H. and J. Nijkamp (2001), *Competition and Economic Performance: Application of SCALES' Sector Model on Competition MOCO*, Zoetermeer: EIM Onderzoek voor bedrijf en beleid.

Nonaka, S. and N. Takeuchi (2003), *De kenniscreërende onderneming; Hoe Japanse bedrijven innovatieprocessen in gang zetten*, (The knowledge creating company: how Japanese companies create the dynamics of innovation), Schiedam: Scriptum.

Noorderhaven, N.G. (1995), *Strategic Decision Making*, Wokingham: Addison-Wesley.

Norton, W.I. and W.T. Moore (2002), 'Entrepreneurial risk: have we been asking the wrong question?', *Small Business Economics*, **18** (4), 281–7.

Nutt, P.C. (1993), 'The formulation processes and tactics used in organizational decision making', *Organization Science*, **4** (2), 226–51.

Nutt, P.C. (2002), *Why Decisions Fail: Avoiding the Blunders and Traps that Lead to Debacles*, San Francisco, CA: Berrett-Koehler.

Nwachukwu, O. (1995), 'CEO locus of control, strategic planning, differentiation, and small business performance: a test of path analytic models', *Journal of Applied Business Research*, **11** (4), 9–14.

O'Regan, N., M. Sims and A. Ghobodian (2005), 'High performance: ownership and decision-making in SMEs', *Management Decision*, **43**, 382–96.

O'Reilly III, C.A. and J.A. Chatman (1994), 'Working smarter and harder: a longitudinal study of managerial success', *Administrative Science Quarterly*, **39** (4), 603–27.

Oerlemans, L.A.G, M.T.H. Meeus and F.W.M. Boekema (1998), 'Do networks matter for innovation? The usefulness of the economic network approach in analyzing innovation', *Tijdschrift voor Economische en Sociale Geografie*, **89** (3), 298–309.

Oh, H., G. Labianca and M. Chung (2006), 'A multilevel model of group social capital', *Academy of Management Review*, **1** (3), 569–82.

Olson, P.D. and D.W. Bokor (1995), 'Strategy process–content interaction: effects on growth performance in small start-up firms', *Journal of Small Business Management*, **33** (1), 34–44.

Palich, L. and D. Bagby (1995), 'Using cognitive theory to explain entre-preneurial risk-taking: challenging conventional wisdom', *Journal of Business Venturing*, **10** (6), 425–38.

Pallant, J. (2005), *SPSS Survival Manual*, Buckingham: Open University Press.

Papadakis, V., S. Lioukas and D. Chambers (1998), 'Strategic decision-making processes: the role of management and context', *Strategic Management Journal*, **19** (2), 115–47.

Parker, S.C. (2006), 'Learning about the unknown: how fast do entrepreneurs adjust their beliefs?', *Journal of Business Venturing*, **21** (1), 1–26.

Popadiuk, S. and C.W. Choo (2006), 'Innovation and knowledge creation: how are these concepts related?', *International Journal of Information Management*, **26**, 302–12.

Porac, J.F. and H. Thomas (1990), 'Taxonomic mental models in competitor definition', *Academy of Management Review*, **15** (2), 224–40.

Post, J.E., L.E. Preston and S. Sachs (2002), *Managing the Extended Enterprise: The New Stakeholder View*, Stanford, CA and London: Stanford University Press.

Poulton, E. (1994), *Behavioral Decision Theory: A New Approach*, Cambridge: Cambridge University Press.

Preble, J.F. (2005), 'Towards a comprehensive model of stakeholder man-agement', *Business and Society Review*, **110**, 407–31.

Prietula, J. and H. Simon (1989), 'The experts in your midst', *Harvard Business Review*, **67** (1), 120–24.

Ray, D.M. (1994), 'The role of risk-taking in Singapore', *Journal of Business Venturing*, **9** (2), 157–77.

Reed, S.K. (2006), *Cognition: Theory and Applications*, 7th edn, Belmont, CA: Wadsworth.

Reger, R.K. (1990), 'Managerial thought structures and competitive posi-tioning', in Huff (ed.), pp. 71–88.

Rerup, C. (2005), 'Learning from past experience: footnotes on mindfulness and habitual entrepreneurship', *Scandinavian Journal of Management*, **21** (1), 451–72.

Reuber, A.R. and E. Fischer (1999), 'Understanding the consequences of founders' experience', *Journal of Small Business Management*, **37** (2), 30–45.

Robinson, R.B. and J.A. Pearce (1983), 'The impact of formalized strate-gic planning on financial performance in small organizations', *Strategic Management Journal*, **4** (1), 197–207.

Robson, P.J.A. and R.J. Bennett (2000), 'SMEs' growth: the relationship with business advice and external collaboration', *Journal of Business Economics*, **15**, 193–208.

Roese, N.J. (1997), 'Counterfactual thinking', *Psychological Bulletin*, **121**, 133–48.

Romijn, H. and M. Albaladejo (2002), 'Determinants of innovation capability in small electronics and software firms in southeast England', *Research Policy*, **31** (7), 1053–67.

Ronstadt, R. (1988), 'The corridor principle', *Journal of Business Venturing*, **3** (1), 31–40.

Rothwell, R. (1991), 'External networking and innovation in small and medium-sized manufacturing firms in Europe', *Technovation*, **11** (2), 93–112.

Rotter, J. (1966), 'Generalized expectancies for internal versus external control of reinforcements', *Psychological Monographs*, **80** (1), 1–28.

Russo, J.E. and P.J. Schoemaker (1992), 'Managing overconfidence', *Sloan Management Review*, **33** (2), 7–17.

Sarmány-Schuller, I. (1998), 'Category width cognitive style and decision-making process', *Studia Psychologica*, **40** (4), 250–54.

Sauner-Leroy, J.B. (2004), 'Managers and productive investment decisions: the impact of risk and uncertainty aversion', *Journal of Small Business Management*, **42**, 1–18.

Savage, L. (1954), *The Foundations of Statistics*, New York: Wiley.

Sawyerr, O.O., J. McGee and M. Peterson (2003), 'Perceived uncertainty and firms' performance in SMEs: the role of personal networking activities', *International Small Business Journal*, **21**, 269–90.

Say, J.B. (1845), *A Treatise on Political Economy*, Philadelphia, PA: Grigg & Elliot.

Schere, J. (1982), 'Tolerance and ambiguity as a discriminating variable between entrepreneurs and managers', in *Proceedings of the Academy of Management Conference*, New York, pp. 404–8.

Schneider, S.C. and A. de Meyer (1991), 'Interpreting and responding to strategic issues: the impact of national culture', *Strategic Management Journal*, **12** (4), 307–20.

Schoemaker, P.J.H. (1993), 'Strategic decisions in organizations: rational and behavioural views', *Journal of Management Studies*, **30** (1), 107–29.

Schröder, H., M. Driver and S. Streufert (1967), *Human Information Processing: Individuals and Groups Functioning in Complex Social Situations*, New York: Holt, Rinehart, Winston.

Schumpeter, J.A. (1934), *The Theory of Economic Development*, Boston, MA: Harvard University Press.

Schwarz, N. (2000), 'Emotion, cognition and decision making', *Cognition and Emotion*, **14**, 433–40.

Schwenk, C.R. (1984), 'Cognitive simplification processes in strategic decision-making', *Strategic Management Journal*, **5** (2), 111–28.

Schwenk, C.R. (1988), 'The cognitive perspective on strategic decision making', *Journal of Management Studies*, **25** (1), 41–55.

Schwenk, C. and C. Shrader (1993), 'Effects of formal strategic planning on financial performance in small firms: a meta analysis', *Entrepreneurship Theory and Practice*, **17** (3), 53–64.

Scott, J. (2000), *Social Network Analysis: A Handbook*, London: Sage.

Sexton, D.L. and N. Bowman (1984), 'The effects of pre-existing psychological characteristics on new venture initiations', paper presented at the annual meeting of the Academy of Management, Boston.

Sexton, D.L and N. Bowman (1985), 'The entrepreneur: a capable executive and more', *Journal of Business Venturing*, **1** (1), 129–40.

Sexton, D.L. and N. Bowman (1986), 'Validation of a personality index: comparative psychological characteristics analysis of female entrepreneurs, managers, entrepreneurship students and business students', in R. Ronstadt, J. Hornaday, R. Peterson and K. Vesper (eds), *Frontiers of Entrepreneurship Research*, Wellesley, MA: Babson College.

Shafir, E. and R.E. LeBoeuf (2002), 'Rationality', *Annual Review of Psychology*, **55** (3), 491–517.

Shane, S., E.A. Locke and C.J. Collins (2003), 'Entrepreneurial motivation', *Human Resource Management Review*, **13** (2), 257–79.

Shane, S. and S. Venkataraman (2000), 'The promise of entrepreneurship as a field of research', *Academy of Management Review*, **25** (1), 217–26.

Shapero, A. and L. Sokol (1982), 'The social dimensions of entrepreneurship', in C. Kent, D. Sexton and K. Vesper (eds), *The Encyclopedia of Entrepreneurship*, Englewood Cliffs, NJ: Prentice-Hall, pp. 72–90.

Shaver, K.G. and L.R. Scott (1991), 'Person, process, choice: the psychology of new venture capital', *Entrepreneurship Theory and Practice*, **16** (2), 23–45.

Shepherd, D.A. (1999), 'Venture capitalists' assessment of new venture survival', *Management Science*, **45** (5), 621–32.

Shepherd, D.A., A. Zacharakis and R.A. Baron (2003), 'VCs' decision processes: evidence suggesting more experience may not always be better', *Journal of Business Venturing*, **18** (3), 381–401.

Siguaw, J.A., P.M. Simpson and C.A. Enz (2006), 'Conceptualizing innovation orientation: a framework for study and integration of innovation research', *Journal of Product Innovation Management*, **23** (1), 556–74.

Simon, H. (1957), *Administrative Behavior: A Study of Decision-making Processes in Administrative Organization*, London and New York: Macmillan.

Simon, H.A. (1965), *Administrative Behavior: A Study of Decision-making Processes in Administrative Organization*, New York: Free Press.

Simon, H.A. (1972), 'Theories of bounded rationality', in C. McGuire and R. Radner (eds), *Decision and Organization*, Amsterdam: North-Holland, pp. 161–76.

Simon, H. (1979), 'Rational decision-making in business organisations', *American Economic Review*, **69** (4), 493–513.

Simon, H.A. (1986) 'Rationality in psychology and economics', *Journal of Business*, **59** (4), 209–24.

Simon, M. and S.M. Houghton (2002), 'The relationship among biases, misperceptions and the introduction of pioneering products: examining differences in venture decision contexts', *Entrepreneurship Theory and Practice*, **27** (2), 105–24.

Simon, M. and S.M. Houghton (2003), 'The relationship between overconfidence and the introduction of risky products: evidence from a field study', *Academy of Management Journal*, **46** (4), 139–49.

Simon, M., S.M. Houghton and K. Aquino (2000), 'Cognitive biases, risk perception, and venture formation: how individuals decide to start companies', *Journal of Business Venturing*, **15** (2), 113–34.

Smircich, L. and C. Stubbart (1985), 'Strategic management in an enacted world', *Academy of Management Review*, **10** (4), 724–36.

Smith, E.R. and J. DeCoster (2000), 'Dual-process models in social and cognitive psychology: conceptual integration and links to underlying memory systems', *Personality and Social Psychology Review*, **4** (2), 108–31.

Smith, J.F. and T. Kida (1991), 'Heuristics and biases: expertise and task realism in auditing', *Psychological Bulletin*, **109** (3), 472–89.

Smith, K.G., M.J. Gannon, C. Grimm and T.R. Mitchell (1988), 'Decision making behaviour in smaller entrepreneurial and larger professionally managed firms', *Journal of Business Venturing*, **3** (3), 223–32.

Smith, N.R (1967), *The Entrepreneur and His Firm: The Relationship between Type of Man and Type of Company*, East Lansing, MI: Michigan State University Press.

Snow, C.C. and D.C. Hambrick (1980), 'Measuring organizational strategies: some theoretical and methodological problems', *Academy of Management Review*, **5** (4), 527–38.

Sorrentino, R.M., D.R. Bobocel, M.Z. Gitta, J.M. Olson and E.C. Hewitt (1988), 'Uncertainty orientation and persuasion: individual differences in the effects of personal relevance on social judgements', *Journal of Personality and Social Psychology*, **55** (3), 351–71.

Spector, P. (1992), 'Behavior in organizations as a function of locus of control', *Psychological Bulletin*, **91** (3), 482–97.

Stanovich, K.E. and R.F. West (2000), 'Individual differences in reasoning: implications for the rationality debate?', *Behavioral and Brain Sciences*, **23**, 645–726.

Stavrou, E., G. Kassinis and A. Filotheou (2006), 'Downsizing and stakeholder orientation among the Fortune 500: does family ownership matter?', *Journal of Business Ethics*, **72**, 149–62.

Stewart, W.H. and P.L. Roth (2001), 'Risk propensity differences between entrepreneurs and managers: a meta-analytic review', *Journal of Applied Psychology*, **86** (1), 145–53.

Stokes, D. (1998), *Strategic Management: A Case Study Approach*, London: Letts.

Storey, D. (1994), *Understanding the Small Business Sector*, London: Routledge.

Streufert, S. and R.W. Swezey (1986), *Complexity, Managers, and Organizations*, New York: Academic Press.

Svenson, O. (1981), 'Are we all less risky and more skillful than our fellow drivers?', *Acta Psychologica*, **47** (2), 143–8.

Swan, J.A. (1995), 'Exploring knowledge and cognition in decision about technological innovation: mapping managerial cognitions', *Human Relations*, **48** (11), 1241–70.

Tan, J. (2001), 'Innovation and risk-taking in a transitional economy: a comparative study of Chinese managers and entrepreneurs', *Journal of Business Venturing*, **16** (4), 359–76.

Taylor, D.W. and R. Thorpe (2004), 'Entrepreneurial learning: a process of co-participation', *Journal of Small Business and Enterprise Development*, **11** (2), 203–11.

Taylor, R.N. (1975), 'Age and experience as determinants of managerial information processing and decision-making performance', *Academy of Management Journal*, **18** (1), 74–81.

Timmons, J. (1990), *New Venture Creation: Entrepreneurship in the 1990s*, Homewood, IL: Richard D. Irwin.

Tversky, A. (1972), 'Elimination by aspects: a theory of choice', *Psychological Review*, **79** (4), 281–99.

Tversky, A. and D. Kahneman (1974), 'Judgement under uncertainty: heuristics and biases', *Science*, **185** (4157), 1124–31.

Tversky, A. and D. Kahneman (1981), 'The framing of decisions and the psychology of choice', *Science*, **211** (4481), 453–8.

Tversky, A. and D. Kahneman (1982), 'Judgments of and by representativeness', in Kahneman et al. (eds), pp. 84–98.

Tversky, A. and D. Kahneman (1983), 'Probability, representativeness, and the conjunction fallacy', *Psychological Review*, **90** (4), 293–315.

Tversky, A. and D. Kahneman (1986), 'Rational choice and the framing of decisions', *Journal of Business*, **59** (4), 251–79.

Tversky, A. and D. Kahneman (1992), 'Advances in prospect theory: cumulative representation of uncertainty', *Journal of Risk and Uncertainty*, **5** (4), 297–323.

Tyebjee, T. and A. Bruno (1984), 'A model of venture capitalist investment activity', *Management Science*, **30** (9), 1051–66.

van Gelderen, M., M. Frese and R. Thurik (2001), 'Strategies, uncertainty and performance of small business start-ups', *Small Business Economics*, **15** (3), 165–81.

van Gils, A. (2005), 'Management and governance in Dutch SMEs', *European Management Journal*, **23** (5), 583–9.

Vandekerckhove, W. and N.A. Dentchev (2005), 'A network perspective on stakeholder management: facilitating entrepreneurs in the discovery of opportunities', *Journal of Business Ethics*, **60**, 221–32.

Vennix, J.A.M. (1996), *Group Model Building: Facilitating Team Learning Using System Dynamics*, Chichester: Wiley.

Verhoeven, W., P. Gibcus and P. De Jong-'t Hart (2005), *Bedrijvendynamiek in Nederland: Goed of slecht?* (The dynamics of companies in the Netherlands: good or bad?), Zoetermeer: EIM Onderzoek voor bedrijf en beleid.

Vermeulen, P.A.M. (2005), 'Uncovering barriers to complex incremental product innovation in small and medium-sized financial services firms', *Journal of Small Business Management*, **43** (4), 432–52.

Veryzer, R.W. (1998), 'Discontinuous innovation and the new product development process', *Journal of Product Innovation Management*, **15**, 304–21.

von Neumann, J. and O. Morgenstern (1944), *Theory of Games and Economic Behavior*, Princeton, NJ: Princeton University Press.

Vossen, R. (1998), 'Relative strengths and weaknesses of small firms in innovation', *International Small Business Journal*, **16** (3), 88–94.

Walliser, B. (1989), 'Instrumental rationality and cognitive rationality', *Theory and Decision*, **27** (1/2), 7–36.

Walsh, J.P. (1995), 'Managerial and organizational cognition: notes from a trip down memory lane', *Organization Science*, **6** (3), 280–321.

Weary, G. and J.A. Edwards (1994), 'Individual differences in causal uncertainty', *Journal of Personality and Social Psychology*, **67**, 308–18.

Weber, E.U., A.R. Blais and N.E. Betz (2002), 'A domain-specific risk-attitude scale: measuring risk perceptions and risk behaviors', *Journal of Behavioral Decision Making*, **15** (1), 263–90.

Weick, K. (1979), *The Social-Psychology of Organizing*, Reading, MA: Addison-Wesley.

Weiss, H.M. and R. Cropanzano (1996), 'Affective events theory: a theoretical discussion of the structure, causes and consequences of affective experiences at work', *Research into Organizational Behavior*, **18** (1), 1–74.

Wells, A. (1974), 'Venture capital decision-making', unpublished doctoral dissertation, Pittsburgh, PA: Carnegie Mellon University.

Wennekers, S. and R. Thurik (1999), 'Linking entrepreneurship and economic growth', *Small Business Economics*, **13** (1), 27–55.

Westhead, P., D. Ucbasaran and M. Wright (2005a), 'Decisions, actions, and performance: do novice, serial, and portfolio entrepreneurs differ?', *Journal of Small Business Management*, **43** (4), 393–417.

Westhead, P., D. Ucbasaran and M. Wright (2005b), 'Experience and cognition: do novice, serial and portfolio entrepreneurs differ?', *International Small Business Journal*, **23** (1), 72–98.

Westhead, P. and M. Wright (1998), 'Novice, portfolio, and serial founders: are they different?', *Journal of Business Venturing*, **13** (3), 173–204.

Wilson, R.A. and F.C. Keil (2002), *The MIT Encyclopedia of the Cognitive Sciences*, Cambridge, MA: MIT Press.

Winn, M.I. (2001), 'Building stakeholder theory with a decision modelling methodology', *Business and Society*, **40**, 133–66.

Winter, S.G. (1987), 'Knowledge and competence as strategic assets', in D.J. Teece (ed.), *The Competitive Challenge: Strategies for Industrial Innovation and Renewal*, New York: Harper & Row, pp. 159–84.

Woo, C.Y., A.C. Cooper and W.C. Dunkelberg (1991), 'The development and interpretation of entrepreneurial typologies', *Journal of Business Venturing*, **6** (1), 93–114.

Woo, C. and F.H. Lochovsky (1992), 'Knowledge communication in intelligent information systems', *International Journal of Cooperative Information Systems*, **1** (1), 203–28.

Wood, R. and A. Bandura (1989), 'Social cognitive theory of organizational management', *Academy of Management Review*, **14** (3), 361–84.

Wyman, B.G. and J.M. Randel (1998), 'The relation of knowledge organization to performance of a complex cognitive task', *Applied Cognitive Psychology*, **12** (3), 251–64.

Zacharakis, A. and D. Meyer (1998), 'A lack of insight: do venture capitalists really understand their own decision process?', *Journal of Business Venturing*, **13** (1), 57–76.

Zacharakis, A. and D. Shepherd (2001), 'The nature of information and overconfidence on venture capitalists' decision process?', *Journal of Business Venturing*, **16** (4), 311–32.

Zhao, L. and J.D. Aram (1995), 'Networking and growth of young technology-intensive ventures in China', *Journal of Business Venturing*, **10**, 349–70.

Index

McGrath, R.G. 2, 5, 23, 24, 101, 102, 119, 135, 197
mediation variables 145
Mediators 20
Meier, R. 5
memory constraint 15
mental (cognitive) frames 74
mental models 74, 151
Messick, D. 25, 27, 100
Meyer, D. 29, 39
Miller, D. 179
Miner, J.B. 45
Mintzberg, H. 3, 15, 29, 30, 31–3, 35, 36–7, 71, 90, 202
Mitchell, R.K. 4, 68, 106, 107, 119, 129, 137, 138, 144
Mitchell, T.R. 6, 101, 108
Moore, D.G. 175
Moore, W.T. 43, 46
Moran, P. 162, 164, 165, 169
Morgenstern, Oskar 12
motivated strategy 59
motivation, entrepreneurial 47–50, 66, 197–8
    cognitive complexity and 67, 85–6, 196, 198–9
Mullins, J. 28, 39
multinationals 5

neoclassical rationality 14–15
net present value technique 15
Netherlands
    cognitive complexity, industry dynamism and risk-taking in entrepreneurial decision-making in 180–89
    distribution of small business population in 203
    employment in SMEs in 6
    entrepreneurial characteristics and innovation in 148, 154–60
    entrepreneurial decision styles and cognition in 109–21
    entrepreneurial decision styles and use of biases and heuristics in 126–34
    entrepreneurial decision styles in 86
    planning in SMEs in 39
    risk, uncertainty and stakeholder involvement in 139–45

SMEs as a percentage of all businesses in 6
social capital, cognitive complexity and innovative performance of SMEs in 168–74
strategic decision-making process in SMEs in 89–104
see also EIM Business and Policy Research
new combinations 20
new industries 169
new markets 153, 169
new processes *see* process innovation
new products *see* product innovation
Ng, H. 32, 33, 121
Nieuwenhuijsen, H. 181, 188
Nijkamp, J. 181, 188
nomothetic mapping techniques 74–5
non-compensating models 36
Nonaka, S. 168
Noorderhaven, N.G. 3–4, 11, 13, 15, 33, 34, 35, 36, 37, 71, 135
Norton, W.I. 43, 46
Nutt, P.C. 29, 30, 34, 36, 37
Nwachukwu, O. 23

O'Regan, N. 144
O'Reilly III, C.A. 69, 70, 107
obstacles to success 112, 113, 115, 116, 120
Oerlemans, L.A.G. 165
Oh, H. 164
Olson, P.D. 38
opportunity recognition 34, 101–2, 136
    cognitive complexity and 151, 154
    entrepreneurial decision styles and 111, 113, 116, 118, 120
    entrepreneurial experience and 151, 183
    heuristics and 151, 153
optimism 24, 58, 125, 133, 134
organizational changes
    decisions concerning 95, 111, 116, 119
    entrepreneurial experience and 146
organizational context 16, 17, 50, 192
organizational culture 112–13, 116–17, 118, 120
organizational structure 112, 116, 119, 146, 163